WALKING IN THE WAYS OF THE LORD

THE ETHICAL AUTHORITY *OF THE* OLD TESTAMENT

Christopher J.H.Wright

InterVarsity Press
Downers Grove, Illinois

© Christopher J. H. Wright, 1995

Published in the United States of America by InterVarsity Press, Downers Grove, Illinois, with permission from Universities and Colleges Christian Fellowship, Leicester, England.

InterVarsity Press® is the book-publishing division of InterVarsity Christian Fellowship®, a student movement active on campus at hundreds of universities, colleges and schools of nursing in the United States of America, and a member movement of the International Fellowship of Evangelical Students. For information about local and regional activities, write Public Relations Dept., InterVarsity Christian Fellowship, 6400 Schroeder Rd., P.O. Box 7895, Madison, WI 53707-7895.

Cover photograph: Cowgirl Stock Photography

ISBN 0-8308-1867-7
Printed in the United States of America ∞

Library of Congress Cataloging-in-Publication Data

Wright, Christopher J. H., 1947-
   Walking in the ways of the Lord: the ethical authority of the Old
Testament/Christopher J. H. Wright.

     p.   cm.
   Includes bibliographical references.
   ISNB 0-8308-1867-7
   1. Ethics in the Bible.   2. Bible.   O.T.—Evidences, authority,
etc.   3. Christian ethics—Biblical teaching.   I. Title.
BS1199.E8W76   1996
241.5—dc20   95-49665
                                  CIP

#33947594

17	16	15	14	13	12	11	10	9	8	7	6	5	4	3	2	1
10	09	08	07	06	05	04	03	02	01	00	99	98	97	96		

Preface

When, in 1983, my first attempt at a survey of Old Testament ethics was published, *Living as the People of God* (*An Eye for an Eye* in North America), I opened the preface with the remark that the field of Old Testament ethics had scarcely any literature to add to. Happily the past decade has rendered that observation quite obsolete. There has been a renewed interest in the ethical dimensions of the Hebrew Scriptures and in the hermeneutical issues involved in discovering their authority and relevance for the modern world. This has produced a steady and encouraging growth of both articles and books in the field, some of which are surveyed in chapters 3 and 4. As well as the constructive work found in the monographs of scholars such as Walter Brueggemann, Walter Kaiser, Bruce Birch, and, most recently, Waldemar Janzen, one hears also of doctoral dissertations in the discipline – a sure sign of renewed health and vitality.

In the years since 1983, including the five during which I lived and taught in India – a fertile environment for the study and application of Old Testament ethics – I have continued to develop the thinking and wrestle with the issues first aired in *Living as the People of God*. This volume collects together a number of articles and booklets, all of which (with one exception, the essay on 'Human Rights') were published after that book. Because they were not originally prepared or published in direct relation to each other, there is bound to be a small amount of overlap and repetition between some of them. Much of this has been

7

removed in editing them for this collection, but I have also thought it best to let each essay retain much of its own original integrity, rather than apply too strict a homogenizing policy upon them.

While the collection has a primarily Old Testament focus, some of the essays do present a wider biblical perspective, and draw on New Testament resources as well. This is particularly so in chapters 1, 2 and 10.

I am grateful to the original publishers for permission to reprint the materials in this form: Inter-Varsity Press, Paternoster Press, Grove Books, Tyndale House, Doubleday Press, and the Theological Research and Communication Institute, Delhi. Details of the original publication are included in the footnotes for each chapter. Similarly, I am grateful to David Kingdon and Inter-Varsity Press for their willingness to make these essays more widely available by publishing them in this collected form. I also wish to express thanks to my secretary at All Nations Christian College, Mrs Carole Hudson, whose labours transferred some of the earlier typescripts on to computer disks and thus made my editing task enormously easier. Like Phoebe, she has been 'a great help to many people, including me' (Rom. 16:2). Like the household of Stephanas, however, it is my wife Liz and family to whom I owe perennial gratitude for the countless ways they 'refresh my spirit' (1 Cor. 16:18).

Ware, England   *Christopher J. H. Wright*
Easter 1995

Chief abbreviations

AS	*Assyriological Studies*
ASTI	*Annual of the Swedish Theological Institute*
BA	*Biblical Archaeologist*
Bib et Or	*Biblica et Orientalia*
BT	*The Bible Translator*
BTB	*Biblical Theology Bulletin*
BZAW	*Beiheft, Zeitschrift für die alttestamentliche Wissenschaft*
CBQ	*Catholic Biblical Quarterly*
CTJ	*Calvin Theological Journal*
EI	*Eretz Israel*
EJT	*European Journal of Theology*
EQ	*Evangelical Quarterly*
ERT	*Evangelical Review of Theology*
HUCA	*Hebrew Union College Annual*
IDB	*Interpreter's Dictionary of the Bible*, ed. J. A. Buttrick *et al.*, 4 vols. (Nashville: Abingdon, 1962)
JBL	*Journal of Biblical Literature*
JBR	*Journal of Biblical Religion*
JCS	*Journal of Cuneiform Studies*
JETS	*Journal of the Evangelical Theological Society*
JNES	*Journal of Near Eastern Studies*
JQR	*Jewish Quarterly Review*
JSOT	*Journal for the Study of the Old Testament*
JTS	*Journal of Theological Studies*
JTSA	*Journal of Theology for Southern Africa*
LXX	Septuagint (Greek version of the Old Testament)

MC	*The Modern Churchman*
NIV	New International Version
REB	Revised English Bible
RSO	*Revista degli Studi Orientali*
RSV	Revised Standard Version
SJT	*Scottish Journal of Theology*
TB	*Tyndale Bulletin*
TDNT	*Theological Dictionary of the New Testament*, ed. G. W. Bromiley, 10 vols. *(Grand Rapids: Eerdmans, 1964–76)*
TSFB	*Theological Students Fellowship Bulletin*
VT(S)	*Vetus Testamentum (Supplement)*

Part One

An approach to
biblical ethics

Chapter One

The use of the Bible in social ethics[1]

Introduction

Nobody doubts that Christian ethics must take account of the Bible. Ethics is applied faith. And Christian faith, of whatever tradition, stems from the Bible, however understood. Nobody doubts, either, that Christian faith has to do with the relationship between people and God. The word 'social', however, reminds us that it unavoidably also has to do with relationships between people – with people as social beings, with the Christian as part of wider human society, and with the Christian church as itself a society within society.

So how do we 'take account of the Bible' in working out our social ethics, in a way that is true to the nature and content of the Bible itself and also appropriate to the world we live in now? This, simply put, is one of the biggest issues facing the church in the modern world – the hermeneutical questions: how do we ascertain what the Bible is saying on current ethical problems? What authority do we give to it and how is it assessed? The answers to such questions have far-reaching effects on the church's understanding of itself and on the effectiveness of its mission in the world. What follows is simply a personal viewpoint on the matter, emerging from having wrestled with the questions in the company of many varied groups over the years.

There are two directions from which one may correlate the Bible with the realm of social ethics. The first (which may be called 'inductive') is to take a specific issue as one's starting-point and then to come to the Bible from it and with it. The second (which may be called 'deductive') is to start from within the Bible, studying in depth its narratives, laws, institutions, *etc.*, and then moving out from them to see how and where they apply to the whole range of issues we face. The first moves from an issue to the Bible; the second moves from the Bible to issues. Ideally, both processes should be in operation together in any serious Christian discussion of social ethics. I have found that the most profitable and effective groups I have been involved with are those where some members are deeply engaged in specific social fields, either professionally or through painstaking research and active involvement, and want to bring that specific concern under the light and authority of Scripture, while others have a deeper and more systematic understanding of the Bible which they are able to apply in a relevant and authentic way. In this essay I want to outline a method of using the Bible in each of these two directions, and then, thirdly, to show how the approaches I suggest seem, to me at any rate, to help 'bridge the gap' between a number of conflicting points of view in this field.

The Bible as story: a linear model

Put any group of Christians together to thrash out a specific social issue and sooner or later they will bring the Bible into the argument. All too often, however, this happens very haphazardly. Someone raises a verse, or an institution, or an event, from the Bible, to support a particular point. Someone else brings in another passage, perhaps quite unrelatedly; a saying of Jesus or a verse from Paul gets emphasized out of all proportion; other parts of the Bible are ignored altogether. Yet at the end, the group may be convinced that they have arrived at a 'biblical view' of their issue, confident that a few quotations amount to 'what the *Bible* says' on it.

The great failing of this practice is that it does not take the Bible seriously for what it is – that is, fundamentally a story, with a beginning, an end and a middle. The Bible begins with creation and ends with a new creation, and in between those two poles it presents the fact and effect of

14

the fall, and the long story of redemption in history. That is the nature of the canonical form of the Scriptures – the form in which God has chosen to give them to us. So if we wish to discover a 'biblical view' on any matter, we must surely seek to let the Scriptures speak as a whole – to respect their form as well as their content. That means bringing the matter into the light of each of the main phases of the Bible's story, in that way illuminating it from several different angles and arriving at a comprehensive and balanced assessment.

I find it helpful to visualize this biblical story as an actual line on which one can plot the different key points. The line might be further pictured as dropping and rising, as on a graph, to represent the fall, and the outworking of God's plan of redemption through history to the end of time, when, at the parousia, it 'leaps' to infinity with the final establishment of the kingdom of God in the new creation. But for our present purpose, a straight line will do. This then functions as a grid on which we can lay out the specific issue we are bringing to the Bible, so that we 'plot' the 'values' that emerge as we take the matter along the line and see what each key point of the story contributes to the total picture. (See diagram 1.) We shall set out the whole length of the line first, and then 'scale up' the redemption section to show its subdivisions.

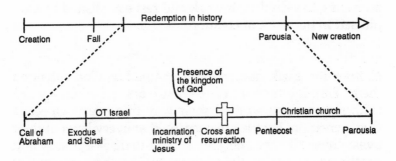

The four major 'co-ordinates' of our linear graph are creation, fall, redemption and the new creation. Let us briefly sketch in the contribution that each will make to an understanding of any issue in social ethics.

a. Creation

Creation is the foundation stone of all biblical faith and ethics. Among the fundamental principles which the early chapters of Genesis lay before us are the following (each with profound and varied ethical implications):

1. That God is sovereign over his whole creation, which he, as sole creator, fashioned with order and design, and in a condition that God called 'good'.

2. That humans, though part of the rest of the animal creation, are unique, having been made in the image of God. As well as the physical and intellectual dimensions of their constitution, therefore, they have a spiritual awareness of, and accountability to, God, and a capacity for social relationship which is also an expression of the image of God, deriving initially from their created sexuality.

3. That God has given the earth into the dominion of human beings. They are accountable to God as stewards both for the earth itself, with all its animal, vegetable and mineral endowment, and for the fair sharing of, access to, and use of, its resources by humankind as a whole.

4. That humans, in fulfilment of this role, are intended to engage in productive work, with all that it will entail, according to a rhythm of work and rest established by God himself in his work of creation.

b. Fall

Neither the earth nor people remained as God intended them. Through human disobedience and rebellion against God, sin and evil worked their way into every aspect of God's creation. People are corrupted at every level of their lives. Physically, they became subject to disease, decay and death; intellectually, they began to use their powers of reason to rationalize and excuse their own evil; spiritually,

16

they became alienated from God, 'dead in sin'; socially, every level of human relationship was fractured and disrupted – sexual, parental, social, societal, international. And the earth itself fell under the curse of God because of the sin of humanity, so that people find themselves at odds with and frustrated by their environment even as they endeavour, inescapably, to fulfil the role God assigned to them. The result is that in no area of ethical concern can we afford to overlook the effects of humanity's fallenness. Biblical social ethics begins with the idealism of creation first principles, but it continues with the realism of a fallen humanity. Mercifully, however, the line does not stop there.

c. Redemption

God chose neither to abandon nor to destroy the creation but rather to redeem it. And God chose to do so, not just by saving individuals out of the world (even the prototype of salvation, Noah, was saved *in* the world, and along with his whole family), but by a process that would embrace the whole of the rest of the history of the world and involve the creation of a new, redeemed community – first of all an actual nation, and then, out of them, a vast multinational community of his own people.

1. The story begins with *the call of Abraham* (Gn. 12). The contrast between the covenant made with him, by which there would be blessing for all the nations through his descendants, contrasts vividly with the story of Babel which precedes it, with its curse of scattering and confusion for the nations of mankind. The covenant with Abraham also included the promise of a land: the earth was not forgotten in God's purposes of redemption. Already we see the outline of a pattern we must study later – God, a people and a land, the first stage of a project of redemption that would bring together again God, humankind and the earth.

2. The next major point on the line of historical redemption is *the exodus* (Ex. 1 – 15). This was not only a demonstration of the incomparable power of Yahweh, Israel's God, it was also a remarkably comprehensive

foretaste of the scope of God's total redemptive purpose. In that one sequence of events God gave to Israel a fourfold freedom: politically, from the tyranny of a foreign, autocratic and oppressive power; socially, from the intolerable interference in their family life; economically, from the burden of enforced slave labour; spiritually from the realm of foreign gods into the freedom of unhindered worship of Yahweh and covenant relationship with him. Through that act, and the covenant and the gift of *the law at Sinai* (Ex. 20 – 24), God began to mould for himself his own people. They would be a 'priesthood' – a model people called out from among the nations, for the sake of the nations, to be a 'light to the nations', as the vehicle and paradigm of God's redemption (*cf.* Ex. 19:4–6). And so the rest of the Old Testament *history of Israel* unfolds before us, replete with the laws, the stories, the prophecy and the worship of the people through whom God eventually sent his own Son. Whenever, therefore, we bring any specific issue to the Bible, we must bring it to the light of the great principles as well as the earthy, concrete specifics of the Old Testament. Indeed, if it is a social issue, it is likely to be the Old Testament even more than the New that provides us with the most instructive and comprehensive range of data for the task of formulating a biblical ethic.

3. The line of history continues until 'when the time had fully come, God sent his Son, born of a woman ...' (Gal. 4:4). With the incarnation of God in Jesus the Messiah, two new factors enter the field of biblical social ethics: *the presence of the kingdom of God*, and the challenge of *the incarnational principle*. In Christ, the rule of God entered human history in a way not hitherto experienced, though long awaited in the eschatological expectation of Israel. The dynamic action of the kingdom of God in the words and deeds of Jesus and the mission of his followers was a power that changed lives, reversed personal standards and values, and presented the radical challenge of a new way – God's way – to the fallen structures of power and authority among humankind. But, in order to inaugurate his kingdom in this way, God had actually entered the world,

18

coping with all the limitations and frustrations of a fallen world as a particular human being. Then he laid his own incarnation before his church as the model for their mission: 'As the Father has sent me, even so I send you into the world.' A biblical social ethic which bears the mark of the incarnation will therefore enshrine a costly love that is identified and involved with the real plight of humanity, but it also takes courage from the knowledge that God in Christ has gone before us.

4. *The cross and resurrection of Jesus Christ* bring us to the centre and climax of the line of redemption in history, though not to its chronological end. Here is God's final answer to the total range of the power and effects of sin and evil. The Christian gospel presents us with an accomplished victory over the effects of the fall in every dimension of our lives – spiritual, intellectual, physical and social, as well in the cosmic realm. This has the crucial implication for our social ethics that in wrestling with the problems and brokenness caused by sin in the social realm, we are not struggling to *achieve* victory but to *apply* a victory already won. This is one of the critical factors which distinguish biblical social ethics from humanist or merely philanthropic principles, even when there is overlap in terms of practical ends and means espoused.

5. Just as the redemptive victory of the exodus led to the birth and moulding of a people for God, so the victory of Easter was followed by *the gift of the Spirit* at Pentecost and the birth of *the church*, God's new community in the world. With the expansion to include the Gentiles, the promise to Abraham was fulfilled – God had indeed brought blessing to all nations through his seed. This section of the historical line (which includes ourselves) contributes two important points to any ethical issue we are pursuing along this biblical grid: first the presence of the Holy Spirit making available to the Christian and the church the same power that filled the life and ministry of Jesus and that raised him from the dead; and, second, the existence of the church itself, the community of those who have responded to and entered the kingdom of God by repentance and faith in

19

Christ, the agent and witness of that kingdom both by the inner nature of its life and by the outward fulfilment of its mission in and to the world.

d. The new creation

The second coming of Jesus Christ will not only bring to an end the section of our line that signifies the redemptive work of God in history, but will inaugurate the complete fulfilment of its purpose – namely the restoration and redemption of God's whole creation. The future hope found in both Testaments of the Bible prepares us to expect that there will be final judgment and destruction of all that is evil and opposed to God's purpose, but also that beyond that judgment there lies a new creation – a 'new heaven and a new earth' – in which there will be righteousness and peace, and in which God will once more dwell with his people (cf. Is. 65:17–25; 66:22; Rom. 8:19–21; 2 Pet. 3:13; Rev. 21:1). This perspective generates within biblically based social ethics an irrepressible optimism; not a naïve optimism based on the illusion of human ability to solve our own problems eventually, but the optimism of faith-certainty that God cannot fail to complete the redemptive work he has already begun. It is an optimism which, without shedding any of the realism induced by a full appreciation of the fall, goes behind it to the will of the good creator and redeemer God. It believes that just as the chaos and brokenness of the fall was not the first word about humanity and the earth, so it will not be the last word either.

This, then, is the grid of the Bible's own story-line, to which we must bring our specific ethical issue. Each point or section of the line then sheds its light and informs our thinking, questions our assumptions, perhaps, and certainly challenges us afresh to action. Very often when, in a group or lecture, I am faced with the question 'Is there (or what is) a biblical position on this or that social issue?' I find myself saying, 'Well, now, let's go back to the beginning ...', and then drawing the issue steadily along the line I have outlined, refusing to be content until the issue rests in the light and perspective of our glorious future hope.

Creation provides our basic values and principles, the fixed points in the matter, by which we orientate the rest of the journey. The fall keeps us earthed in the reality of human stubbornness and a world under curse, preserving us from crippling disillusionment when things go wrong as they always do. The history, law and traditions of Old Testament Israel show us how God sought to work out his moral will in a specific historical and cultural context and provide us with a wide variety of actual responses to social, political and economic circumstances within the framework of theological assessment and critique.[2] The incarnation brings God right alongside us in our struggle, especially with the knowledge of the presence of the kingdom of God in the world. The cross brings the power of genuine reconciliation and a shalom (a state of peace and well-being) that breaks down the most intransigent social barriers (cf. Eph. 2:11–22). The life and mission of the church keep our eyes on the corporate nature of God's redemptive purpose and prevent us sliding into an individualistic frame of mind. Our future hope of the new creation sets a constant goal before us as a standard for our values and policies, and is the guarantee that our labour is not in vain, for the future belongs to the kingdom of God.

Benefits of this method

There are four main benefits in using the Bible in this way when bringing an issue inductively to it.

The first benefit is that this method is *canonical*; it respects the form, order and structure of the Bible itself. We have the highest example for such a method – that of Jesus himself on the road to Emmaus. Granted, it was not a matter of social ethics as such, but certainly it was a problem: the question of the identity, mission and destiny of the Messiah. Jesus takes the problem to the Scriptures, and works methodically and canonically through them, 'beginning with Moses ...' (Lk. 24:27). By the time he finished 'opening the Scriptures' in that way, their

Christology must have looked very different, even before they recognized their teacher. He had made himself the unitive, central focus of the whole canon. And this is not so far removed from social ethics as might be thought at first sight. For the calling of the Messiah was to embody Israel. His mission, as the Servant of the Lord, was identical to Israel's and included the bringing of righteousness and peace to humankind. He was the 'end-point' of the people of God in the Old Testament, and the 'beginning-point' for the messianic community of the New Testament people of God. He is the focal centre of the Israel of God in both Testaments. But the existence and mission of the people of God is an essential constituent in biblical social ethics. So by adopting a canonical approach we are able to keep in tune with the Christ-centred unity of the Scriptures which is just as important for ethics as it is for soteriology.

The second benefit of this approach is that it is *comprehensive*; it makes use of the whole range of the Scriptures and is thus much more likely to arrive at a balanced conclusion. In my experience, groups which are enabled to work out a biblical view on a specific issue in this way end up much more satisfied that they have achieved a balanced and truly biblical result. There are less likely to be dissenting quarrels that the Bible has been twisted, or some bits blown up out of proportion to fit in with a preconceived position.

Take, for example, the question of a Christian attitude to the state and secular forms of authority and power of all kinds. Some Christians' view on this matter begins and ends with Romans 13 – submission to authorities because they are appointed by God. Our approach would begin with the created diversity of the nations of humankind (*cf.* Acts 17:26; Dt. 32:8). But it would also analyse the extent of the infiltration of evil into human social organization, as typified in the corporate arrogance of the builders of Babel and the prophetic exposure of the oppression and injustice of personified empire states (Babylon, Tyre and Egypt especially) – with more than a hint of the spiritual, demonic forces at work within these political systems. It would include a study of the subtle and ambivalent assessment of monarchy in Israel – the fascinating interplay between divine anointing and human feet of clay – and the variety of responses that we find when the kings of Israel became virtually 'pagan' in their rejection and persecution of the true faith of Israel. Contrast, for example, Elijah's implacable hostility with Obadiah's political service (1 Ki. 18).[3]

We would then go on to examine the range of responses articulated within Israel when she faced life under the political authority of an external power, a position analogous to that of the church, namely as the people of God over against a third-party state. That would include Jeremiah's prayer for the peace of Babylon, the experience of Daniel in political office (compared, perhaps, with that of Joseph in Egypt), the opportunism of Nehemiah and Esther – all showing us that there is no single, clear 'biblical attitude' to the state, but a range of responses which depend on the nature of the situation.

Only then would we come to the New Testament, and first of all to Jesus, to see the impact of his message and example in the highly charged political world of his day, and of his own confrontation with political authority in his trial. Then Acts would show us the actual attitude and behaviour shown by the early Christian community towards both the Jewish and Roman authorities. The teaching of Paul and Peter is thus set in its practical and historical context. Finally, we would take account of the eye-opening eschatological vision of the kingdoms of humankind in Revelation (which draws much of its content and imagery concerning the destiny of the nations from the Old Testament). There we see the full potential horror of the demonic control of the state and the certainty of its judgment. But beyond the judgment, we would also see the breathtaking vision of all the riches and achievements and glory of the kingdoms of humankind being taken up, redeemed and purged, into the glory of the kingdom of our God and his Christ. This, of course, is merely an outline sketch of what would have to be a thorough and detailed study.[4] But the end result of such a study will be a biblically based social ethic concerning the state which, on the one hand, will be much more wholly and authentically biblical, and on the other, much more 'muscular' and usable in the complex world of wrestling as a Christian with the issues of political power and policy.

The third benefit of this approach is that it is *community-oriented*. It keeps us geared in to God's central purpose throughout the whole span of biblical history, which is the calling and creation of a people for his own possession, a new, redeemed humanity with whom he can dwell in his new, redeemed creation. Biblical ethics are therefore inescapably social, for the people of God exist as a society within society. And their reason for existence is to bear witness to the kind of social relationship between persons that God desires and, in the eschatological vision, will ultimately create in perfection, under the headship of Christ and through the reconciling power of his cross.

Westerners like myself have to undergo a certain reorientation in our habitual pattern of ethical thought in this matter if we are to see things from a biblical perspective. We tend to begin at the personal level and work outwards. We think of ethics as the means to the goal of a good and happy life. So our emphasis is to persuade people to live a certain kind of life according to this and that moral standard. If enough individuals live up to such a morality, then, almost as a by-product, society itself will be improved, or at least maintained as a safe environment for individuals to pursue their personal goodness. This is the kind of person you must be; that kind of society will result as a bonus.

However, the Bible tends to place the emphasis the other way round: here is the kind of society that God wants. His desire is for a holy people, a redeemed community living under his kingship according to his standards, a model society in whom he can display, as far as is possible in a fallen world, a prototype of the new humanity of his ultimate redemptive purpose. Now, then, if that is the kind of society God wants, what kind of person must you be to be worthy of your inclusion within it, and what must be your contribution to the furthering of these overall social objectives?

This is really just another way of expressing the fact that biblical ethics are *covenantal*. The covenant is between God and his whole people, but its moral implications affect every individual. In fact, our distinction between personal and social ethics is not always appropriate or helpful in biblical ethics, for personal ethics are 'community shaped', and the ethic of the redeemed community is that of a 'priesthood' – for the sake of the rest of human society. It is the nature of the community God seeks which governs the kind of person he approves. This community-orientated ethic must not, however, be taken in any way to diminish or replace the moral challenge to the individual to live uprightly before God – any more than the knowledge that God is saving a people for himself lessens the challenge to the individual to personal repentance and faith in Christ.

The fourth benefit of this approach is that it enables the Bible to be *contemporary*. This is so because we ourselves, like every generation of Christians, standing as we do between Pentecost and the parousia, are part of the Bible's own story-line. We are not detached observers striving to make sense of an alien ethos. We stand in organic spiritual continuity with the biblical people of God in both Testaments, a continuity which transcends the varying degrees of cultural discontinuity. Our story is part of their story. This was the principle by which New Testament writers could apply the ethics of the Old Testament to their Christian readers, even before the formation of the New Testament canon. This was Paul's understanding (*cf.* Rom. 15:4; 1 Cor. 9:9f.; 10:6, 11), and even more so, Peter's (*cf.* 1 Pet. 2:9ff.). Thus, by setting ourselves within the line of the Bible's story, we see that the great principles based on the ways and deeds of God with his people in the period of canonical history also apply to us.

The Bible as story is like a great 'unfinished symphony'; not the kind where the whole last movement is missing, for the last movement of God's symphony has already begun.

We live in the 'last days'. The decisive chords and theme have already been played in the victory of the cross, resurrection and ascension of Jesus Christ. Furthermore, the Bible also gives us the composer's own sketch of the grand finale, so that we know what the end will be like, though we do not know precisely when the composer (who is also the conductor) will intervene to bring it upon us. Meanwhile, he has commissioned us to continue the symphony, under his guidance, until he does so intervene. In the Bible we have the full score of the earlier movements, with such a wealth of recurring themes and variations, played on such a variety of human instruments, that it is quite sufficient to enable us work out the music of our own ethics according to the mind and will of the composer, confident in the assurance that the final resolution lies in his hands.

God, humanity and the world: a triangular model

We turn now to what is usually called the deductive method of biblical hermeneutics, that is, starting from within the Bible with detailed study of its content, and then moving out to see how and where the understanding so gained applies in contemporary social issues. There are two main problems here. One is the sheer quantity and variety of the biblical material before us; how do we go about bringing some kind of integration and organization into what we have to study? The other is to ensure that the way we apply it is valid, so that when we claim a biblical basis or justification for a particular stance or policy or action, we do so legitimately.

Again, it seems to me that our approach needs to be essentially simple and based on the pattern of primary relationships that we find in the Bible. I like to envisage these in the shape of a triangle formed by the interrelationships between God, humanity and the earth. (See diagram 2.) This triangle can be used not only as a framework for organizing the biblical material, but also, when the shape of the biblical material is appreciated, a model for expressing the relationship between the Testaments and for applying the biblical ethic to the contemporary world.

a. The creation triangle

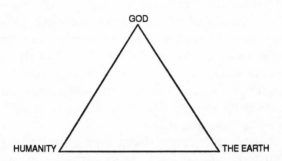

God, then, created the material earth and he saw that it was 'good'. The relationship between God and his non-human creation, animal, vegetable and mineral, is something we cannot rationally comprehend. But that a relationship of some kind does exist seems to be clearly implied in the Bible, by the delight of God in his creation, by its express dependence on him, by his involvement in the suffering of its lowliest members, according to the words of Jesus about sparrows and those of Paul about the frustration and labour pains of nature. And God created man and woman, an integral part of creation, but also, as the image of God, given dominion over the rest of it. Then God dwelt, 'walked and talked', with these persons in the midst of the earth he had given to them – a triangle of relationships that God saw as 'very good'.

The fall distorted and fractured the three relationships but did not destroy their underlying pattern. Thus, although the earth now labours under the curse of God and has been subject to (temporary) frustration by him, it is still actively sustained by him in the unfailing regularity of its seasons; animal and vegetable life is still fed and watered by his hand; the whole creation still bears its silent witness to its creator, declaring his glory and showing his handiwork. Likewise we humans, though alienated from

27

God in our sin and rebellion, find that we are still inescapably answerable to our maker, both for ourselves (as Adam found: 'Where are you?'), and for our neighbours (as Cain found: 'Where is your brother?'). Meanwhile God, in his grace, continues to provide for fallen humanity, sending his sun and rain on the just and the unjust, and preventing the sin of humans from reaching such global and corporate dimensions as to render life on earth intolerable (the lesson of Babel). And thirdly, humans remain committed to the task of subduing the earth, however much sweat it exacts from one's brow, while the earth, however reluctantly and stubbornly, still yields inexorably to their dominion.

This triangle then, comprising humanity (fallen) on the earth (cursed) under God, who remains in sovereign control, is the basic conceptual framework within which the Bible's portrayal of history, providence, redemption, faith and ethics operates. It is the foundational structure of the biblical worldview.

b. The redemption triangle (Old Testament)

Old Testament ethics are built around Israel's understanding of who and what they are, of their relationship to God, and of their own land. There is a triangular framework – God, Israel and the land – which corresponds to that which we have just seen between God, humankind and the earth. The laws, institutions, history and traditions of Israel – all that goes to make up their ethics – can be studied from three angles: theological, social and economic.[5] (See diagram 3.)

The *theological angle* reminds us that God is very much the apex of Old Testament ethics. God takes the initiative in grace and redemption and calls on men and women to respond, so that right from the beginning ethics are a matter of gratitude and response, not of legalistic obedience or merit. God also sets the agenda as far as the content of ethics is concerned: it is a matter of imitation of the character and ways of God. And it is God's redeeming grace and moral judgment which provide the motivation

28

and sanction behind the ethical commands. The moral sovereignty of God as redeemer is only an expansion and deepening of his moral sovereignty as creator. It is the same God at the apex of both triangles. This is worth remembering when some writers tend to drive a wedge between the creation and redemption aspects of biblical ethics – a point to which we must return later.

The *social angle* reminds us that God's plan of redemption, operating *within* the world of fallen humankind, was to choose and call out Israel, as a nation, among the nations, for the sake of the nations. Israel, the redeemed people, was a human society in every normal sense of the word – political, judicial, military, economic, *etc*. Right from the call of the father of the nation, Abraham, their life was lived on a very open stage indeed, at the crossroads of civilizations already ancient, unavoidably entwined with the affairs of international politics. Yet at the same time they were a distinctive nation, both in the sphere of their own religious self-consciousness as a 'holy nation', and in the realm of actual sociological fact. In many observable ways Israel's social system was distinct from, and in some cases apparently a deliberate reversal or rejection of, the accepted social norms and systems of their contemporary neighbours. Furthermore, this distinctive social shape of Israel was inseparably bound up with the nation's theological beliefs about their relationship with God and their role and mission as his people in the world.[6] The

29

social shape of Israel was not just a historical accident; it was in itself part of the pattern of redemption. Israel was not to be merely the vehicle of redemption, but a 'working model' of a redeemed community in a fallen world – 'a light to the nations'. They, the medium, were themselves part of the message.

The economic angle draws our attention to the very prominent place that the land occupies in the historical and theological traditions of Israel. The covenant with Abraham, which sets the pattern of the covenant of redemptive grace in both Testaments, includes it. The story of the fulfilment of that promise in the conquest and control of the land of Canaan occupies a substantial part of the Pentateuch and historical narratives up to the united monarchy. The gift and possession of the land was the largest single, tangible proof of Israel's covenant relationship with God, monumentally demonstrating his faithfulness to his promises, effectively signalling their total dependence on him, as regularly as each year's harvest. On the other side of the same coin, however, was the belief that the land was still owned by God (*cf.* Lv. 25:23). He therefore retained his moral authority over how it was allocated, used, shared, transferred, *etc.*

This principle of divine ownership of the land affected a very wide range of laws and institutions within kinship units; redemption procedures; sabbatical year laws; jubilee; harvest and gleaning rules, *etc.* It was a principle of great comprehensiveness, for it entailed the fact that anything you did on, with or to your land fell under God's moral inspection. The whole of life was there. This accounts for the very practical 'earthiness' of the Old Testament ethics.[7]

Now, with these three keystones of Old Testament ethics – God, Israel and the land – understood and in place, we can bring a measure of organizational coherence into our study of specific laws or institutions. So when we take up a particular case, we do not immediately jump to asking the question, 'How does this apply to me, or to the contemporary social scene?' Rather, we seek to set it within its own Israelite context, this framework, and assess its relevance and contribution to the overall model of Israel as God intended her to be. It is that whole model, and the principles drawn from it, which we must apply to our social ethics; the individual item is evaluated from the function it has (which will vary and may be quite limited) within the wider framework of Old Testament life and thought.

Supposing we take the *jubilee* (Lv. 25), which has been much used by evangelical social ethicists, and seek to work deductively from it. To what issues and in what ways can we 'apply' it?[8] By placing it within the triangular framework, the first thing we avoid is a 'one-track' interpretation which confines it to an economic instrument of alleged equalization of wealth. We might want to begin from the *social* angle, from which we would see that the jubilee is part of, and presupposes, a *kinship* system of social organization which, among other things, resulted in a wide distribution of social power and authority. Indeed, *the jubilee is primarily concerned with the family, not simply wealth*. Its provision for the restoration of land was for the sake of restoring social freedom and continued economic viability to the family units. That in turn opens up to us the fact of, and the reasons for, the centrality of the household unit within the Israelite social, theological and economic framework. Already the angle of our field of view, the field of deductive applicability, is widening considerably.

Then we might move round to the *economic* angle, from which we would see the jubilee in the context of the theology of the land, as briefly outlined above. We would be careful to analyse accurately the actual provisions of the jubilee institution, noting that it does not describe redistribution or equalization of wealth, but, more precisely, a restoration to an original *status quo*. That in itself, however, was very significant, because the original division of the land, by clans and families, had been designed to spread the ownership of land as widely as possible (*cf.* Nu. 33:54, and the division of the tribal lands 'according to their families' in Jos. 13ff., *e.g.* 15:1; 16:5; *etc.*). It was a kind of egalitarianism: not the sort which said that everyone must have exactly *the same* amount of property – an impossible geographical ideal – but that every family should have *sufficient* property to preserve its freedom and viability, and to enjoy to the full the tangible blessings of the inheritance that God had given to his whole people. We would see in the jubilee a restraint on economic growth that was really callous aggrandizement; a serious attempt to limit the destructive accumulation of debt; a mechanism to restore the dignity of meaningful social participation to those afflicted by poverty.

However, our deductions and application will be incomplete, and we shall have seriously undersold the full Old Testament understanding of the issue, unless we also move round to the *theological* angle. From there we see that the jubilee was one of a range of *sabbatical* institutions which were 'to the LORD' (Lv. 25:2, 4, *cf.* 12, 17). Their combined effect was to witness to the *sovereignty of God* in every sphere of life – over creation, time, history, nature and economic affairs. The jubilee would be kept only by those who were prepared to submit wholly in trust to the *providence of God* (Lv. 25:20–22). We also see that the text of the jubilee law in Leviticus 25 is shot through with references to the experience of *historical redemption* from Egypt, as motivation for obedience to a law which would require considerable material sacrifice for the sake of the less well-off (Lv. 25:38, 42, 55; 26:13). But the theological ethos of the jubilee was more than just historical memory; it included personal experience of *God's forgiveness*, for it began on the Day of Atonement (Lv. 25:9), and it attracted to itself an eschatological expectation, based on its twin themes of release and return, which fed into later messianic hopes (*e.g.* Is. 35:10; 61:1–2).

So then, if our deductive application of the jubilee is going to be faithful to the total Old Testament framework in which it is set, it will not only give rise to a range of desirable socio-economic objectives, though it certainly does do that. Applying the jubilee also includes laying before men and women the challenge of the total sovereignty of God, leading them to personal appropriation of atonement, and giving them the living hope of God's ultimate restoration. The jubilee, in other words, can function as a remarkable model of holistic concern for human need, theologically relevant to evangelistic endeavour as well as socio-economic reform.

c. Paradigmatic application

In applying the Old Testament in this way, we are taking it as a model or paradigm which can legitimately be brought to bear on issues of our contemporary world, with all appropriate allowances for cultural and historical differences. This paradigmatic approach is one which I believe is very useful as a means of releasing the message and potential of the Bible into our social ethics, and it is the methodological key to most of the essays in this book. It is explained further in chapters 2 and 4 below. In the context of the present argument, I would seek to justify it on two further grounds.

The first reason for advocating this method of applying the Old Testament was hinted at above in our discussion of the 'social angle' of our triangular framework – namely, the fact that the Old Testament itself asserts that part of God's purpose in bringing the nation of Israel into existence and in ordering their social life was in order to make visible his moral requirements on the rest of the nations. This understanding of Israel's role is expressed in God's address to them in the preface to the foundational Sinai covenant:

> Now if you obey me fully and keep my covenant,
> then out of all nations you will be my treasured
> possession. Although the whole earth is mine,
> you will be for me a kingdom of priests and a
> holy nation.
>
> (Ex. 19:5-6)

They were to be a priestly nation. A priest, in Old Testament thought and practice, stood between God and the people, a mediator in both directions. He represented God to the people, both in his own person and example of life and especially in his role as teacher of the law (*cf.* Dt. 33:10; Ho. 4:6; Mal. 2:5–7). Through the priests the word and will of God were to be made known to the rest of the people. Now if Israel as a nation were to be a priesthood, the implication is that they were to represent God to the nations in an analogous way. God's character, word and ways would be made manifest in their life as a nation. That is why the role for Israel expressed in verse 6 is linked so closely to the call for obedience to the covenant law in verse 5. It would be as they lived out the quality of national and social life demanded by the law they were about to receive, with its great chords of freedom, justice, love and compassion, that they would function as God's priesthood among the nations (*cf.* Dt. 4:5–8).

A second justification for this paradigmatic approach is triangular again! (See diagram 4.) It is the unmistakable correspondence between the 'redemption triangle' of Israel's faith (God, Israel and the land) and the 'creation triangle' (God, humanity and the earth). The latter, larger, triangle embraces the whole ongoing story of people on earth, and therefore includes ourselves 'on the bottom line', so to speak. The former, which was God's redemptive response to the disruption of his creative purposes, embraced the canonical history of Old Testament Israel and

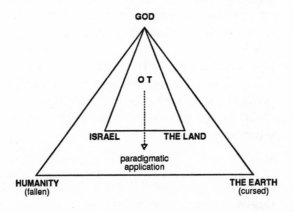

operated within, and still applies to, the outer, creation triangle of the fallen world.

The correspondence is not just a matter of contrived geometry. We have already seen that the choice and creation of Israel were for the sake of the nations of humankind, and that the promise of the land was included within the covenant with Abraham – that point at which God began the reversal of the global effects of sin illustrated in the story of Babel. In the case of the land, there are interesting similarities between the ethics generated by its relation to both God and Israel and those explicit or implied in the creation narratives about the earth as a whole. The twin themes of divine gift and divine ownership apply to the earth and to the land. The land was expressly God's gift to Israel on the one hand, the earth to humanity on the other (cf., on the latter, Ps. 115:16). Both are therefore a blessing meant to be enjoyed, shared, used and made fruitful. But at the same time, both are still owned by God. It is God's earth (Ps. 24:1); it was God's land. Humans are stewards of the earth, morally account-able to God for their use of it, just as Israel was accountable at every turn for what they did with their land. The earth fell under God's curse, and fallen humanity lives there in rejection of God. The land of Israel was to be the place of his abundant, luxuriant blessing and his redeemed people would live there with his presence dwelling in their midst. The correspondence is very evident.

Furthermore, the paradigmatic link between the two triangles is indicated by the fact that God worked out his redemptive purpose in the midst of the earth. He did not whisk those whom he redeemed off to another, unpolluted planet, still less to heaven itself. Israel (like the church, too, of course), though redeemed, was still part of fallen humankind; and the land of Israel was still part of the whole cursed earth. Unavoidably, therefore, we are led to see that what God did in and to them, what he demanded of them, is intended to relate to the wider stage of God's creation. Paradigmatic application of Israel's social and economic life is simply to reason thus: 'If that is what God required of Israel as a society, if that is how he demanded that they should use the portion of his earth that he gave to them, then, assuming his moral consistency, we can argue for social objectives and policies which are comparable in principle to Israel's, even in the wider world of fallen humanity around us.'

This way of assessing and applying the social life and institutions of Israel protects us from two opposite dangers. On the one hand, it means that we do not think in terms of literal imitation of Israel. We cannot simply lift the social laws of an ancient people and transplant them into our vastly changed modern world and try to make them work exactly as written. That would be like taking the paradigms of a grammar book as if they were the only words you could use in that language! The paradigms are there, not to be the sole means of communication ever after, but to be applied to the infinite complexities of the rest of the language. There has to be adjustment and imaginative reflection on what modern realities correspond in principle to realities addressed by Israel.

But on the other hand, a paradigmatic approach prevents us taking the view that the social system of Israel was relevant only within the confines of historical Israel and is therefore inapplicable in any way beyond that. There are those who argue that since the Old Testament laws and institutions were given to a redeemed people they cannot be extended in any valid way to unredeemed people; that is, they can be applied in the church, but not in the world. Now it is certainly true that the ethical thrust and challenge of the Old Testament needs to be directed at those who have come to share with Israel the title and responsibilities of God's redeemed people, namely that community of believing Jews and Gentiles we call the Christian church. I do not accept, however, that God gave us the Old Testament just so that its social challenge should be locked up in past history or within the confines of the church. On the contrary, if Israel was meant to be a 'light to the nations', then that light must be allowed to illuminate; the paradigm must be allowed to exert its authority over all our ethical 'inflections'.

d. Other methods of application

The reader may by this stage be wondering if I have forgotten that the title of this essay speaks of the 'use of the Bible', since I have, for some time, been engaging only with the Old Testament. This has been deliberate, because the nature of our use of the Bible itself in social ethics is very largely dependent on our assessment of the relevance of the Old Testament and our method of applying it (or our reasons for failing to do so). However, I also believe that once the patterns of relationships outlined above have been accepted and understood, they can be extended in a way that embraces the relevance of the whole of Scripture. I can do no more than mention two further points without development.

In addition, then, to the paradigmatic application of Old Testament texts, there is, secondly, the *typological* application of the Old Testament in the New. Certain events, persons, institutions, even objects, in the Old Testament are seen to have prefigured the new action of God in Jesus Christ. But there is a typological correspondence in the sphere of social ethics too. On the one hand, the church as the messianic community stands in organic continuity with Israel, and, as Peter most clearly saw, inherits the same role and responsibility in relation to the rest of the world. On the other hand, while the land as a slice of actual territory is given no further explicit theological significance in the New Testament, all that the land stood for in Israel's theology (tangible experience of God's blessing, inclusion and security within the covenant people, the inheritance of sonship, practical responsibility in fulfilling the socio-economic demands of brotherhood, equality, justice and compassion) finds its counterpart and fulfilment in the richness of Christian experience of fellowship 'in Christ'. *Koinōnia* in its full New Testament sense has some very concrete economic implications with deep roots in Old Testament land theology and ethics.[9] Yet another triangle serves to express this! (See diagram 5.)

There is, thirdly, the *eschatological* dimension of our

37

application, without which, as we emphasized in our first section, our biblical interpretation is incomplete. Both the Old and the New Testaments set before us the conviction that God's redemptive purpose, initiated through Israel

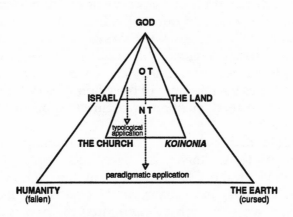

and their land, continued through the church and its life and mission, will ultimately embrace all nations and the whole earth in a redeemed, transformed and perfect new creation. The world of nations will turn to acknowledge the God of Israel and the Father of our Lord Jesus Christ, and live in peace and righteousness under his rule; the world of nature will be freed from the frustration of the curse and transformed by his miraculous power into the arena of blessing, harmony and fulfilment. There will, in short, be perfect shalom on the other side of divine judgment.

In terms of our diagram (one last triangle! See diagram 6), this means that the redemptive triangle will ultimately break through, or 'transcend' the triangle of fallen creation and the history of fallen humankind. That vision then 'rebounds', so to speak, back to our present life in the midst of this world. It provides a goal and incentive for our social ethics, just as in a comparable way, our expectation of the resurrection of the body has its retroactive effect on our

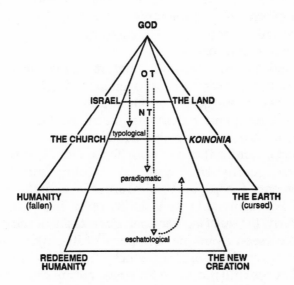

personal ethics in respect of our present life in the flesh.

I would offer this threefold framework of interpretation – paradigmatic, typological and eschatological – as a useful conceptual tool which enables us to release the potential of biblical ethics into the whole range of Christian concerns - for the world, the church, and for the ultimate future of both.

Bridging some gaps

The current revival of evangelical interest in social ethics is a matter of rejoicing, but one's joy is tempered by the divisions which still exist in various quarters over certain issues. There will always, of course, be a perfectly healthy spectrum of responses to various questions, but it seems to me that some of our differences are sadly due to an unnecessary polarizing in matters where a wholly biblical understanding demands inclusiveness: both-and, rather than either-or. This chapter has only sketched a personal approach, and makes no claim to resolve deep theological debates. However, as we look back over the two models I have outlined as a framework for inductive and deductive biblical ethics, we can already pinpoint a number of well-worn alleged opposites or dichotomies which our approach helps to reconcile.

We noticed, for example, that *the corporate and the individual* thrust must be held together, and not opposed to one another, in our gospel or our ethics. God's redemptive purpose throughout history has been the building of a people for his own possession, which, as we have seen, has wide social ramifications in both Testaments. But both the 'entrance requirements' and the ongoing 'membership requirements' (gospel and ethics) are alike addressed to the personal decision and responsibility of the individual.

Similarly, *the social and the evangelistic* tasks of the church have to be seen as inseparable parts of its single mission. On the one hand, evangelism which is faithful to the whole biblical gospel must include the social nature of the human constitution, the effects of sin in the realm of social life and relationships, and a challenge to repentance and conversion which has profound effects on that realm. The evangelistic preaching of the prophets and Jesus' own proclamation of the demands of the kingdom of God both include this social challenge. On the other hand (and this is the more neglected side of the matter), Christian social ethics cannot evade an evangelistic dimension if it is being true to the total biblical basis, motivation and goal of its operations. We hinted at this when we set the jubilee within all three angles of its Old Testament ethics framework.

The jubilee, because of its network of links with Israel's theology and ethics of land, family and social structure, is one of the richest sources for deriving biblical objectives over a wide range of socio-economic issues, and we are quite right to apply it paradigmatically in that sphere. But the jubilee was based on God's universal sovereignty and motivated by his acts of redemption. A full biblical application of it, therefore, must involve bringing men and women to face and accept the sovereignty of God and to experience the totality of his redemption – which is nothing short of evangelism. Precisely such a unified and integrated adoption of the jubilee characterized the public ministry of Jesus: socially effective evangelism; evangelistically effective social action.

How many wasted and fruitless hours of argument in Christian gatherings, especially in missionary councils and conferences, over the imagined competing claims of evangelism and social action would be saved, if it could be seen not only that a fully biblical understanding of mission includes them both, but that in fact each necessarily involves the other in biblical thought?

This leads to reflection on another unfortunate dichotomy in some evangelicals' thinking – that between *the Old and the New Testaments*. It was in a missionary gathering that I heard the view expressed that the church should have nothing to do with the socio-political or socio-economic spheres, on the grounds that there was no mention of such things in the mission given to the church in the New Testament. Passing over my first reaction (which was that that was a very superficial view of the New Testament itself and of the impact of the mission and message of Jesus, and that even if it were true, what did God give us an Old Testament for, then?), there is a much weightier reason for refusing to allow the Old Testament to be cut adrift from the New in that way. It is, simply, that Jesus was the Messiah.

As we saw earlier in our linear model, the Messiah is the focal point of unity of both Testaments. As the Servant, he embodied Israel, the people of God. He thus inherited, *and*, by implication, passed on to the new messianic community founded by and 'in' him, the social role and *raison d'être* of Old Testament Israel. Even if we took the Old Testament as nothing more than a quarry of messianic proof-texts, as is still the habit of some, we have to take account of the fact that the messianic prophecies include much more than predictions of the birth and death of Christ. Some of them are detailed descriptions of the *content* of his mission also,

41

which is said to have an explicitly social dimension. He will bring justice, overthrow oppression, dispense knowledge of, and create obedience to, the law of God, build lasting peace among people as he brings them to acknowledge God, *etc.* Now although Jesus himself (Lk. 4:18f.) and the evangelists (*cf.* Mt. 12:17–21) saw this as a dimension of his mission, clearly the fulfilment of such prophecies was not exhausted in his earthly life. To what, then do we refer them? Should we postpone their relevance only to his second coming, when, of course, they will be perfectly fulfilled? Is there not a strong case for seeing in them a programme and objectives for the ongoing messianic community whom he sent into the world as he had been sent, who 'have the mind of the Messiah' and the same Spirit as anointed him? In other words, our concern for justice and peace, indeed all our social ethics, must be messianic – as messianic as our gospel itself. In that way we shall preserve the proper unity and integrity of both Testaments of the Scriptures.[10]

Finally, I believe that the approach I have suggested may help to bridge a divide among evangelicals which, to my mind, is one of the saddest and most unnecessary: that is, between the advocates, respectively, of a *creation approach and a kingdom of God approach* to social ethics.[11] 'Creationists' (nothing to do with evolution, in this context!) argue that in the creation ordinances and the basic moral law God has given us a sufficient basis for formulating our social ethic. Furthermore, because they are creation-based 'maker's instructions', as it were, they apply to all persons and can therefore be advocated by Christians to secular society, not on overtly Christian grounds, but simply because they work best for the good of society. 'Kingdomists' argue that the arrival of the kingdom of God among people in the ministry of Jesus introduced a radical challenge to the whole present world order with its myriad social, economic and political structures, of every level. Christians, as followers of Jesus who have 'entered the kingdom of God', are meant to bear witness to it by a corporate lifestyle and by programmes of social involvement which embody a rejection or reversal of the values and standards of the world; that is, to 'live the life of the kingdom of God' in the midst of the present world.

Creationists then complain that the kingdomists exaggerate the importance of the idea of the kingdom of God in the New Testament, and that they take an unduly pessimistic and negative attitude to human society and the structures of authority within it. Because the ethics of the kingdom of God really apply only to those who have entered it, creationists claim that kingdomists are unable to give a convincing content and rationale to a 'kingdom ethic' as addressed to a mixed and secular society, except in terms that are drawn from, and would be better kept in, a creation context.

Kingdomists, in return, complain that the creationists do not take seriously enough the radical effects of the fall on the whole of human social order. They do not give sufficient weight to the centrality of the kingdom of God in the self-understanding and teaching of Jesus or to the role of the church as the agent of the kingdom of God in the world. They, also, are unable to build a complete and coherent 'creation ethic' without drawing in material, such as the Ten Commandments, which actually comes within a redemptive context in the Bible – that is, material given to the redeemed people of God who, covenantally, have accepted his sovereignty; in other words, from a 'kingdom' context canonically.

My complaint is that both sides are unhelpfully polarizing the unity of the Bible in an attempt to align its support with their own emphasis and vision. Generalizations are always very dangerous, of course, but I think it would be fair to say that advocates of 'creation ethics' *tend* to lean to the conservative end of the political spectrum, while advocates of 'kingdom ethics' *tend* to espouse more radical ideals of changing the structures of society itself. Now I am not suggesting that such diversity of conviction is in itself regrettable. The Bible both allows and illustrates a variety of responses, within limits, to fallen human society and its authorities and powers. I have nothing against spectrums! But I do believe it is fundamentally a theological misuse of the Bible, however unwitting, to pursue one's own perceptions by exalting either of these important aspects of the biblical revelation (or any other aspect) to a dominant status which excludes or diminishes the relevance of the other. That it is mistaken to try to do so is shown by the impossibility of carrying either emphasis through consistently without 'borrowing' from the other side. As we saw, each approach inevitably implicates the other when it comes to giving practical content to its position. But this is hardly surprising, since it is obvious, though one fears it is overlooked, that the God who is creator is the same God who is redeemer-king. So there is bound to be considerable continuity and overlap between the ethical content of both spheres, given the moral consistency of God and the fixity of his moral purpose for humanity.

There is a weightier consideration than that more or less formal point. The redemptive work of God, running through both Testaments, is a restorative response to the failure of humankind to fulfil God's creative purpose for them. The full tragedy of the fall is that men and women are not only unwilling, but also unable, to live by the creation ordinances, though they remain as perpetually valid moral guidelines for human life on earth. The purpose of the ethical provisions given in the context of redemption, which include both the covenant law of the Old Testament and the ethics of the kingdom of God in the New, is to restore to humans the desire and the ability to conform to the creation pattern – God's original purpose for them. (This brings in 'image Christology': Jesus being the perfect image of God and believers being formed into his image – *i.e.* restored to our true humanity. It is also evident, as we saw, in the correspondence of the redemptive and creative triangles: redemption, including the operation of the kingdom of God, is the restoration of creation by the reversal of the effects of the fall.) Thus, for example, the economic laws of the Old Testament are full of values and ideals that we associate with creation –

44

stewardship, sharing, equality, *etc*. But at the same time they reckon with the socio-economic effects of the fall, the inroads of injustice, inequality and poverty. Therefore they include restorative measures and attempts to reverse undesirable economic forces, coupled with a demand not simply for sharing, but for material sacrifice where necessary, motivated by the experience of redemption. Only thus could creation ideals actually be approached. Similarly, the kingdom of God teaching on social relationships enshrines creation values – the worth of each individual, mutual love, harmony between individuals, fundamental human structures of relationship such as the family, *etc*. But, in view of our fallen nature, it presupposes the need not only for the experience of redemption (new creation in Christ), but also for the 'reversal virtues' – self-denial, mutual service, leadership by servanthood, forgiveness, forbearance, *etc*.

So the two themes interpenetrate each other. We cannot advocate the 'maker's instructions' in fallen human society without at the same time both proclaiming and living out the 'redeemer's commands'. Otherwise we set up an unbiblical dualism between our social ethics and our evangelism. Nor can we strive to advance the kingdom of God without acknowledging that our redeemer-king is also the sovereign creator, preserver and disposer of all people, whose providence still governs the affairs, structures and history of his fallen creation.

God as creator makes our biblical social ethics credible, workable and applicable to all persons and all creation. God as redeemer-king gives our social ethics the only sufficient motivating force, the only efficient power to achieve real and beneficial moral change in conformity with God's will, and the only unfailing guarantee that, in this sphere too, 'our labour is not in vain in the Lord'. For the future belongs to the kingdom of God, which, in its consummation, will be nothing less than a new creation.

Chapter Two

The authority of Scripture in an age of relativism

Old Testament perspective[1]

Introduction

This essay is not an attempt to rewrite a doctrine of Scripture by redefining its authority, but is more a personal testimony as to how I see that authority functioning in two areas with which I am professionally concerned. The phrase 'the authority of Scripture' is commonly used in a prescriptive sense, namely that the Scriptures tell us what we must believe and what we must and must not do. They have an authority over our minds and our actions because they come from the one who is Lord of both.

A somewhat different, though doubtless complementary, perception of authority stimulated my thinking through reading Oliver O'Donovan's programmatic survey of evangelical ethics, *Resurrection and Moral Order*. He defined authority as that which constitutes a sufficient ground for acting.

> Authority is the objective correlate of freedom. It is what we encounter in the world which makes it meaningful for us to act. An authority, we may say, is something which, by virtue of its kind, constitutes an immediate and sufficient ground for acting. If someone listens to music, joins a club, or reads philosophy, his action requires no explanation. Beauty, community and truth are sufficient grounds for action in themselves. They make action undertaken in relation to them immediately intelligible.[2]

O'Donovan argues that the created order itself, coming from the hand of God, provides that range of authority within which we are free to act in a great variety of ways, for authority is the precondition of freedom. The authority of the Scriptures lies, at least in part, therefore, in their revelatory witness to that created order and the God who stands behind it.

I was led therefore to ask myself in what ways the Scripture 'authorizes' my own action in God's world. It happens that I teach the Hebrew Scriptures with particular emphasis on ethics and mission, in a college which specializes in training people for cross-cultural Christian life and mission. Both of those activities – assessing and evaluating ethical stances and seeking to understand and critique divergent cultures – raise questions of authority. Both of them, I hope to show, find adequate authority in the Old Testament.

1. In an age of moral relativism

Any course of study on ethics has to spend considerable time on the analysis and critique of the varieties of moral relativism in the air today. From the pop culture's 'If it feels OK and nobody gets hurt, who can say it's wrong?' to the more sophisticated forms of subjectivism, existentialism, situationism and utilitarian consequentialism, the common dogma is that there is no transcendent authority by which absolute right or wrong, good or evil, can be determined *a priori*. Morality is relative. 'It all depends ...' on any number of things. Against this climate of moral relativism, the Christian affirms the authority of Scripture. But the simple affirmation by itself will not get us very far, since the issue of what the authority of Scripture (especially of the Old Testament) actually means in practical ethical decision-making has dogged the church since its beginnings.

a. Authority in relation to history

The Scriptures give us authorized grounds for acting, not merely because they tell us what Israel or the early

Christians thought or how they articulated their own moral perceptions, but because they claim to record what God has actually done in history. This is how the Hebrew Scriptures characteristically underwrite the authority of particular laws: 'This is how you must act because this is what Yahweh has done.' The Ten Commandments begin that way – with a historical indicative referring to God's action in delivering Israel from Egypt. The 'motive clause', so distinctive a feature of Israelite law, regularly cites historical precedent or model for the particulars of the law.

The point here is not that there are vague moral lessons to be learned from the past (a truth which probably all human cultures would endorse in general), but that certain specific moral distinctions are made between some kinds of behaviour which are mandated and others which are prohibited on the authority of concrete historical events which are attributed to the action of Yahweh. If one meaning of authority is that which provides a sufficient ground for acting, then we are right in referring to the authority of history, provided it is interpreted (as of course it is in the Scriptures), within a theological framework which discerns the action of God. Thus the law is not content to remain on the level of moral ideals such as 'You shall be holy', even backed up by the theological affirmation, 'for I Yahweh your God am holy', but concretely commands, 'You shall love the alien (with all concomitant rights and privileges that flow from that stance) because I Yahweh your God love the alien, and (in effect) proved it by the historical act of delivering you from Egypt' (cf. Lv. 19:33f.; Dt. 10:19ff.). God's action creates the authority by which it is right to behave in certain ways to aliens. Conversely his action is what makes it wrong to behave otherwise to them. In other words, the moral authority of biblical history is not just that it happened (for, as O'Donovan points out, all historical events are unique and would have no compelling moral authority in themselves), but rather that in it God chose to act in a way which gives meaning and purpose to all history (climaxing in the resurrection) and to reveal the meaning and implications of

49

his action for our moral guidance.

The importance of the concrete historical basis of biblical faith and ethics has often been contrasted with abstract, cyclical, or pantheistic religious worldviews. For that reason it has become increasingly relevant in facing the challenge of New Age thinking. Recently I was conducting some seminars on the Old Testament theology of the land, and the observation was made how apparently similar many of the scriptural assertions and imagery concerning the land were to the way New Age philosophy talks about the earth. Examples abound in the Hebrew Scriptures of the personification of the land. It rejoices, it mourns, it can vomit, it can be addressed and respond, it suffers but can be refreshed and enjoy sabbath rest. But are we dealing here with the personal world spirit, or the divine 'Gaia'? Nothing could be further from the Hebrew conception. The reason the land could be spoken of in personal terms was not that it in itself was personal or because of any magical or mythological view of it, but because it was the stage on which the personal relationship between Yahweh and Israel was enacted in specific historical events that took place upon it. [3]

In our seminars we observed that even the festivals of Israel which were most closely linked to the land and its fruitfulness were consistently given a historical reference or justification. That is, the recurrent cycle of nature was celebrated as it ought to be, but it was attributed to the God who, more importantly than the harvest he had just given, had at a specific point in the past acted in justice and redemption to give them the land on which they could have harvests of their own at all (Dt. 26). Similarly, all the moral requirements which we might broadly label ecological – relating to land use, harvests, concern for animals, trees and resources – were based on the authority of Yahweh's action in history, not on some innate divine properties in the soil itself. In fact, by being rooted in history rather than in the soil they proved much more morally durable, both in resisting fertility cults which tend to dominate when the religion of the soil is divorced from response to the God of justice in history, and in surviving the loss of particular turf (as Brueggeman calls it),[4] in the exile.

So the insistence of the Scriptures that God himself has acted in history and has thereby constituted moral criteria for human action in history is a major feature of biblical ethics, which sets it against the hyper-individualism of existentialism in which every individual must reinvent the moral wheel for himself in each moment of decision, and the hyper-corporatism of New Age super-consciousness which virtually dissolves personal morality as most pantheisms ultimately do.

b. Authority in relation to creation

At the same time as we stress the centrality of the scriptural affirmation concerning the moral authority of God's action in history, we need to give adequate attention to its portrayal of God as creator, with all its implications for our worldview. An emphasis on history alone, without the safeguards of the biblical creation faith, could deliver us into the kind of historial relativism which puts all things, morality included, at the mercy of the historical process. This is a danger which O'Donovan also warns us of, insisting that the only proper protection from it is the biblical affirmation of a given order of creation which, though disturbed by the fall, is still the order within which we live, and which will finally be restored to its perfection and glory through God's redemptive action. That redemption of creation has already been anticipated in the resurrection of Christ and will be completed at his return.

> That which most distinguishes the concept of creation is that it is complete. Creation is the given totality of order which forms the pre-supposition of historical existence. 'Created order' is that which is not negotiable within the course of history, that which neither the terrors of chance nor the ingenuity of art can overthrow. It defines the scope of our freedom and the limits of

51

our fears. The affirmation of the psalm, sung on the sabbath which celebrates the completion of creation, affords a ground for human activity and human hope: 'The world is established, it shall never be moved'. Within such a world, in which 'The Lord reigns', we are free to act and can have confidence that God will act. Because created order is given, because it is secure, we dare to be certain that God will vindicate it in history. 'He comes to judge the earth. He will judge the world with righteousness and the peoples with his truth' (Ps. 96:10, 13).[5]

The importance of keeping a firm grasp on the creation base is to be seen first of all in its anchoring of the gospel itself. An immense amount has been written and said in recent years about the need to see how the gospel takes root in different historical and cultural contexts. In fact, the gospel cannot be understood and responded to apart from the context within which it is heard. We cannot escape our existence in some context or other. But while culture and context will assuredly shape our understanding, reception, response and formulation of the gospel, they do not in themselves determine its fundamental content. This is so for two reasons at least.

First, because the gospel is in essence good news about something, which has happened. It is not an ideology or even a theology, but simply the announcing of an event: namely, the birth, life, death and resurrection of Jesus of Nazareth. The culture and context of the person or group to whom that announcement is made will shape their perception of it and their response to it, but cannot change the factual reality of it. We will discover in ever-changing contexts what the good news *means* for specific peoples, but we will not rediscover what actually happened which makes it to be good news in the first place.

52

Second, because the gospel is in fact the restoration, redemption and reconciliation of *creation* by God and to God. And the creation is something *given*. That is, there is a reality, an order to human life on the earth under God which we did not invent. In our human history we have messed it up by our sin and rebellion. But it is still 'there', and we cannot escape it or change it any more than we can get outside our own createdness. And it is that given reality which is the object of God's restoration (because it has been spoiled), his redemption (because it is enslaved and lost), and his reconciliation (because it is broken, divided and alienated). There is, therefore, a *givenness* about the gospel also, derived from the givenness of creation. Our evangelism and social action together must be culturally and contextually *relevant* in any historical location, but they are not *dependent* on culture, context or history. We did not invent creation, but we are called to live responsibly within it. Neither did we invent the gospel or discover it, but we are called to live obediently to it ... If there were nothing given and universal about the gospel, we would not be able to recognize it when it impacts a particular context.[6]

What is true of the gospel is true of the ethic which is integral to it. And what is true in New Testament terms was true also in the Old Testament. The levels and dimensions of meaning in the exodus event, for example, could be appreciated in different ways through Israel's history, but nothing could affect the basic historicity of the event itself.

Similarly, whatever the culture or whatever the juncture of history, we all have to live in God's created world as his human creatures. There is a basic shape to that world which we did not invent, and therefore a corresponding shape to the moral response required of us if we are to live within it with the kind of freedom which, by God's so ordering, it authorizes. Morality, in biblical terms, therefore, is preconditioned by the given shape of creation, which underlies and precedes the relativity of cultural responses to it within history.

The heart of our complaint, then, against those who assert that morality is historically and culturally relative *per se* is that they themselves absolutize that which is relative, (the historical process), and relativize that which is absolute (the order of creation).

> Classical Christian thought proceeded from a universal order of meaning and value, an order given in creation and fulfilled in the kingdom of God, an order, therefore, which forms a framework for all action and history, to which action is summoned to conform in its making of history. Historicism denies that such a universal order exists. What classical ethics thought of as a transhistorical order is, it maintains, itself a historical phenomenon. Action cannot be conformed to transhistorical values, for there are none, but must respond to the immutable dynamics of that history to which it finds itself contributing.[7]

The biblical authority, then, for our ethics in a world of moral relativism, is based on its twin affirmation of creation and history: creation as the fundamental order that shapes our existence in history, and which is destined for restoration in the new creation of the kingdom of God; and history as the stage on which we observe the acts of the God whom we are commanded to imitate by 'walking in his ways'.

2. In an age of cultural relativism

We live in a multicultural world. That was always true, of course, but it is now much more a part of modern self-consciousness than before. Our cities are polychrome and polycultural. Television, coffee-table books and travel

54

to more exotic holiday locations, all bring us into contact with cultures previously unknown. The effect on the popular mind has been a greater awareness of the plurality of human culture and a questioning of the assumptions of the superiority of any one culture. True, Western culture still seems determined to flood the world, but the motive is probably more nakedly commercial self-interest than the self-conscious cultural superiority that characterized previous eras. Then, colonial exploitation accompanied the assumption of a duty to spread 'civilization'. The exploitation continues but our consciences are soothed by a feeling that at least we respect other cultures more now – or we would like to think we do.

a. Relativizing the relativizers

Or at least, we have become highly critical of those whom we suspect of not respecting other cultures, or worse, of destroying them, whether by destroying their habitat (as in the current concern for the rainforests and their inhabitants) or by religious conversion. Thus, the BBC television series *Missionaries* started out from its opening footage with the unqualified assertion that missionaries ever since Paul have been marked by an 'arrogance' which confidently sees all cultures other than (Western) Christian culture as both sinful and inferior and therefore to be attacked and replaced.

Now if we take the missionary expansion of the church as a test case, we may agree that in many instances missionaries made judgments about other cultures which were based not so much on essential Christian and gospel values as on their own cultural assumptions.[8] But were they mistaken in making any judgments at all? Their judgments may have been faulty and laden with unexamined assumptions of Western superiority, but is it illegitimate to criticize any features of a culture on any grounds? The underlying assumption of series like *Missionaries* seems to be that it is. No culture has the right to criticize another, and to do so in the guise of religion is both arrogant and destructive.

However, even before going on to see whether the Bible gives us authority for a critical examination of cultures, it is worth pointing out that the stance of those who produce a series like *Missionaries* is not itself culturally neutral. These critics of the criticizers of other cultures are themselves the children of a particular culture, with hidden and unexamined assumptions, namely those of post-Enlightenment secular humanism, which, having relegated religion to the realm of the subjective and out of the realm of factual reality, itself affirms the dogma of religious relativism and rules out *a priori* as arrogant and self-righteous any claim to ultimate truth. For devotees of *these* enormous assumptions to criticize those who criticized other cultures on the basis of *their* assumptions of what cultural dress was appropriate for Christianity is rather like the blind criticizing the blind.

As Richard Niebuhr has helpfully clarified, there are a variety of ways in which the relationship between the Christian gospel and human culture may be expressed, in theory and practice.[9] Evangelicals committed to the authority of Scripture will affirm that in whatever way the relationship is nuanced, the basic order is that it is the gospel which judges the culture. All culture is a human product and therefore manifests both the dignity of the image of God and the depravity of human fallenness. So while we may not be in a position to make judgments upon other human cultures from the horizontal viewpoint of our own (we may at least be grateful to the relativizers for challenging and undermining all forms of cultural or racist superiority), the revelation of God in Scripture and Christ gives us an elevation (which of course is neither of our own creation nor to our own credit), from which such a critique can be made.

At this point, however, we will be told that the Bible itself is culturally contextual. The Scriptures we take as our authority come from not one but several cultures over a vast span of history all very remote from ourselves. How then can religious responses in a remote cultural context carry the authority for us to stand in judgment on modern cultures? For some scholars, such as D. E. Nineham, the culture gap is too great for even Jesus to have the kind of moral authority traditionally attributed to him.

Our answer has to begin with the same two points that were stressed in the first section of this chapter. The Scriptures claim that God has acted in history. The faith of Israel, therefore, was not just a cultural feedback but a response to objective events which they witnessed and participated in. The Scriptures which grew within their cultural context were therefore not merely (though inevitably) shaped by that culture (in language, background, imagery, *etc.*), but stood in constant dialogue, and often conflict, with it, shaping and moulding it in terms of the values of Yahweh himself. And the God who thus acted within the historical development of that culture was none other than the creator of humanity and the world. Hence, the direction in which God acted to shape or refine the historical culture of God's people was in line with the structure of created order underlying God's will for all human life in his world.

b. Israel as a paradigm for evaluating cultures

It is at this point that the relevance of Israel as an actual historical society becomes most apparent. God chose to act through a human community, which, from its beginning in the election of Abraham, was to be a distinctive people, committed to God's own way in the midst of a world going its own way.

> I have chosen him, so that he will direct his children and his household after him to keep the way of the LORD by doing what is right and just, so that the LORD will bring about for Abraham what he has promised him (Gn. 18:19).

God's purpose of blessing for humanity as a whole is the goal and purpose both of the election of Abraham and also of the moral requirement upon Abraham's descendants (and this was said before Isaac was even conceived!).

Similarly, at the point of the constitution of Israel as God's own covenant people, at Sinai, their identity and mission to be a priesthood in the midst of the nations of the whole earth are linked to the moral demand to be a holy (distinct) community through obedience to the covenant law (Ex. 19:6). God chose, therefore, to make a people the locus of God's historical revelation and saving activity. And that people was intentionally and self-consciously to be a light to the nations.

Elsewhere I have used the word 'paradigm' to describe this feature of biblical Israel.[10] It seems to me both to sum up what God intended in creating Israel and then giving them laws and institutions that shaped their culture, and also to be a fruitful concept in helping us work from the Hebrew Scriptures to our own situation. When I first used the term, I had in mind its usage in grammar. Paradigm verbs or nouns may be used to show how other words behave in different syntactical arangements within a language. The paradigm then functions to enable the language learner to achieve grammatical correctness in the use of all the other words he may want to use. The words and contexts will be of infinite variety, but the shape of the paradigms can be seen in each new sentence.

Recently I came across the use of paradigms in a very different context, but one which struck me as helpful in developing further the point I wish to make. Vern Poythress, in his study of *Science and Hermeneutics*,[11] makes use of Thomas Kuhn's seminal work, *The Structure of Scientific Revolutions*,[12] in which he rejected the classic view of the progress of science, the view associated with Baconian scientific method. Kuhn argued that science did not advance merely by a step-by-step inductive method.

> Research on specific problems always took place against the background of assumptions and convictions produced by previously existing science. In mature science, this background took the form of 'paradigms', a cluster of beliefs, theories, values, standards for research, and

58

exemplary research results, that provided a framework for scientific advance within a whole field.[13]

Poythress goes on to distinguish two senses in which Kuhn uses the word 'paradigm'. On the one hand it can denote 'the entire constellation of beliefs, values, techniques, and so on shared by the members of a given community'. On the other hand, it designates 'concrete puzzle-solutions', that is, actual results of experimentation that provide models for further research by suggesting ways of problem-solving for a large number of unsolved problems. Poythress prefers to distinguish the two by using 'disciplinary matrix' for the first and 'exemplar' for the second. It seems to me that both senses of the word 'paradigm' can be fruitfully used in understanding how the Old Testament functions authoritatively for us, particularly in the matter of evaluating human cultures.

In the first place, the emergence of Israel introduced a new paradigm of beliefs and values into the ancient Near Eastern world. This is not to suggest that somehow Israel was exotic, with no religious or cultural links in its own environment. Vast amounts of comparative scholarship have shown the extent of the interaction between Israel and her contemporary world – as one would expect. Nevertheless, it is equally apparent that in certain key areas Israel was *different*, consciously and deliberately. The requirement that they should be a 'holy people' emphasized this distinctiveness. Among the features of this revolutionary new worldview one could include, as a bare minimum list:

1. Israel's monotheism, emerging first perhaps as mono-Yahwism, but certainly developing into a fully-fledged commitment not merely to the uniqueness of Yahweh, but also to his sole deity.

2. The characteristics of Yahweh as the God described above – *i.e.* one who is Lord of creation and also acts in history.

3. The values expressed through Yahweh's action in history, made explicit through the exodus and then

consolidated in Israel's own law – concern for the vulnerable and oppressed, commitment to justice, rejection of idolatry and its associated social evils.

4. A covenantal conception of social structure with remarkable effects in the political sphere – especially the way Israel translated their belief that Yahweh was their king (a common enough belief among ancient nations, as Millard Lind has shown)[14] into the practical rejection of human kingship for several centuries and a theoretical limit on its power when it did emerge.

5. A belief in the divine ownership of the land which produced a drive towards economic justice and inverted the dominant pattern of land ownership.

6. A belief in Yahweh as creator and sustainer of the natural order which desacralized whole areas of life such as sexuality, fertility (of land, herds and wives) and even death.

These are just some of the contours of the paradigm. This was the overall matrix of beliefs, values and assumptions which shaped historical Israel.

In the second place, Israel itself was a paradigm, in Kuhn's second sense; *i.e.* a concrete model, a practical, culturally specific, experimental exemplar of the beliefs and values they embodied. Now nobody would want to deny what the Hebrew Scriptures themselves make very clear, that Israel failed to be all that they believed themselves called to be in terms of their own covenant, law and social institutions. Nevertheless, it is a simple historical fact that in the transition from Bronze to Iron Age in Canaan a society emerged with some radically different forms of social, economic and political life, integrally linked to a very distinctive form of religious belief. They called themselves Israel and the people of Yahweh, and they succeeded for several centuries to prove, for example, that a theocracy could actually work without a human king; that land could be possessed and enjoyed to the full without being treated merely as a commercial asset, to be bought, sold and exploited through absolute ownership; that a broad equality of families with built-in mechanisms for the prevention or relief of poverty, debt and slavery could be maintained; that the people's spiritual needs could be met without a highly consumptive, land-owning, cultic élite.[15]

As history progressed, this historical experiment went through a lot of change in itself. As Goldingay points out so clearly, the people of God from Abraham to the return from exile went through several major metamorphoses, yet in each era there were the constants, the underlying fundamental ideals of what it was to be Israel, of what was or was not 'done' in Israel.[16] In other words, the people of Israel themselves were called to an ongoing self-check against the paradigm of their own 'constitution'. The settlers in the land were no longer pilgrims in the wilderness, but they still had to manifest the paradigm of Sinai in their new context. And the role of the prophets was to point out precisely where they were failing to do so. Indeed, it could be said that the main canonical function of the negative critique of the prophetic word (both the prophetic historical narratives and the books of the prophets) is to throw into clearer relief precisely what the paradigm of Israel was – i.e. Israel as God intended. By exposing the failures one highlights the ideals.

Another feature of Kuhn's second use of a paradigm in science, as described by Poythress, is intriguing for our purpose. The 'concrete exemplar' provided by a specific piece of scientific research and its results functions as a model of 'puzzle-solving' for attacking other or subsequent puzzles. That is, scientists working within a certain 'disciplinary matrix' (paradigm in the first sense) assume that a model which successfully solves one problem (paradigm in the second sense) is likely to produce results if applied to other problems in the same general field. The exemplar in fact functions as an *authority* in the field, as long as it demonstrably fits the facts and confirms the wider matrix of perception of the nature of reality. Newton's theory of gravitation served that purpose, and held that authority within the overall field of physics until Einstein showed that it no longer could be seen as a total or adequate representation of the nature of the universe as our expanding knowledge explores it.

Now the analogy with science becomes inadequate at this point, because, on an evangelical view of Scripture, the paradigm provided in the Bible is the result not of human enquiry and experiment but of divine revelation and historical redemptive action. Its truth is not provisional but final. On the one hand, the overall matrix of belief that we find in the Scriptures, as regards the person of God, the created world, and humanity in relation to both, is God's own revelation of the way things truly are. Cultural worldviews, therefore, which incorporate false views of *God* (*e.g.* idolatry, polytheism, pantheism, *etc*), or false views of *creation* (deifying it, or rejecting it as illusory, or destroying it for greed, *etc.*), or false views of *humanity* (oppressive discriminations, *e.g.* by race or caste, or reductionism, self-deification, *etc.*) are exposed as untrue (*i.e.* as failing to correspond with reality) when tested against the paradigm of the biblical worldview. On the other hand, the specific, concrete paradigm of Israel as exemplar can also function both negatively and positively in our evaluation of other human societies and cultures, on the assumption that the laws and institutions God gave to Israel accurately reflected, within that particular historical and geographical context, God's desire and design for human life in the world in general.

Elsewhere I have tried to analyse the various responses found in Old Testament Israel to different aspects of surrounding culture.[17] Some features were accepted and absorbed, others were tolerated but with criticism and limiting factors, and others were utterly rejected and banned in Israel. If we examine the aspects of contemporary culture which Israel opposed, they fall into several fairly clear categories. These include idolatry and related social practices; morally perverted practices, including sexual perversion, bestiality, *etc*; practices which were destructive of persons, such as child sacrifice and cultic prostitution; the whole realm of the occult, divination, sorcery, mediums, *etc.* (the above feature mainly in the critique of Canaan); and economic or political systems that oppress or neglect the poor (the brunt of the critique of imperial cultures such as Egypt, Tyre and Babylon).

Israel's rejection of such things provides a paradigm for our evaluation of comparable elements in cultures we encounter in our own day.

Another way of giving content to the paradigm would be to look at Israel's penal system and the values it embodies, in comparison with the surrounding legal systems known to us from that era. Points of interest would include the valuing of human life above property in the scale of offences and in the forms of punishment; the absence of imprisonment as a legal penalty; the almost total absence of forms of bodily mutilation as punishment, very common in other law codes; strict limits on corporal punishment; and particular legislative concern for the protection of the weak and vulnerable, including unparallelled legal rights for slaves.

Since in several cases these aspects of Israel's legal system are directly distinct from the common legal conventions of surrounding culture, we can discern a consciously articulated distinctive ethical stance.[18]

To affirm that Israel functions as a paradigm (concrete exemplar) for our task of cultural critique in our own day is not to say that somehow Israel was a 'normative culture' in any static sense. It has already been noted that even the culture of Israel itself changed and developed over the centuries recorded in the Hebrew Bible. All culture, being human and historical, is fluid. What is being said is that within the parameters of ancient Near Eastern macro-culture God brought into being a society through whom he both revealed a new paradigm of understanding God, the world and humanity, and actually modelled a framework of laws, institutions, conventions and customs, which experimentally demonstrated the truth of that revelation. The Old Testament thus provides us with both the matrix of belief and understanding which corresponds to reality (*i.e.* it governs the shape of our worldview) and it shows us a historical exemplar of what that meant in practice for one human community – both through its achievements and in its self-conscious and self-critical failures. It thus provides a paradigm in both Kuhn's senses.

The scientific idea of paradigm as puzzle-solution is stimulating here too. Newton's gravitation theory did not in itself solve all the puzzles in physics, but it set the pattern by which scientists set about the remaining problems, including ones which the original paradigm had not faced. Likewise, historical Israel articulated a comprehensive corporate response to a wide range of economic, social and political issues in their day. We cannot chide them for not solving all the problems of the human race. That is not the purpose of a paradigm. The whole point of a 'puzzle-solution' lies in its specificity. It says to us, 'This is how this particular experiment works out.'[19] The hermeneutical and ethical task, like the scientific one, is to approach the problems we face within the framework of assumptions and actual experimental results that the paradigm of Israel affords us, with the reassurance that, unlike Newtonian physics, both the wider conceptual paradigm and the concrete historical paradigm as recorded in Scripture come to us with the status of divine revelation, not as provisional human theory.[20]

Conclusion

How then does this shape my concept of the authority of Scripture, particularly the Old Testament? I have argued that the Old Testament, by its revelatory witness to the creation order and to the God who has acted within history, provides authority for commitment to definable and abiding moral values in an age of moral relativism, and by its provision of a paradigm (both conceptual and practical) in Israel gives us authority to evaluate and critique contemporary cultures, without succumbing either to the temptation of cultural arrogance or to the paralysis of cultural relativism.

Having, I hope, justified my job in teaching biblical ethics in a cross-cultural context, one final piece of self-defence may be forgiven, to bring this essay to a close.

Frank Anthony Spina, in an otherwise warm review of my book, *Living as the People of God = An Eye for an Eye*, concludes by raising the question whether my paradigmatic approach to the application of Old Testament ethical teaching diverges from the traditional view of the authority of Scripture. 'For many Evangelicals, authority means a specific, final, irrefutable answer to a particular (ethical or theological) problem. Wright seems to advocate a somewhat more open-ended system ...'[21]

Well, yes, I do, but it is certainly not in conflict with a full acceptance of the authority of Scripture. My point is rather that I do not think the authority of Scripture can be earthed in quite the way Spina says many evangelicals would like, when it comes to the complex moral issues with which we have to contend in the modern world. Does the Bible give 'specific, final, irrefutable answers' to issues it did not address? If such answers were available, why do Christians, including those fully committed to biblical authority, differ over the moral interpretation of the biblical evidence on many issues? The reason, it seems to me, is that the authority of the Bible is such as to allow room for divergence of moral conviction on some issues, but within the constraints of a definite paradigm. So, for example, a moral critique of a government's economic policy might give variant responses to actual policy proposals on welfare mechanisms designed to relieve or remedy poverty, *e.g.* by fiscal arrangements, or loan schemes or direct benefits. The Bible may not directly sanction one or another as policy options, but it certainly endorses the intention of doing something designed to assist the poor and preferably to restore them to full participation in the community. On the other hand, certain economic policies would be ruled out, not because some 'specific, final and irrefutable' text in the Bible prohibited them, but because their intention or likely effects would contradict the whole paradigm set before us in Scripture. To use the Hebrew laws and the whole of Israel's life as based upon them as our ethical paradigm, far from being so 'open-ended' as to let blank-cheque moral relativism in by the back door, is actually immensely demanding and sharpens one's whole use of the wide range of scriptural texts. For the paradigm is itself very sharp and specific in its own context, and therein lies both its strength (in preventing Old Testament ethics from being little more than vague generalities) and its ever-changing challenge, in facing us with the task of checking all our culture's values and our own against the authority of God's given paradigm of how people should live in his world.

Part Two

A survey of
Old Testament ethics

Chapter Three

The ethical authority of the Old Testament

A survey of approaches, part 1[1]

The question of what authority the Scriptures of the Hebrew Bible have for Christians and how they should be used for ethics is, and always has been, difficult and divisive. The purpose of this chapter and the next is primarily to survey a few representative approaches to the problem, both ancient and modern, examining their assumptions and methods, and then finally to sketch a personal strategy for the ethical use of the Old Testament.

1. The early church

In a brief but stimulating article, Richard Longenecker suggested that there were three major positions or traditions of biblical hermeneutics (specifically on handling the Old Testament) in the early centuries of the church and that these three approaches have continued to be influential all through Christian history.[2] His classification provides a useful starting-point and grid for our survey.

a. Marcion

No writings of Marcion have survived so he is known only through those who opposed him, especially Irenaeus and Tertullian. Writing in the mid-second century AD, his starting-point was Galatians, which he understood as directed against Judaism and all things Jewish. The revelation of God in Jesus was totally different from the work of the Jewish creator God. He thus saw a radical discontinuity between the Jewish Scriptures and the Christian New Testament. The Hebrew Bible had no relevance or authority for Christians and should be regarded as having no place in Christian Scripture – along with several parts of the New Testament which he judged to be seriously infected with Jewish concerns. Not surprisingly, any ethical authority of the Old Testament for Christians is rejected *a priori*. Marcion's radical rejection of the Hebrew Scriptures was itself rejected by the church. His attack, however, was indirectly one of the factors which led to the clarification and defining of the canon of Christian Scripture, with the Old Testament firmly included.

b. The Alexandrian fathers

Christian scholarship at Alexandria flourished from the late second to mid-third century. The most notable figures there were Clement and Origen, Origen being the more prolific and influential. Origen distinguished between the 'letter' and the 'spirit' of the Old Testament, with priority given to the spiritual meaning and purpose of the text. He did not deny the historical and literal meaning of the Old Testament, but argued that often the literal sense of a story or command was simply *impossible* and concluded that the Spirit must have *intended* the reader to look for a hidden spiritual meaning. The Word could use historical stories to teach spiritual truths, but could also weave into the narrative things which did not happen, or into the law things which could not be obeyed. The reader is thereby forced to seek the higher sense worthy of God.[3]

Origen also made a distinction between two parts of the law – the ceremonial and the moral (though in fact in his commentary on Romans he listed six ways in which Paul talks about law!). The first part came to an end in Christ, but the second part was retained and amplified by Christ. This distinction, subsequently expanded by the identification of a third category, namely Israel's civil or judicial law, has remained as a major hermeneutical framework for handling Old Testament law right down to the present day.

Since the main characteristic of the Alexandrian school was the belief that there was a spiritual meaning already there, intentionally hidden in the text of the Old Testament by the Spirit, they had to devise a method for getting at this hidden meaning and expounding it. The allegorical method of exegesis and interpretation was their solution. Though it has become that for which Alexandria is most famous, it should be remembered that this allegorical method was essentially just a tool, and was later discarded or modified by the heirs of their tradition. The more important legacy of Alexandria in relation to Old Testament hermeneutics was the presupposition of continuity and harmony between the Testaments. The Hebrew Scriptures, since they had come from the same Spirit who had inspired the New Testament, must also have Christian spiritual significance. This led to a fairly static conception of the Bible, with little weight given to historical development between the Testaments.

c. The Antiochene fathers

The rival school of Antioch flourished in the fourth and fifth centuries, and includes such names as Chrysostom, Theodore of Mopsuestia, Theodoret, and Diodore of Tarsus in its broad tradition.

Whereas Alexandria subordinated the literal, historical sense of the Old Testament to a higher, moral and spiritual sense (the *allegoria*), Antioch gave priority to history, and looked for higher principles only secondarily. They used the term *theoria* or *anagōgē* for such secondary principles. They strongly and vociferously rejected the allegorical methods of Alexandria, and also questioned the twofold division of the law that stemmed from there.

Chrysostom argued that a whole new dynamic had entered the world with the arrival of the gospel in Christ. In the light of that, he did not accept that the Old Testament law had ongoing moral authority for Christians. Even things which had been allowed by the law in the Old Testament could be rejected by Christians because of the newness of life in Christ. He applied this argument to slavery – being one of the earliest to suggest that although the Old Testament allowed it, that did not of itself justify

71

the practice for Christians who must take Galatians 3:28 into consideration.[4]

Diodore of Tarsus, in his commentary on the Psalms, however, did see the ethical value of the Old Testament, provided it is carefully grounded in historical reality and a literal reading of the text. He refused all allegory.[5] Theodore of Mopsuestia, in his commentary on Galatians, emphasizes the two covenants, through Moses and through Christ, and sets up a very clear law–gospel contrast.[6]

The Antiochene school thus emphasized the historical development within the Scriptures and the importance of redemptive fulfilment of the Old Testament in the New. This led to a less static and more dynamic approach to biblical authority, in which Old Testament perspectives could be set aside in the light of the 'new thing' of the incarnation and kingdom of God in Christ. Both Alexandria and Antioch believed in the continuity between the Testaments, but whereas Alexandria saw sameness and made the Old Testament say Christian things, Antioch saw development and allowed the New Testament to override the Old where necessary.

Longenecker suggests, then, that these three attitudes and approaches to the Old Testament have surfaced in different traditions in the church ever since. Though officially rejected by the church, the ghost of Marcion has haunted the hermeneutical house down through the ages, making its appearance in the antinomian tendencies of the radical wing of the Reformation, the ahistorical existentialism of Bultmann and kindred spirits, and (for very different theological reasons) in modern dispensationalism. And those are only the theological movements. Many churches are in practice Marcionite in their abysmal neglect of the Scriptures that Jesus himself used, refusing to read them in worship even when lectionary provision is made for it. Small wonder there is such confusion over whether and how the Old Testament has anything ethical to contribute to the Christian's resources for practical living.

The influence of Alexandria lives on in Calvin and the Reformed tradition – not in its allegorical treatment of the Hebrew Bible, which Calvin definitely rejected in favour of a careful historico-grammatical exegesis, but in the commitment to the unity and continuity of the Testaments such that the Old Testament is read as unquestionably Christian Scripture to be interpreted and obeyed in the light of Christ. Its influence can be seen in the Puritans' emphasis on the 'third (moral) use' of the law in the Christian's life. A static kind of unity is pushed to its ethical extreme in the theonomist movement which asserts that the moral authority of the Old Testament applies with as much force as the law did for Israel, since it is God's law for all time for all humanity. Whereas, however, the Alexandrians made Hebrew law relevant by allegorizing it, theonomists wish to make it relevant by literal application as far as possible.[7]

The Antiochene antipathy to allegory surfaced again in Luther's bold rejection of medieval scholastic theology. Luther was also more Antiochene than Calvin in allowing the new wine of the gospel to dispense with the old wineskins of the Old Testament wherever he sensed a conflict. Where Calvin sought consistency and harmony, Luther was content with a very free and sometimes inconsistent handling of the Old Testament ethically, which arose from his dynamic and ebullient glorying in the primacy of the gospel as over against the law. As for modern examples of the Antiochene spirit, I think I would point to the heirs of the radical Reformation, such as those Mennonites who are concerned about and active in social issues, who stress a radical discipleship and have a strongly New Testament, messianic orientation in both theology and ethics, while emphasizing the importance of the distinctiveness of the people of God, which is a value most strongly inculcated in the Hebrew Scriptures.

2. The Reformation era

a. Luther

Martin Luther, as a biblical expositor, inherited the medieval tools of exegesis, which included the allegorical method among others that had been developed in the Western church, particularly in North Africa. The early editions of his Galatians commentary show that Alexandrian influence. However, he came to reject entirely (in principle, if not always consistently in practice) the allegorical method, and swung to a much more Antiochene approach – theologically as well as exegetically. This, of course, was directly related to his own experiential rediscovery of the New Testament gospel. The tremendous experience of liberation by the gospel from the burdens of conscience which he felt were imposed upon him by the law and wrath of God led him to a fundamentally Christocentric and gospel-centred approach to everything, including biblical hermeneutics. This entailed a dynamic, historically differentiated, use of the Old Testament, which never relinquished it as essential to the Scripture and the Christian faith, but certainly subordinated it to the New Testament and his own understanding of grace and salvation. This led to a not always consistent use of the Old Testament. At times he can teach certain duties from Old Testament laws and stories. At other times he can urge Christians to be free from certain scruples (*e.g.* in relation to monastic vows) precisely because they (vows) *are* in the Old Testament, and Christians need not behave like Jews![8]

Luther saw the law as having had a civil use; like a hedge, it functioned as a political restraint upon human sin in Israelite society. He also saw its spiritual use; like a mirror, it exposes sin and thus drives us in terror and condemnation to repentance and the gospel. This second use, for Luther, is its primary purpose as far as Christians are concerned. There is debate over whether Luther ever accepted a 'third use' of the law – namely as a moral guide for Christian living now, with ethical authority over believers. It seems that he rejected such moral authority for the law, in the sense of Christians being bound to obey it. And yet, in practice, he made extensive use of the Old Testament in his *catechisms* when dealing with the requirements of Christian behaviour. Much of his teaching there is based on the Decalogue. He 'dejudaizes' the commandments and freely reinterprets them in Christian terms, but the assumption is clearly that the Ten Commandments still function authoritatively in guiding Christian behaviour, even though Luther insists that the Christian is not bound – even by the Decalogue. So when it comes to the grounds for finding moral authority in Old Testament law, Luther locates it in natural law. That is, at those points where the Christian is bound by moral authority in the law, it is not by the law *qua* given by Moses, but by the law as simply reflecting the wider moral will of God in creation.

Fundamentally, however, the law precedes and stands in final contrast with the gospel (as remains the case for Lutheran theology and ethics ever since). The Antiochene model is there; the new events of salvation history in Christ override and supersede all that went before. Thus Luther can be very free in handling not only the laws but also the narratives of the Old Testament. He can engage in curious defence of the morally questionable actions of great heroes of the Old Testament (*e.g.* Abraham's lying to Abimelech about Sarah), if he can show that they were acting out of faith in God's promise. In that sense, grace covers a multitude of sins in more ways than one.

b. Calvin

Calvin represents a swing of the pendulum towards a more Alexandrian approach to the Old Testament, *not* in the sense of allegorical exegesis (which Calvin renounced as much as Luther), but in seeing the unity and continuity of the Testaments. Calvin affirmed a single covenant of saving grace – the Abrahamic promise – running throughout the Bible, and thus saw the gospel in the Old Testament and made great efforts to display a greater harmony and consistency between the law and the gospel.

75

Calvin took very seriously Christ's affirmation of the continuing validity of the law and the prophets (Mt. 5:17ff.), so he not only accepted the 'third use' of the law, but regarded it as in fact the most important. The law functions as a practical guide for Christian conduct, to shape and prepare us for good works in response to saving grace. So, whereas Luther, though he was aware of the threefold use of the law, affirmed that the principal use was the second (*i.e.* to accuse and condemn and terrify us so that we are driven to Christ), Calvin emphasized the third use.

> The third and principal use [of the moral law], which pertains more closely to the proper purpose of the law, finds its place among believers in whose hearts the Spirit of God already lives and reigns ... Here is the best instrument for [believers] to learn more thoroughly each day the nature of the Lord's will to which they aspire, and to confirm them in the understanding of it ... And because we need not only teaching but also exhortation, the servant of God will also avail himself of this benefit of the law: by frequent meditation upon it to be aroused to obedience, be strengthened in it and be drawn back from the slippery path of transgression.[9]

The law, in fact, provided 'a perfect pattern of righteousness', which applied in all ages, not just to Israelites. Its historical and contextual particularity was of course to be taken into account, but that did not destroy its relevance to the people of God of later ages. Even Christ did not *add* to the law, but rather 'he only restored it to its integrity'.[10]

With this more positive perspective, Calvin argues that the way to derive benefit from the law (and he is principally expounding the Decalogue) is to look for the *purpose* of each commandment. He constantly seeks a

76

positive use, somewhat in the same way that Jesus often went to the heart of a matter by seeing the point of a law – why it was given and for whose benefit. Likewise Calvin regards it as legitimate to expand the force of the literal words themselves by presupposing that any law prohibits the opposite of what it commands, or commands the opposite of what it prohibits.

One can detect, therefore, a difference between Luther's and Calvin's handling of the law which is almost as much psychological or intuitive, as theological. Whereas Luther often sees what the law *prohibits*, in order to emphasize its role as a 'killer' from which one must flee to the grace of the gospel, Calvin looks for what the law *promotes*, using it as a model or primer which he applies to all kinds of issues of Christian living in the world of his day. When either of these approaches (both of which can claim New Testament precedent) are taken to extremes they can, of course, become unbalanced in opposite ways. Thus the danger of Lutheranism is a slide into practical Marcionism or antinomianism, while the danger of Calvinism has always been a slide into legalism. But neither of these extremes can be charged against Luther or Calvin himself.

In the *Institutes* Calvin is mainly expounding the Decalogue. However, in his *Commentaries on the Last Four Books of Moses* (*Harmony*) he comments not only on the Ten Commandments themselves, but on all the other laws, which he arranges in relation to their connection with the Ten Commandments.[11] He makes a further distinction in these latter laws between *exposition* – *i.e.* laws which simply clarify or apply the main thrust of the Decalogue commandment, and therefore belong to the essence of the law and share the continuing moral validity of the Decalogue; and *political supplements* – *i.e.* civil or ceremonial provisions that were applicable to Israel. This last category of laws need not be imposed in the laws of other societies, so long as the basic purpose of the Decalogue is preserved. Thus, for example, in his handling of the eighth commandment (against stealing), he includes in the 'exposition':

Prompt payment of wages (Lv. 19:11, 13; Dt. 24:14f.; 25:4)

Care and impartiality for aliens (Ex. 22:21–24, Lv. 19:33f.; Dt. 10:17–19)

Honesty in weights and measures (Lv. 19:35f.; Dt. 25:13–16)

No removal of boundary markers (Dt. 19:14)

Duties in respect of pledges for loans (Ex. 22:26–27; Dt. 24:6, 10–13, 17–18)

Laws against taking interest (Ex. 22:25; Lv. 25:35–38; Dt. 23:19f.)

Recovery of lost possessions (Ex. 23:4; Dt. 22:1–3)

Restitution for theft (Nu. 5:5–7)

Denunciation of bribery and corruption (Ex. 23:8; Lv. 19:15; Dt. 16:19f.)

Prohibition on partiality, for or against the poor (Ex. 23:3, 6)

He then includes the following laws in the category of 'political supplements':

Gleanings for the poor (Lv. 19:9f.; 23:22; Dt. 24:19–22)

The sabbatical year (Ex. 21:1–6; Dt. 15:1–18)

The jubilee and redemption regulations (Lv. 25)

Ban on destroying fruit trees in war (Dt. 20:19f.)

Exemptions from military service for certain categories of people (Dt. 20:5–8)

The levirate marriage duty (Dt. 25:5–10)

The question obviously arises in relation to Calvin's categorizing as to how and why certain laws are assigned to his two sub-Decalogue categories, and no easy answer can be given. The point is, however, that he is refusing to allow that only the Ten Commandments themselves are of any relevance to Christians. The principles they express are also to be found in other laws which stand to a greater or lesser degree in relationship to them. Thus, while a modern state may differ greatly in its civil and political arrangements from the specific laws of Israel, that does not matter, provided the modern laws serve the same purpose and safeguard the same basic principles. What matters is that the 'general equity' which characterizes Israel's civil law should be preserved even if the literal form no longer is binding. If the essential principle of the Decalogue commandment is taken seriously, then matters of practical justice, fair treatment of the poor, protection of boundaries, *etc.*, will fall into place with appropriate legislation, just as they did in Israel.[12] To this extent, then, Calvin took the authority of the Old Testament law very seriously, and sought to show its relevance from a wider perspective than just the Ten Commandments. He was not, however, a 'theonomist' in the latter-day sense of seeking to apply the whole Old Testament law as it stands to post-biblical societies. The modern theonomist movement, since it stands closest to the Reformed theological worldview, often claims Calvin as patron saint. But there is no doubt that he would not have endorsed its assertion of literal application of Old Testament law in modern society, since he explicitly distinguished between permanent moral or natural law and temporary political laws.[13]

c. The Anabaptists

The radical wing of the Reformation produced a remarkable variety of writings – remarkable in view of the pressures and prejudice they faced. It is harder to make general classifications of their position on a given subject than one can do for a single Reformer such as Luther or Calvin, but there are some significant common features. On the matter of biblical interpretation and the specific use of the Old Testament, we can point to certain areas of broad agreement between the Anabaptists and the mainline Reformers before identifying key areas of disagreement.[14]

The Anabaptists were in full agreement with the other Reformers that the Bible was the authoritative Word of God; that it could be understood clearly by the common person; that interpretation was to be free from bondage to ecclesiastical tradition; that special hermeneutical techniques were necessary to elucidate certain difficulties; and that in the end the Bible was meant to be obeyed. However, disagreement focused on three major matters.

1. *The scope of biblical relevance.* The question was whether the Bible as a whole was to be applied to public, civil life or

whether the New Testament applied to Christian personal behaviour only. The Reformers' position generally was that the Old Testament law could be related to civil affairs (thus permitting Old Testament sanctions and penalties in judicial and military matters), whereas the teachings of Christ were essentially for personal relationships between Christians. The Anabaptists asserted that the rule of Christ should govern the whole of life, including civil life also. This had the effect of rejecting, or at least relativizing, the authority of the Old Testament for civil life and government.

2. *The nature of the church and its relation to the state.* The mainline Reformers are sometimes called 'magisterial' because of their conviction that the church and state were bound together in the purposes of God, and that the Reformation of the church was part of the responsibility of the civil magistrate. Though they advocated different patterns of how that relationship should work, they were commonly committed to a broadly theocratic understanding of 'Christendom'. The Anabaptists, on the other hand, regarded the church as the separated and gathered community of true believers, clearly and visibly distinct from all secular institutions and certainly not part of the state. They rejected the 'Christendom' notion, and along with it the theocratic presuppositions derived from the Old Testament. The church was precisely *not* a nation state like Israel in the Old Testament, and therefore should not behave as if she were. This distinction is seen in two fundamental Anabaptist convictions.

First, baptism. For the Reformers, infant baptism was part of Christian citizenship in a Christian state, and was justified partly through affirming its equivalence to Old Testament circumcision. To refuse it, or to deny its validity by 're-baptism', was, in the religio-political context of sixteenth-century Europe, tantamount to sedition or rebellion against the foundations of the state itself. For the Anabaptists, baptism is clearly commanded in the New Testament only for believers, and has nothing to do with citizenship, and therefore the Old Testament was irrelevant to the question. The strength of Anabaptist conviction on this matter, coupled with the intense heat and severe cost of the controversy, probably led to a sharper devaluation of the Old Testament than would have been intended otherwise. That is, if the mainline Protestants justified infant baptism on Old Testament grounds, and then ruthlessly persecuted and slew Anabaptists for rejecting it (justifying the action again on Old Testament grounds), it is hardly surprising to find the Anabaptist counter-polemic seeking to undermine the Old Testament foundations of their enemies' position.

Second, pacificism. The Reformers argued that since civil authority was appointed by God, Christians were bound to obedience, which included bearing arms on behalf of the state in war. Again, the Old Testament was widely used in support of the legitimacy of war in certain circumstances. The major tradition of the Anabaptists (there were some groups who took an opposite and extreme view) took Jesus' teaching on non-violence with total seriousness and therefore argued that Christians could not participate in violence or war. Again, since this was an issue that was so dear to them and so anathema to their opponents, it affected the hermeneutical argument. In order to highlight Christ's non-violence they had to put the Old Testament and its wars in the shadows – either by careful relativizing in relation to Christ, or by a less careful rejection of its authority which led in some cases to the charge of Marcionism.

So we can see that, in the Reformation era, to a considerable degree the question of the ethical authority and use of the Old Testament was affected by the prior question of ecclesiology, particularly in relation to the state. It would be possible to point to a comparable dynamic today. The extent to which Christian groups are prepared to use the Old Testament at all, or, if they are, the use to which they put it, is certainly partly affected by how they understand the nature of the church and its role in society in general.

It is also interesting to note that the Anabaptist relegation

81

of the Old Testament was partly a reaction to what they perceived as the continuing legalism and 'Erastianism' (using the term anachronistically) of the mainline Protestant movement. This was also true, though in a very different ecclesiastical climate, of the origins of dispensationalism, as we shall see below.

3. *The absolute priority of obedience to Christ.* This could probably be regarded as the guiding principle of Anabaptism in many respects. Christianity was a personal, spiritual experience of salvation through Jesus and thereafter of simple committed discipleship. What he said must be done. This could sometimes lead to a new kind of literalism and legalism of its own, but it certainly meant that the Old Testament was decidedly secondary to the New in moral priority. (Again, there were exceptions, such as Thomas Muntzer and Jan of Leyden, who resorted to Old Testament apocalypticism as justification for violence and other excesses.) Sometimes this led to virtual Marcionism, and indeed, when coupled with claims for direct contemporary revelations of the Spirit, could lead to the abandoning of the New Testament as well among some on the radical spiritualist wing of the movement. But among the more careful and significant exegetes and leaders, it was still the position that the advent of Christ and the New Testament relativized the Old.

Menno Simons, an Anabaptist leader with the most enduring legacy, held the Old Testament in high regard, but believed that Christ enables Christians to go far beyond it.

> According to Menno, Jesus Christ really did bring something new. The Old Covenant was displaced by the radical newness of Christ's kingdom. The mainline reformers stressed the continuity of the two testaments; for them there was really only *one covenant in two dispensations.* This principle enabled them to justify infant baptism by analogy to its Old Testament counterpart, circumcision. They also found in the

Old Testament a pattern for church–state relationships. The Anabaptists denied the legitimacy of this appeal to the Old Testament by pointing to the *normative* status of the New Covenant.[15]

Menno's superior evaluation of the New Testament was but the corollary of his basic affirmation – the centrality of Jesus Christ ... When Christ came he fulfilled the Law and enabled man to 'realize' fully what God wanted of him. Menno says that men can now go beyond the Old Testament Law, for they are directed to Christ. Moses served his day, now Christ has given a new commandment ... Menno was fully aware of the ethical issues which stemmed from his theological concerns. His statements about warfare and the use of the sword grew out of his position of seeing the difference between the Old and New Testaments. Any vindictive approach to a person is ruled out because the New Testament forbids revenge, and the law of love must motivate the believer. Christ's command is too clear to be ignored, and wherever the Old Testament stipulations are not in accord with the teachings of Jesus and the apostles they must give way.[16]

Menno, like some other Anabaptists (*e.g.* Pilgram Marpeck),[17] insisted that the Old Testament was still part of the Christian Scripture, and made extensive use of it for devotional and spiritual exhortation. But the overwhelming priority in moral authority was given to the New Testament.

These hermeneutical debates of the Reformation era over the ethical authority and use of the Old Testament are fascinatingly relevant and alive today, though thankfully shorn of the vitriol and bloodshed that accompanied them in the sixteeth century. Do we give the Old Testament equivalent moral authority to the New, or a relativized and secondary authority, or none at all? Does obedience to Christ *endorse* the Old Testament or *relegate* it?

3. The modern period

In the twentieth century the field of Old Testament ethics has been subject to the same uncertainties and intro-spection as the field of Old Testament theology. Scholars have turned to asking whether there is such a category and if so, by what methodology it can be identified and presented. This led to a dearth of substantial writing on the subject in mid-century, which is happily giving way to a more fruitful period in these last two decades.

In terms of our initial threefold classification, modern critical scholarship could be described as Antiochene by virtue of its desire to see the historical depth and perspective of the biblical writings, including not only the crucial difference between the Testaments, but also the internal variety of historical, literary and religious traditions in the Old Testament itself. Attempts to present systematized or diachronically unified accounts of the subject matter have been criticized on much the same grounds as similar attempts in Old Testament theology, such as Eichrodt's. Indeed, Eichrodt's classic model for structuring Old Testament theology included a major section on the ethical teaching of the Old Testament as well.[18] Hempel likewise, one of the few to write an Old Testament ethic in that era, while obviously fully aware of the historical-critical issues of biblical scholarship, sought to present an overview of what could be seen as Old Testament ethics as a whole.[19]

Both these works are critiqued by Barton,[20] who argues that, in contrast with the systematic, diachronic approach, we can only satisfactorily make progress in the discipline of Old Testament ethics if we take into account all the sociological, chronological and traditio-critical depths and nuances of the material. We need to distinguish between what some Israelites believed and did at various times, what certain Old Testament authors and traditions held regarding what Israelites should believe or do, and what kinds of behaviour the Old Testament as a whole may be said to condemn or endorse. We cannot assume that our construction of the last of these would have coincided with popular ethics in Israel – in theory or practice – at any given time. Yet neither can we reduce Old Testament ethics merely to a descriptive history of Israel's behaviour, any more than Old Testament theology can be reduced to a history of Israel's religion. We can discern an 'ethos' or 'general drift' of the moral worldview of ancient Israel. There was a pattern of life lived in the presence of God and pleasing to him which has a number of constant factors through the whole period. 'The [Old Testament] law affords an insight into the contours of God's own ideal will for his people and for all mankind.'[21] Barton lists at least three fundamental elements in this 'ethos': (1) obedience to the divine will; (2) conformity to a pattern of natural order; (3) imitation of God.

Rogerson[22] also relates Old Testament morality to a natural order. He finds much in common between Israelite law and the laws and other moral texts of contemporary ancient Near Eastern societies, and thus sees the moral norms of Israel as reflecting that natural morality of the time. This is not the same as 'natural law' in the dogmatic sense, since it is clearly historically conditioned. But the modern Christian (or non-Christian) can still learn from these ancient texts when we observe their moral consensus and weigh it up in its historical context. There are principles, but they are not timeless or unique to Israel. However, if we are to take the Old Testament's moral demands seriously *as Christians*, we have to do so in the light of the Old Testament's imperatives of redemption. We are reminded by it of our total dependence on God, our constant need for his grace, and our need for the vision of his kingdom which the Bible alone supplies.

Another critic of the attempt to derive absolute moral norms from the Old Testament material is R. R. Wilson.[23] He points out how the narratives of the Deuteronomic historians appear quite inconsistent in applying Torah norms to some of the central characters in Israel's history (such as David). So if pentateuchal laws did not exclusively govern the ethical evaluation even of biblical authors, why should they be considered binding on us in any direct way?

R. E. Clements also recognizes the historically contextual limits on the ethical material of the Old Testament, and observes how even phrases which have passed into the fundamentals of the Christian ethical tradition (such as 'Love your neighbour as yourself') come in contexts which are 'occasional' and sometimes syntactically incidental. It is questionable, in his view, whether the Old Testament gives us, in its own words and by its own intention, any timeless moral principles. Nevertheless, Clements is impressed with the breadth and durability of Old Testament moral insights. 'Overall, the Old Testament literature appears to be feeling its way towards the formulation of universal principles of morality.' Certain moral priorities and demands are so repeatedly apparent that they achieve a 'sense of "primacy" as regards importance [which] readily lends itself to a sense of "principle", as regards universal applicability'.[24] Clements also observes how the long history of Israel in the Old Testament period gave ample opportunity for the fundamental insights and values of her society to be tested and refined in an amazing variety of historical situations. Since Israel had to adapt and yet preserve essentials, the norms and values they expressed through law, prophecy, narrative, worship and wisdom, likewise manifest that quality of adaptability.

> The Old Testament has provided a system of *tora*-instruction, which has proved to be remarkably adaptable to a vast range of human social and political systems. Societies of dramatically different economic, political and cultural types have found within the Old Testament a richly viable source of social and moral teaching.[25]

Birch and Rasmussen[26] take a somewhat different approach and argue that the Old Testament, while it cannot be prescriptive or normative for the Christian, can help to shape the Christian's moral identity and character. Birch has emphasized particularly the power of biblical narrative to this end.[27] The Old Testament narratives have moral power in exposing reality, shattering or transforming worldviews and challenging the reader to response. They therefore have to be read as wholes within their canonical context, and not just by the methods of historical criticism. The canonical approach also underlies Birch's most recent book, in which he seeks to apply the broad themes of the Old Testament, arranged in the historical pattern of the canon, to the ethical task facing the Christian and the church in the modern world. This is welcome, even though it is not finally clear what actual moral authority the Old Testament bears for the Christian. It has *power*, but not *authority*. 'Authority is not a property inherent in the Bible itself ... it is a recognition of the Christian community over the centuries of experience that the scripture is a source of empowerment for its moral life in the world.'[28]

One of the most prolific advocates of unleashing the ethical power and challenge of the Old Testament has been Walter Brueggemann. His handling of the text has an almost 'kerygmatic' force, as he constantly strives to see how the great themes of biblical theology address modern issues. He finds in the narratives of Israel, in the message of the prophets, in the passion for justice on the land, *etc.*, material that exposes the dynamics of human relationships, personal, social and international, and calls for new ways of bringing God's word into a veritably 'missionary' engagement with contemporary realities.[29]

The goal of bringing the Old Testament texts to bear on contemporary issues, however, can become overlaid with a heavy dose of ideology. Gottwald's overtly Marxist reading of the Hebrew Bible is a case in point, though other examples from various liberationist or advocacy stances could be given.[30] Gottwald, perhaps the best-known figure in the recent upsurge of sociological study of the Old Testament, sees ethical relevance in the Old Testament, not in the sense of a revelation of God with ethical norms inherent in it, but rather in its portrayal of the historical struggle of Israel. According to Gottwald's sociological explanation, Israel is a remarkable historical case study of a people committed to a great experiment in social freedom, equality and justice, an experiment which generated a supporting and sanctioning religion – mono-Yahwism. Any authority it may have lies in the realm of historical precedent and contemporary challenge, not in the spiritualizing idealism of claiming Yahweh as our own God.[31] Gottwald's sociological positivism and critical methodology will be unacceptable to those committed to any view of divine authority in Scripture, and have not gone unchallenged in the wider world of critical scholarship also. But in my view he has made the significant contribution to Old Testament ethics of establishing the importance of studying Israel as a total social organism, so that we no longer simply try to quarry out ethical 'gems' from isolated texts, but rather see the relevance of all that Israel tried to be and achieve in their historical context.[32]

In seeking to evaluate the recent work in the field by scholars such as those briefly sampled above, one can begin with several points of positive appreciation. First of all, there is no doubt that the emphasis on history and context in studying the moral teaching of the Old Testament keeps us rooted in reality. There are many helpful perspectives on Israel's actual response to the ethical issues and dilemmas that bristled in her own world. As we see how they articulated an understanding of themselves in relation to God and the world around them, and how they so acutely perceived the tension between the ideals of their faith and the realities of their history (in narrative, prophecy and worship), we are given an abundance of resources in the task of transferring their ethical values and priorities out of their cultural context and into our own. This is not, of course, an obvious or easy transference. But at least the historical and sociological depth of recent study enables us to understand much more clearly what it is we are seeking to make relevant. It also warns us of the danger of moving too quickly from a possibly incidental feature of the Old Testament text to an alleged universal principle of Christian ethics.

Secondly, there is a much deeper understanding of how literary texts of widely differing *genres* actually function in shaping our ethics. Newer literary-critical approaches have alerted us to the importance of reader response. Though not without its problems also, as we shall see in the next chapter, this new emphasis has made us aware of the need to be more nuanced in what we mean by 'moral authority' in a given text. If it can be difficult to express precisely what the authority of an Old Testament *law* is for Christians, when at least the text is in the imperative mood to start with, how much more difficult it is to clarify how (if at all) a narrative functions authoritatively, or a poem.

But that difficulty is precisely something which is not adequately tackled in recent critical scholarship, in my view. As mentioned above, it is possible to talk about the *power* of the text without really coming to grips with the question of its *authority*. The question is whether the Old Testament carries, for Christians, an authority which *requires* us to hear and respond to its texts as the word of God. Perhaps Clements comes close to that when he suggests that the Old Testament's ethical development tends towards a clear affirmation of the 'autonomy of the moral realm', but that in itself needs unpacking! So the challenge of the Old Testament texts is certainly there, and can be very eloquently expressed. Yet it seems somehow ungrounded in any view of prescriptive normativity. If the Old Testament text is not telling us what we ought to do directly, is there any way in which it is telling us what to do at all? And how can we find that out and articulate it?

In the following chapter, the second part of this essay, we shall examine some contemporary evangelical attempts to answer these questions.

Chapter Four

The ethical authority of the Old Testament

A survey of approaches, part 2[1]

In the last chapter, the first part of this essay, we traced some lines of approach to the ethical use of the Old Testament, from the early church, through mainline Reformation and Anabaptist writings, to recent critical scholarship. In this part we look at a variety of evangelical approaches to the question, concluding with an outline of my own presuppositions and method in handling the Old Testament for Christian ethics.

1. Walter Kaiser

In 1983 a long silence was broken. After more than half a century when no book had been published in English on the subject of Old Testament ethics, two arrived almost simultaneously, their authors quite unaware of each other's work. One, my own *Living as the People of God=An Eye for an Eye*,[2] sets out a way of understanding the ethical thrust of the Old Testament in general terms and then illustrates its method in several applied areas. It is referred to more fully in the closing section of this chapter. The other, *Toward old Testament Ethics* by Walter C. Kaiser, Jr, is a much more wide-ranging work.[3] Kaiser devotes a major first section to a survey of the field itself, its definition, scope and methodological problems, and also a classification of such approaches as were advocated in various scholars work on biblical ethics in general. After an exegetical survey of the major sections of the law, he organizes his material around the central theme of holiness, and proceeds with an exposition of the second table of the Decalogue. Finally, he tackles some of the moral difficulties frequently raised by readers of the Old Testament.

Kaiser is thus among those who affirm two things about the Old Testament: first, that it can be handled in some systematic, unified way, in spite of its manifest diversity; and second, that it does still hold moral authority for the Christian. On both counts, he finds much current writing on the subject deficient. In a recent article,[4] he regrets the absence of a sense of coherence or a central principle in writing on Old Testament ethics over the last decade or two, such as characterized the work of Eichrodt. He is well aware of the reasons for this, as expressed by John Barton,[5] but points out that even where a scholar like Barton is willing to see several dominant motifs (such as conformity to natural order, obedience to divine will, imitation of God), he does not regard these as normative or prescriptive. There is, in other words, a marked resistance to a deontological understanding of ethics in treatments of the Old Testament.

In the same article, Kaiser also regrets the effect on ethics of the paradigm shift in Old Testament hermeneutics from concern for author intention to theories of reader response. While there is much to learn and great potential in the newer literary criticism, it can undermine any objective authority the text had in normative ethics. Some practitioners of a reader-response approach to the text, of course, would say that no such thing as objectivity exists anyway. There is certainly a shift from attempting some kind of objective, cognitive understanding of the text, to a more subjective, intuitive stance.

> More and more, the Bible functions in modern thought as a catalyst suggesting ways in which former communities faced problems, but imposing no categories, no norms, or principles of its own – especially in an objective, cognitive, or regulative way.[6]

There is little scope here for a revelation-based authority in actual ethical decision-making.

Kaiser himself wants to insist on the moral authority of the Old Testament, and does so first by calling for a fresh appreciation of the classic division of the law into moral, civil and ceremonial categories.[7] This ancient scheme – partly perceived by Origen, given clear shape by Calvin, enshrined for Anglicans in Article 7 of the Thirty-nine Articles of Religion and for the Reformed tradition in the Westminster Confession of Faith, and influential until comparatively recent years[8] – has fallen into disfavour. The main attack upon it is, first, that it serves no exegetical purpose, in that it is impossible to make clear divisions into such categories when actually studying Old Testament legal texts, and second that it is foreign to the thought of either Old or New Testament.[9] However, it could be argued against the first point that it was never intended as an *exegetical* tool, but as a self-consciously post-biblical hermeneutical means of applying the law in a Christian context. And against the second, Kaiser shows that there is more evidence than one would think for an awareness of some such distinction in the minds of New Testament authors, and indeed that the Old Testament itself prepares the way for it when some of the prophets clearly set up priorities as between the sacrificial and other ritual laws on the one hand and the demands of social justice on the other (and not only the prophets, *cf.* Pr. 21:3). In calling for a fresh understanding and application of this way of handling the law, Kaiser is waging a polemic against the 'all-or-nothing' banner of the theonomist/reconstructionist school – that is, either the whole law applies today, or none at all. This position is examined below.

Having reinstated the idea of moral law, Kaiser is keen not to confine it merely to the Ten Commandments alone, as has often been done. Rather, there is a breadth of moral *principles* that inform the whole core and meaning of the Torah, and can be drawn on as we seek to apply them to contemporary issues. The law was given, not solely for Israel, but purposely to be of moral relevance to the nations, as the prophets implicitly affirm in their moral evaluation of the nations' behaviour. Kaiser advocates a 'ladder of abstraction' approach,[10] in which the precedents and specifics of Old Testament law are applied to modern situations by way of intermediate moral principles.[11]

In affirming the moral authority of the Old Testament mediated through moral principles derived from the text, Kaiser declines to see Israel as a *model* for the nations.[12] This again is because he is resisting the theonomist scheme, particularly as advocated by Greg Bahnsen, in which the expression 'Israel as a model' is used to imply fairly literal and total application of Israel's law, including its penalties in the civil realm. However, in my view, the expression need not be taken in the theonomists' fashion, but can be a useful means of encapsulating the relevance to contemporary ethics of Israel as a total society. It was Israel as a whole community that was to be 'a light to the nations'. It was Israel as a holy nation that was to be a priesthood in the midst of the nations. I believe there are ways in which we can use the idea of Israel as a model in applying Old Testament laws and institutions paradigmatically that avoid the theonomist extreme while preserving their commendable enthusiasm for the abiding ethical relevance of the law. This is the focus of the concluding section of this essay.

2. John Goldingay

Like Kaiser, Goldingay wishes to affirm the normative authority of the Old Testament in Christian ethics, and also sees the importance of derived or intermediate principles (sometimes called 'middle axioms') as a way of moving from the specifics of the ancient text to the specifics of our modern context. Otherwise the 'specificness' of the Old Testament commands (not to mention its stories and other genres) could induce a kind of ethical paralysis in which one is so aware of the cultural and historical particularity of Israel's laws that one despairs of finding any modern relevance at all, let alone a normative ethic. Against such a negative view, Goldingay points out that the specificity of commands to a context need not spell irrelevance to other contexts, since they can be the concrete expression of some general principle which is being applied. There are also human constants that survive cultural discontinuities, as well as the moral consistency of God himself.[13]

However, in exploring the necessity of some such procedure, he warns against making the derived principles themselves the locus of authority. It is the text of Scripture itself which remains normative.

> If we are concerned with interpreting the Bible itself, it is nevertheless not these hypothetical principles which are normative or canonical. The Bible itself remains the norm. The principles we find in it are part of our interpretation, not the object of our interpretation. They are limited by our blind-spots, and can be the means of missing aspects of the whole message of Scripture or of evading the meaning of the text itself, rather than of serving it.[14]

This is an important caveat. But it might seem to impale us on the horns of a dilemma, namely that on the one hand we have an authoritative text which we cannot directly apply, or which does not actually address the specific moral problem that confronts us, while on the other hand we have derivative moral principles which we can use but which have no intrinsic authority. Nevertheless, it seems to me that we have no alternative but to derive intermediate mechanisms of some kind, which I would prefer to call paradigms (as discussed below), or else the Bible will be ethically gagged and bound. The vital thing, therefore, is that we constantly submit those intermediate means – call them principles, axioms, paradigms or whatever – to revision in the light of the biblical text. Our ethical agenda must be as *semper reformanda* as our ecclesiology or theology.

In later work, Goldingay examines the importance of historical *context* in understanding and relating Old Testament laws and narratives. The Bible itself shows how changing contexts called forth different responses and different priorities, and we ought not merely to flatten all that diversity into alleged timeless truths, except in cases where the Bible itself explicitly does so. As a case study in this, Goldingay traces the idea of 'the people of God' through its long historical journey in the Old Testament. He shows how each major period found the people of God in sometimes radically different forms, and facing new challenges and ethical tasks, as they move from the ancestral wandering clan, through theocratic nation, institutional state, afflicted remnant to the post-exilic community of promise. There is continuity and yet obvious diversity as well, and ethical principles drawn from the texts which relate to any of these periods must take into account the interwoven patterns of this historical tapestry. As Goldingay explores this continuity in diversity, he makes it very clear that he sees definite ethical challenges and resources for the Christian church in such a study of just one theme of the Hebrew canon.[15]

In the same book, Goldingay puts forward what he calls the 'pastoral strategy' of Deuteronomy. After surveying the book's behavioural values and theological perspectives, he points out that apparent moral tensions between high ethical ideals and some laws which appear less than ethical to us may be resolved by realizing that the legislator was concerned both to set out the highest possible standards of covenant loyalty and behaviour, and yet at the same time to take into account the reality of a sinful, rebellious people and their ambient culture. You have to start where people are – then as now. So the law necessarily made concessions to the facts of sin and of undesirable aspects of historical culture. In noting this, Goldingay takes his cue from the way Jesus handled the divorce controversy. Jesus contrasted the creation ideal with the Mosaic permission. Yet both texts, of course, are part of the same Torah. The Bible itself, therefore, gives us precedent for moral evaluation of some parts in the light of others.[16]

The authority of the Old Testament, therefore, is not simply flat and even and equal in every text. While the whole text has its canonical authority, some parts are clearly prescriptive in a way that moves quickly towards application now, while others are more in the nature of 'case studies' of God's engagement with Israel in situations of greater or lesser obedience to God's will.

> Thus either the Bible's statements tell us how to live, or (when they do not do this) these actual statements are the model for and the measure of our attempts to state how we are to live. This means we do not ignore the particularity of biblical commands (and apply them to our own day as if they were timeless universals). Nor are we paralysed by their particularity (and thus unable to apply them to our day at all). We rejoice in their particularity because it shows us how the will of God was expressed in their context, and we take them as our paradigm for our own ethical construction.[17]

3. Dispensationalism

Dispensationalism traces its roots to J. N. Darby (1800–1882) in nineteenth-century Britain, though the premillennialism which it also espouses has a much longer history in the church. Darby found himself frustrated and depressed with the ineffective legalism of Anglican church life in Ireland at that time. It was ineffective because, although it was deeply moralistic in theory, it was abysmally lax in practice. A conversion-type experience liberated him into an experience of the grace of God and a realization of the fullness of the gospel in Christ. This simultaneously engendered a strong antipathy to 'works', and thence also to what he perceived to be an over-reliance on the Old Testament in the church's moralizing.[18]

Darby went on to develop a system of biblical understanding which stemmed from his desire to preserve the utter priority of grace over law. The most straightforward way to do this, in a sense, is to separate them altogether. Darby and those who followed his lead[19] did this by arguing that God's dealings with human beings in the course of redemptive history have proceeded by entirely separate dispensations. The precise number of these varies in different schools, but the most fundamental divide is between the dispensation of the law through Moses and that of the present age of grace through Christ. The next most significant will be the millennial earthly reign of Christ. This entails also a complete separation between national Israel and the church. God deals with them differently, and the distinction will be preserved eternally. The moral teaching of the Old Testament law was for the dispensation before Christ alone, and will be the standard again in the millennial age when Christ reigns on earth among a converted Jewish nation. But in the age of the church, it has no continuing authority. In the twentieth century, dispensationalism has softened somewhat under the onslaught of so-called covenant theology, and is prepared to recognize that there was grace in the Old Testament also and that salvation was never simply by keeping the law. But its hermeneutical and eschatological system has remained largely intact.

Norman Geisler has provided a helpful statement of a dispensationalist approach to biblical ethics.[20] He points out that all Christians, including theonomists, know that Christians are not bound to obey every single law in the Pentateuch since in practice they do not do so and do not urge that others should. 'So even those who claim that Christians are still under the Old Testament Law do not agree that every point is still applicable. The question then is not whether the Mosaic Law is still in force, but *how much* of it is still binding on Christians.'[21] Geisler dismisses the attempt to preserve some part of the law as authoritative by distinguishing between moral, civil and ceremonial categories, arguing that it is not borne out by the New Testament. He cites a list of New Testament passages where the law, as a whole, is regarded as at an end, or that Christians are no longer under it.[22]

According to Paul, with the Law it is either all or

nothing at all. So on the one hand, if any of the Law is binding on Christians, then all of it is, but even theonomists cringe at this suggestion. On the other hand, if some of the Mosaic Law does not apply to Christians then none of it does. This is precisely what Paul argues in Galatians.[23]

Geisler is well aware that many Old Testament laws are quoted in the New Testament, along with other uses of the Old Testament there. But he insists that the force of the texts as authoritative law is not carried over. Rather it is the principles that are being applied, sometimes (as in the case of the sabbath or adultery) with significant modifications in the actual law. 'There are many similar moral principles in both Old and New Testaments, but it by no means follows that there are the same laws,'[24] and certainly not the same penalties. So the Old Testament can provide guidance on social holiness and personal righteousness, but it cannot be applied either theocratically or theonomically today. The law of Moses was never intended as a guide for civil government other than in Old Testament Israel. For that, God has given the unwritten 'natural law' of general revelation.

> From this discussion it should also be clear that the law of God (divine revelation) is not the basis for civil law today. God does not presently rule the world's governments by divine law. He desires that they be ruled by civil law based on natural law. Divine law is only for the church. Natural law is for the whole world (Rom. 2:12–14).[25]

It is clear from Geisler's discussion in this article that his main target is the theonomists and their insistence on applying the laws of the Old Testament as rigorously as possible (including their penalties) in modern society.[26] He is not denying the relevance of the moral principles exemplified in the Old Testament, but is rejecting its

99

authoritative normativity as law. This is apparent also in his later monograph on Christian ethics, which examines different ethical stances in relation to specific contemporary issues.[27] There Geisler makes plenty of use of Old Testament texts in framing what he regards as appropriate Christian responses. So in practice he seems to assume the moral relevance of the Old Testament, while theologically declining to accord it normative authority.

In evaluating the dispensationalist approach to Old Testament ethics, one can first of all express a positive appreciation for the emphasis on the priority of grace, and for the proper insistence on the centrality of Christ and New Testament fulfilment theology in any Christian interpretation of the Old Testament.

However, in my view the approach is flawed by the theological questionability of the whole dispensationalist scheme, in its severance of the Old from the New Testament redemptively, its denial of the organic spiritual continuity between Israel and the church through the Messiah, and its over-emphasis on the contrast between law and grace. These major distinctives of the theology of dispensationalism appear to demote the Old Testament in a way which makes its ethical use more or less redundant. My impression is that Geisler himself is somewhat exceptional in paying the attention he does to the moral value of the Old Testament. On the whole, the teaching that Old Testament law has no relevance to the present dispensation of the church leads to a kind of practical Marcionism. If the law does not apply until the millennium, the task of finding out what it might mean to us now hardly seems worth the effort. On such a view, the New Testament offers sufficient moral authority and guidance without the Old. It is also my impression that the pre-millennial eschatology of dispensationalism has a heavily dampening effect on the relevance of the Old Testament to social ethics in the present context. Since the realization of justice and peace will be features of the millennial earthly reign of Christ, they need not be the focus of Christian striving here and now. The primary (if not only) task of the church is evangelism, conceived as rescue from a perishing world order. Inevitably this produces a sceptical (sometimes hostile) assessment of the value of Christian involvement in the social, economic, political, educational and legal structures of the present world order. The Old Testament, therefore, with its strong concern for such issues, suffers corresponding neglect.[28]

4. Theonomism

At the polar opposite extreme from the dispensationalist demotion of the Old Testament as regards ethical authority lies the theonomist exaltation of it as the permanently valid expression of God's moral will for all societies. The difference could be expressed at its simplest by saying that whereas dispensationalists say that *no* Old Testament law is morally binding since the coming of Christ, unless specifically endorsed and re-commanded in the New Testament, theonomists argue that *all* Old Testament laws are perpetually morally binding, unless explicitly abrogated in the New Testament. Theonomists have the same essentially 'all-or-nothing' approach to the law as dispensationalists, except that whereas the dispensationalists answer 'nothing' to the question, 'How much of the Old Testament law is authoritative for Christians?' the theonomists answer, 'All – and not just for Christians.'

The theonomist movement has emerged from the Reformed wing of the church, and claims legitimate descent from the teaching of Calvin, the Westminster Confession of Faith, and the Puritans. These claims are strongly resisted by other Reformed scholars who do not accept the validity either of theonomist hermeneutics or of reconstructionist social and political prescriptions, and who say that Calvin and the classic Reformed theologians were by no means theonomist in the modern sense of the word.[29]

The movement emphasizes the essential unity and continuity of the Old and New Testament and espouses a form of covenant theology. Based on that, its writers argue that the Mosaic law was given by God as divine revelation not merely for the guidance of Israel, but to provide a perfect model of justice for all societies – ancient and modern. The ceremonial aspects of the law have been fulfilled by Christ and are therefore not binding on Christians – though theonomists argue that they *would be* were it not for Christ having fulfilled them for us (to this extent theonomists accept differentiation within the law). But all the rest of the law is binding, including its penalties. Laws which older traditions had regarded as 'civil' and distinguished from 'moral' laws are thus included by theonomists in their 'moral and binding' category. Civil authorities in all societies are thus obligated to enforce the laws and penalties of the Mosaic law, and are in a state of sin and rebellion to the extent that they fail to do so. Enforcing the Mosaic law, for theonomists, would include a mandatory death penalty for homosexual offences, rebellious young people, *etc.* On the penalty for sabbath-breaking there are differences of opinion.

'Christian reconstructionism' is the name chosen by the leaders of the movement which believes that the church should be preparing to reconstruct society and to exercise rightful 'dominion' (another favourite term in theonomic vocabulary), to institute a theocratic government which embodies the lordship of Christ in every realm of society. The optimism of this vision easily degenerates into triumphalism. Theologically it is closely allied to a postmillennialist eschatology which characterizes and shapes reconstructionism as much as premillennialism does for dispensationalism. The founding father of the movement is Rousas Rushdoony, but its growth has largely been due to the theological writings of his disciple, Greg Bahnsen, and the popularizing, and more economics-inclined writing and speaking, of Gary North.[30]

A helpful starting-point for getting to grips with the theonomist approach to Old Testament ethics is Bahnsen's companion article to Geisler's in *Transformation*.[31] In it he sets out his case that the general continuity of the moral standards of the Old Testament applies legitimately to the socio-political realm as much as to personal, family or ecclesiastical ethics and that the standing civil laws[32] of the Old Testament are God's revealed model of perfect social justice for all societies (though he allows for necessary modifications to accommodate changing cultures). He justifies the non-applicability of those laws which made Israel distinctive symbolically from the nations on the grounds that the New Testament redefines the people of God to include Gentiles as well as Jews, so the old marks of separation are no longer necessary, though their *point* (separation from ungodliness) is still a Christian concern. He stresses the importance of Matthew 5:17 and other New Testament texts pointing to the abiding importance of the law, much as dispensationalists point to texts which speak of its 'end'.

In evaluating theonomism's approach to the ethical authority of the Old Testament, one can begin, as with dispensationalism, with some (probably more) words of positive appreciation. I have nothing but applause for theonomists' concern to restore the validity and authority of the Old Testament as an integral part of the whole canon of Christian Scripture to the life and witness of the church. There is no doubt that a contributory factor to the social ineffectiveness and moral confusion of the modern church is the practical Marcionism that besets it. Anything which corrects that imbalance is to be welcomed, but one fears that the perceived extremism of the reconstructionist platform may well reinforce rather than reform popular depreciation of the Old Testament.

Secondly, I agree with the theonomists' premise that the Old Testament law was given by God for a purpose that had a wider ethical relevance than solely the shaping of Israel. Nothing less satisfies the assertion of 2 Timothy 3:15ff. that all Scripture is God-breathed *and profitable* ... I believe that such wider, abiding ethical significance is anticipated and expressed in the Old Testament itself, as we shall see below.

Thirdly, it is my view that the Reformed, covenantal understanding of the unity of the Testaments and of the fulfilled, redefined nature of Israel in the New Testament[33] is a more adequate framework for biblical interpretation than dispensationalism, so again I find myself in agreement with a theological premise of theonomy.

Fourthly, one appreciates the overriding desire to see the lordship of Christ recognized and realized in all of life on earth, though I confess to a theological rejection of the postmillennial framework in which reconstructionists expect it, and to a more subjective rejection of the triumphalist rhetoric with which some reconstructionist writers portray it.

In spite of sharing some of theonomy's theology and concerns, however, there are various criticisms to be made.[34] First, from the perspective of the sociology of law, it is arguable that theonomists misunderstand the function of law, especially in ancient societies. In biblical ancient Israel and contemporary cultures, law was not always in the form of hard and fast statutes intended to be applied to the letter in formal courts. Judges operated with precedents and paradigms guided by *tôrâ* (which means 'guidance' or 'instruction'). The fabric of Israel's judicial system included local elders, levitical priests, individual 'circuit judges' like Samuel, and after Jehoshaphat's reform, royally appointed judges in fortified towns and an appeal court in Jerusalem (2 Ch. 19). The emphasis was on the imperative to do justice and act fairly without bribery or favouritism, but much was left to the discretion and judgment of those responsible (Dt. 16:18–20; 17:8–13).[35]

Secondly, the theonomists' preoccupation with enforcing the penalties of Old Testament law for equivalent modern offences attaches too much importance to the literal (and literary) form of the biblical penalties and fails to reckon with two points: (1) that in many cases it is probable that the penalty specified was a *maximum* penalty which could be reduced at the discretion of the elders or judges handling the matter. This is clear in the law governing the use of the whip as punishment (Dt. 25:1–3). Forty strokes was the *maximum* penalty; the law assumes that fewer than that, at the judges' discretion, would be normal. The fact that in a few specific cases the law prohibits any reduction of penalty (for deliberate murder, Nu. 35:31; idolatry, Dt. 13:8; and false testimony in court, Dt. 19:19–21) suggests that lesser penalties were permissible in other cases. Wenham has suggested that the death penalty for adultery may have been allowed to be commuted to monetary compensation, though would-be adulterers should not count on it (Pr. 6:32–35).[36]

(2) What is important about the penal system of Israel's law is the scale of values it reflects rather than the literal prescriptions themselves. Careful study of Israel's penology shows that the range of offences for which the death penalty was applied had to do with the central concerns of protecting the covenant relationship and the family/household unit within which the relationship was preserved and experienced.[37] The gradation of penalties also shows a clear priority of human life over property and other priorities which challenge the sometimes distorted values of our modern judicial systems.[38] It is certainly possible to set the scale of moral values reflected in Israel's penalties over against those of our own society and then to observe shortcomings and suggest reforms in order to bring our own system of law and justice more in line with biblical priorities. But this need not take the form of seeking to re-impose Old Testament penalties as they stand. This point seems to be reinforced theologically by the fact that in the New Testament it appears that neither Jesus nor Paul wanted to apply the full weight of the Old Testament penal system, for adultery or for false teaching.

Thirdly, it seems to me that theonomy overstates the importance of the pentateuchal laws within the overall balance of the Old Testament canon. Now it is obvious that the Torah (as a whole; it should always be remembered that the word includes narratives as well as law codes) has a foundational role, and is celebrated in the Psalms and held up against the people of Israel by the prophets. Nevertheless, it seems significant that the historical narratives and prophetic texts (and certainly the Wisdom literature) do not often quote specific laws or call for their implementation, or for specific penalties to be enforced.

Not as often, that is, as one would expect if the written, standing law had had quite the central importance in Israel's everyday social affairs as theonomists imply. In fact, if the law was as definitive as theonomists claim, then the narratives portray apparent inconsistencies – the most notorious being the lack of capital punishment on either Cain or David. It is arguable that a truly prophetic response to the needs of society would not place quite the emphasis that theonomy does on law and punishment. The Old Testament seems aware of the limitations of that approach.[39]

Fourthly, the theonomist agenda seems to me oddly selective in what it says modern civil rulers *must* apply and enforce from Old Testament law and what it says they *must not*. According to Bahnsen, the realm of the economic marketplace is out of bounds for civil rulers, legislatively or coercively, on the grounds that Old Testament law did not prescribe such intervention. Outside those areas where God's law prescribes their intervention and application of penal redress, civil rulers are not authorized to legislate or use coercion (*e.g.* the economic marketplace).[40]

But the pentateuchal law, by any criterion, is deeply concerned about the economic marketplace and prescribes a whole raft of mechanisms designed to preserve or restore justice: in relation to the distribution of land, the payment of workers, lending and debt, alleviation of poverty, *etc*. By whom were these laws and mechanisms administered if not by the civil authorities (the elders)? By whom was coercion to be brought to bear on those who tried to evade them? What was Nehemiah, the civil governor, doing when, on behalf of the debt-impoverished farmers,he confronted the nobles who took interest illegally (Ne. 5)? To argue that since Old Testament law does not prescribe explicit *penalties* related to infringement of its economic legislation, modern civil authorities are therefore *excluded* from any form of intervention in the economic marketplace, betrays both the inadequacy of theonomism's preoccupation with penalties and also, in my view, its ideological bias towards a free-market economic conservatism.

5. The Jubilee Centre

American-style theonomic reconstructionism has not generated a large British following. There is, however, a movement under the auspices of the Foundation for Christian Reconstruction, begun in 1987, directed by Stephen Perks. It is dedicated to the 'rebuilding of Christian civilisation ... on the belief that Christ has called His disciples to subject every aspect of life ... to the authority of God's word'. It shares the same Calvinist Reformed background as American reconstructionists, as well as their theonomic presuppositions and postmillennialist eschatology. It distributes theonomist literature and produces occasional papers and a journal.[41]

More significant in the British scene is the work of the Jubilee Centre in Cambridge, whose work in bringing a biblical perspective to the public arena of social policy, legislation and reform has been recognized both in Parliament and the secular media. The director, Michael Schluter, in collaboration with Roy Clements, has provided the theological and biblical basis for the Centre's various programmes aimed at social reform in Britain.[42]

Prominent in their theological position is their use of the Old Testament as a normative authority for Christian social ethics. On the basis of New Testament texts such as Matthew 5:17ff. and 2 Timothy 3:16f., they argue that Christians are obliged to search the Old Testament Scriptures for ethical guidance and that to confine the relevance of Old Testament law to Israel BC is fundamentally misguided. Thus far, they would endorse the stance represented by Kaiser and Goldingay above. However, they are dissatisfied with the proposal that the only way to move from Old Testament text to modern context is by way of a list of derived intermediate principles. The problems they perceive regarding such a 'principles approach' include the following. How does one determine the 'right' principle when different interpreters derive different principles from the same text or texts? Deriving principles involves a process of abstraction and generalization, the so-called 'ladder of abstraction'. How far 'up the ladder' should one go, what steps are appropriate for descending again into concrete proposals in our own context, and who decides such issues? How do we organize or prioritize our derived principles if they come into conflict with each other? How can we avoid our selection of derived principles being nothing more than a subjective statement of our own biases tangentially linked to the biblical text?

Schluter and Clements argue[43] that the only way to avoid these difficulties (or at least to mitigate them) is the holistic approach which regards the whole social system of Israel as a normative model. That is, rather than take isolated laws and attempt to derive moral principles from them, we need to see how individual laws, and whole categories of law, as well as the many social, economic and political institutions of Israel, *functioned* together. God did not just give arbitrary laws to an otherwise 'neutral' community. God *created* that community, moulding them out of an unpromising crowd of escaped slaves into a people with distinctive structures of social life in relation to the historical and cultural context in which they lived. It is this total community that was to serve as God's model for the nations. Therefore, any principles we derive from different parts of the model must be integrated together and consistent with the whole. So, for example, the law banning interest will not be generalized merely into an abstract principle about curtailing greed, but will be understood in relation to Israel's system of land tenure and economic objectives, which in turn are bound up with the importance and role of the extended families, which in turn relate to other features of Israel's judicial and social life. Since so much of Israel's law has to do with creating or restoring a community of justice and compassion in family and societal life, Schluter and Clements have begun to use the term 'relationism' to describe the social ethical system they wish to build from this biblical base.[44]

By advocating this method, they claim to avoid some of the problems inherent in taking as a starting-point for

Christian social ethics either a creation mandate approach or a kingdom of God approach, while preserving the essential truths of each.[45] In their work they endorse and carry further the concept of Israel and its law as a 'paradigm' which I developed in *Living as the People of God = An Eye for an Eye* and refer to further below. It is this overall paradigm, the social shape of Israel in all its dimensions, that acts as a guiding, organizing and prioritizing control on our expression and application of derived principles. Thus, while they share the theonomists' insistence on the relevance and normativity of the Old Testament and its law, they do not share the reconstructionist agenda of enforcing Old Testament laws and penalties through modern legislation. Nevertheless, they are prepared to step out of the world of biblical research into the complex world of actual social policy and legislation. They are prepared, that is, not only to go up the ladder of abstraction, but to come down again with concrete proposals in the public arena. Not everyone will agree with the specifics of all their agenda. Nor do they expect everyone to do so, still less to compel them to do so. The point is that there comes a time to move from principles to practice, from questions to answers, from debate to action; and the Jubilee Centre at least seeks to do these things from a clearly stated hermeneutical approach to the biblical text.

6. Messianic Judaism

Before concluding with an outline of my own approach, it is worth noting the approach of a unique and growing Christian group that is often overlooked, but by its very identity ought to have something to offer on a Christian approach to the Old Testament law – namely messianic Jews. There have always been Jewish believers, since the days of the New Testament itself, of course. Paul accords high theological significance to their existence as the believing remnant of prophecy, in Romans 9 – 11. Over the centuries the tendency has been that those few Jews who became Christians simply assimilated into the predominantly Gentile churches. There was little other option.

However, since the Second World War not only has the number of Jewish believers in Jesus as the Messiah increased dramatically, but also there has emerged the movement known as messianic Judaism. Numbering approximately 100,000 in America and several thousands in other parts of the world, messianic Jews are Christian believers who wish to preserve and affirm their identity as Jews and to live and worship in culturally Jewish ways.[46]

One might have thought that Jewish believers committed to preserving their Jewish heritage and choosing to live their lives as far as possible in accordance with the Torah would adopt a more or less theonomic approach to the Hebrew Bible. But this is not the case. As regards the Torah as understood within Orthodox Judaism – including both the written law of the *Tanakh* (Hebrew Bible, Old Testament) and the oral rabbinic law – the messianic Jewish position is that a Jewish believer *may* observe it as a matter of choice.[47] Thus he or she may observe the *kashrut* (food laws), the sabbath and other festivals, and circumcise male infants, *etc.* There may be two valid reasons for such observant lifestyle. It may be a matter of ethnic and cultural identity. The messianic Jew is saying, 'I *am* a Jew, so let me live as one.' Or it may also be a matter of evangelistic integrity, choosing, with Paul (1 Cor. 9:20), to live a Jewish lifestyle within a Jewish context in order to avoid unnecessary offence while witnessing to Jesus. But such laws are not binding. The messianic Jew may choose to keep them and do so enthusiastically, but he is not obliged to, nor are they in any way linked to salvation.

However, messianic Judaism argues further that in the light of the New Testament, the very idea of Torah must be redefined. It cannot be confined to (though it still includes) the Old Testament Torah, but now encompasses, for the Christian, 'the Torah of the Messiah'.[48] This includes not only the specific commands of Jesus, but also the total way of obedience and practical holiness to which Christians are called in the New Testament. But the full understanding of New Testament moral teaching actually requires knowledge of Old Testament law which forms the basis for so

110

much of it. Thus, messianic Judaism agrees that the Old Testament law retains its moral authority for believers, but that it must be set within its total Christian canonical context as part of the new messianic Torah of the new covenant.[49] As regards specific application of Old Testament laws in social ethics, the view seems to be that even though they may not be literally binding, they do provide a primary guide as to how God wants people to live. In other words, when necessary cultural and historical adjustments have been made, the law still retains its moral force in principle by way of concrete example.[50]

Conclusion: a personal approach

My own approach to the ethical use of the Old Testament is worked out in greater depth elsewhere,[51] so I propose to offer here simply a summary of the theological assumptions and hermeneutical methods by which it operates.

a. Assumptions

1. *The authority and relevance of the Old Testament for Christians.* I take 2 Timothy 3:15–17 as an axiomatic starting-point. This text affirms that the Old Testament law is part of the Scriptures which, being God-breathed, are salvifically effective and ethically relevant. The question, therefore, is not *whether* the Old Testament law has authority and relevance for us as Christians, but *how* that given authority is to be earthed and that relevance applied.

2. *The unity of Scripture.* This is not to affirm a flat, Alexandrian-style identity between the Testaments, or to overlook the diversity within the Testaments. Rather, it is my belief that the organic unity and continuity of God's work of revelation and redemption in history, from the call of Abraham to the return of Christ, constitute a greater reality than, and exercise hermeneutical priority over, the historical discontinuities, covenantal articulations and changing cultural contexts at each stage of its outworking. By analogy one might point to the unity and continuity of a single human life as of greater importance than the differences of context, understanding, behaviour, *etc.*, that

mark each period of a person's life – infancy, childhood, adolescence, adulthood, old age. What God said and did in Old Testament Israel therefore matters to us as Christians because it is part of the way we have been saved; it is part of our story and part of the story of the salvation of humanity and the creation itself. Similarly, what God required of Israel ethically must speak to us also, because of the moral consistency of God and the continuity of the people of God to whom we belong with them.

3. *The priority of grace.* The foundation of biblical faith and ethics in *both* Testaments is God's grace and redemptive initiative. So while I have a stronger affinity with 'covenant theology' than dispensationalism (as may have become obvious above!), I prefer not to speak of a so-called 'covenant of works', even hypothetically.[52] The law was never given as a means of salvation (again, even hypothetically), but as a gift of grace to those already redeemed. Thus I cannot accept a rigid separation of law and grace as a valid way of categorizing the Old and New Testaments, still less the setting of one against the other – except in terms of the specific argumentation of Paul against a *distorted* view of both.

4. *The mission and purpose of Israel.* To understand the purpose of the law it is vital to enquire first about the role of Israel in God's purposes. God created and called Israel to fulfil his purpose of blessing the nations. The covenant with Abram in Genesis 12:1–3 has this as its climax, and the phrase is repeated throughout the book of Genesis. Genesis 12, therefore, has to be read in the light of Genesis 1 – 11. There was a universal goal to the very existence of Israel. God's covenant commitment to Israel served God's commitment to humanity as a whole, and therefore what God did in, for and through Israel was ultimately for the benefit of the nations. And furthermore, what God ethically required of Israel served the same purpose. Genesis 18:19 states this clearly, when it links together in one sentence God's election of Abraham, the ethical demand to walk in the way of the Lord by doing righteousness and justice, and the ultimate 'missionary'

goal – blessing the nations as promised. In other words, the very election of Israel, in all its particularity, not only has a universal missionary goal, but also leads to a clear and distinctive ethical agenda in the world for God's people as part of the condition of that goal being accomplished. Genesis 26:4f. reinforces this by again linking the universal promise of blessing to the specific moral obedience of Abraham, expressed in terms normally used of the Sinai law even though it had not been given.

5. *The function of the law in relation to the mission of Israel.* Exodus 19:1–6 is a key text at this point. Coming at the hinge between the exodus and the actual giving of the law and making of the covenant, it looks both backwards and forwards. It points to the initiative of God's redemptive grace ('You have seen what I have done …') as the essential context for obedience to the law (as the Decalogue also does), and it gives to Israel an identity and role as a *priestly* and *holy* people in the midst of 'all the nations' in 'the whole earth', which is God's. Obedience to the covenant law was thus to enable them to be holy – *i.e.* different, distinctive *from* the nations. But at the same time, as a priesthood, they were to be teacher, model and mediator *for* the nations. Keeping the law, then, was not an end in itself for Israel, but related to their very reason for existence – God's concern for the nations. Deuteronomy 4:5–8 sets Israel's social righteousness in the same context – the public stage of the world of nations. If we ask, then, whether the law was given specifically to Israel with particular relevance to them, or was meant to apply to the nations, the answer is 'Both', but this needs qualification. The law was not explicitly and consciously applied to the nations. But that does not mean it was irrelevant to them. Rather, the law was given to Israel to enable Israel to live as a model, as a light to the nations, such that, in the prophetic vision, the law would 'go forth' to the nations, or they would 'come up' to learn it.

6. *Israel and its law as paradigmatic.* Given, then, Israel's role in relation to God's purpose for the nations, and given the law's function in relation to that mission of Israel, we

can see that the law was designed (along with many other aspects of Israel's historical experience) to mould and shape Israel in certain clearly defined directions, within their own historico-cultural context. That overall social shape, with its legal and institutional structures, ethical norms and values and theological undergirding, thus becomes the model or paradigm *intended* to have a relevance and application beyond the geographical, historical and cultural borders of Israel itself.[53] The particularity of Israel then does not hinder universal application, but serves it. There is no need to repeat the explanations of my understanding of 'paradigm' (see chapters 1 and 2 above). My point here is that this paradigmatic nature of Israel is not just a hermeneutical tool devised by *us* retrospectively, but, theologically speaking, was part of God's design in creating and shaping Israel in the first place.

b. Method

1. *Distinguish the general categories of Old Testament law.* This is not just a matter of the classic distinction between moral, civil and ceremonial. Whatever importance and value that retains, it is not adequate to understand the law from an internal Israelite perspective. We need to see the different ways that law functioned in Israelite society, the different kinds of law that operated, and the different patterns of judicial administration. Elsewhere I have suggested five different categories of law: 'criminal', civil, family, cultic and compassionate.[54] Even within these the distinctions are not always clear-cut, and other sub-categories could be suggested. The point is that in order to make ethical use of the Old Testament we must first step inside it and understand the law from Israel's own social perspective. It is immediately clear that we do not find a separate, textually isolated, category of 'moral law' as such. But we do find moral motivation and principle expressed or implied in every category we turn to. In order to articulate those moral principles more sharply we need to go further.

2. *Analyse the functions of particular laws and institutions.*

114

When dealing with any particular law, we need to ask how it related to and functioned within the overall social system of Israel. Is it central or peripheral to the dominant themes and social objectives that we find in the rest of the material? Does it reinforce other primary legislation, or is it a modification, or a secondary application? This is where the importance of seeing the overall social shape of Israel really counts. It prevents us from treating every single text with flat equality and enables us to discern those which in Israel itself had priority. As Schluter and Clements rightly say, it is our awareness of this total picture which helps us organize and prioritize any derivative principles we may draw from specific texts. It also helps us avoid the tendency to jump straight from a particular text to the question, 'How does this apply to modern society?' But such analytical and descriptive work does not come cheap. It calls for an awareness of the breadth of scholarly work being done in the fields of Old Testament economics, politics, sociology, legal history, *etc.*[55] In this respect, Old Testament ethics has to take into account the whole social world of Israel in the same way that New Testament ethics now looks not just at the biblical text alone but the whole social, economic and political context of the first Christians.[56]

3. *Define the objective(s) of the law.* Laws in any society are made for a purpose. They protect interests. They restrict power. They promote social objectives. So, in the light of our understanding of Israelite society, we need to articulate as precisely as possible the objective of any specific law. This can best be done by seeking answers to a number of questions, such as the following: In Israel's society, whose interests was this law trying to protect? Whose power was it trying to restrict? What kind of behaviour did it encourage or discourage? What kind of state of affairs was it trying to promote or prevent? There are times when the obscurity of some laws defeats even such questioning. But often these questions generate a nuanced understanding of the purpose of Israel's laws which enables a much more targeted application of them when one moves to the final step.

115

4. *Preserve the objective but change the context.* Moving from the Old Testament world back to our own, we can ask a parallel set of questions about our context, seeking to identify analogous situations, interests, powers, behaviours, *etc.*, that need to be addressed. Then in that new context we ask how the objectives of Old Testament laws can be achieved, or at least how we can bring our own social objectives to point in the same direction. At this point, of course, we are 'descending the ladder of abstraction' into the realm of specific policy and action in our world. But we are doing so, not merely with highly generalized principles, but with much more sharply articulated objectives derived from the paradigm of the society God called Israel to be.

Such a procedure may help to bridge the gap between, on the one hand, an authoritative text which cannot be directly applied, and on the other hand, applied principles which have no intrinsic authority. The authority of the Scripture is that which authorizes us to develop our ethical stances, policy choices and decision-making in new contexts not directly addressed by the Bible. The authority of the Old Testament for ethics does not pre-define every choice we have to make. But the more closely and sharply we can perceive and articulate the very particularity of Israel, the more confident we can be in making choices which are 'authorized' – that is, that are legitimate within the contours and limits of the paradigm God has given us. This view also allows for a degree of variety and disagreement among Christians over the details of ethical decisions and social policies. Like the Ten Commandments themselves, the authority of the Bible sets limits to our behaviour without telling us in specific terms what we must do in every situation.

Chapter Five

Ethical decisions in the Old Testament[1]

The original full title which I was given for the paper reprinted in this chapter, 'How Were Ethical Decisions Made in the Old Testament?', reminded me of examination questions where you had to spend most of your answer interpreting and defining the question. Such a question could be approached in at least two ways. A *canonical* approach would be to look at the ethical teaching of the major sections of the Old Testament to enquire what they have to offer us as usable material that we can theologically synthesize into our own Christian ethical agenda. An *empirical* approach would be to ask how Mr and Mrs Average Israelite came to make ethical decisions in daily life, asssuming that the Hebrew Bible affords the kind of evidence we need to answer that. After trying several possible ways of juggling the material I have finally opted to organize it on a canonical basis, and to illustrate each main section with whatever empirical evidence seems appropriate to that dimension of the subject.

It is something of a truism to say that biblical ethics is theistic. That is to say, it assumes the existence of one living personal God and sets the whole of human life in response to him. Ethics is not an agenda, a means to an end, an inflexible law, self-fulfilment, or any of the other terms that may secondarily describe various human formulations of it. It is primarily response to God, who he is and what he has done. In the Hebrew Bible that response is first set in the context of God as creator, so that is where we begin. Secondly, we meet the revelation of the God of covenant purpose whose commitment to blessing the human race leads him to initiate a special relationship with Israel within which their ethical response is a central feature. Thirdly, we find that purpose given concrete historical form as we meet the God of redemptive action who delivers his people and then gives them land to live in and law to live by.

1. Responding to the God of created order

a. 'The fear of the LORD ...'

The assumption of monotheism in the opening chapters of the Bible is so obvious that we easily miss its ethically revolutionary character. The creation narratives almost effortlessly exclude polytheism and dualism, and the pervasive ethico-cultural edifices that go with them. Only one God created the heavens and the earth. Human beings are answerable only to that one God. Whether walking and talking with him in the garden in Eden, or fleeing from him in the restless land of Nod, east of Eden, it is one and the same God with whom we have to do. This immediately introduces a fundamental simplicity into biblical ethics. Commitment to love and obey the one living God rescues us from the fear of offending one god by trying to please another, from the confusion of moral requirements, or from the moral cynicism that arises when people feel that it really does not matter in the end how you live because you cannot win; the gods will get you in the end.

For Israel, the fear of Yahweh alone was the first principle not only of wisdom, but of ethics. 'Fear him, ye saints, and you will then have nothing else to fear' (from Tate and Brady's hymn, 'Through all the changing scenes of life') is not quite the words of the psalmist (34:9), but he would doubtless have agreed heartily. Certainly, in Psalm 33 the thought moves directly from the sole creative word of Yahweh to the universal challenge to all human beings to fear him (6–8), since he is the moral adjudicator of all human behaviour (13–15). The same universal ethical thrust is found in some of the psalms celebrating the kingship of Yahweh (e.g. 96:4f., 10–13).

To say that ethics in the Old Testament was simple is not to say that obedience was easy or that ethical decision-making was a matter of black-and-white choices. It is to say that the task of living in this world is not complicated by divided allegiances to competing gods, or obscure philosophies which demand religious or 'expert' élites to interpret them for us. Sometimes this essential simplicity is referred to by way of encouragement to act in accordance with God's will. 'Now what I am commanding you today is not too difficult for you or beyond your reach', says Moses. '... No, the word is very near you; it is in your mouth and in your heart so that you may obey it' (Dt. 30:11–14). 'He has showed you, O man, what is good. And what does the LORD require of you? To act justly and to love mercy and to walk humbly with your God' (Mi. 6:8). Although these texts were spoken to Israel, they can be relevant to humanity at large inasmuch as Paul generalizes the requirements of the law as something written on the hearts even of those who never heard it (Rom. 2:14f.).

b. 'The earth is fixed ...'

Another unmistakable feature of Genesis 1 is its presentation of the creation as a place of order, system and structure. We live in a cosmos, not a chaos, and we do so because of the creative word and action of God. This is not only affirmed in Genesis 1 but celebrated in Israel's worship and used by prophets to exalt the power of Yahweh as over against the gods of the nations (Is. 45:18ff.). This created order has two effects on biblical ethics.

1. *As a bulwark against relativism.* The most important effect of this truth as regards ethics is that it provides the objective basis and authority for the exercise of moral freedom, while exposing the wrongheadedness of moral relativism. Oliver O'Donovan has reinstated the importance of the creation basis for evangelical ethics in his programmatic study *Resurrection and Moral Order.*[2] At the same time as we stress the centrality of the scriptural affirmation concerning the moral authority of God's action in history, we need to give adequate attention to its portrayal of God

as creator, with all its implications for our worldview. An emphasis on history alone, without the safeguards of the biblical creation faith, could deliver us into the kind of historical relativism which puts all things, morality included, at the mercy of the historical process. This is a danger which O'Donovan also warns us of, insisting that the only proper protection from it is the biblical affirmation of a given order of creation which, though disturbed by the fall, is still the order within which we live, and which will finally be restored to its perfection and glory through God's redemptive action, which has already been achieved in the resurrection of Christ and will be complete at his return.

The biblical authority, then, for our ethics in a world of moral relativism, is based on its twin affirmation of creation and history: creation as the fundamental order that shapes our existence in history, and which is destined for restoration in the new creation of the kingdom of God; and history as the stage on which we observe the acts of the God whom we are commanded to imitate by 'walking in his ways'.[3]

2. *As a basis for legitimate consequentialism.* In Christian evaluation of different ethical stances, 'consequentialism' usually gets a bad press. This is the view that moral choices should be evaluated in terms of their likely consequences, not in terms of *a priori* moral principles which might be regarded as absolute and necessary (the latter view being termed 'deontological'). The most influential secular brand of consequentialism is utilitarianism, which at its simplest argues that the correct ethical choice in any matter is that which is likely to achieve the greatest happiness of the greatest number of people. This is not the place to enter into a critique of it.[4] What I would like to show is that among the effects of the biblical teaching on the established order of creation is a degree of confidence in the reliability and predictability of life in this world. This is not, of course, to suggest that nothing untoward ever happens unexpectedly (see the discussion of Ecclesiastes below), still less to endorse an unbiblical fatalism. It is simply to

note that the Hebrew Bible does move from the observation of regularity, consistency and permanence in creation itself (*e.g.* in Je. 31:35ff.) to affirmations of the same characteristics in God, and thence to the assumption that certain consequences will always follow from certain actions. There are causes and effects in the moral realm, as in the physical, and it is part of wise living in this world to take note of them and behave accordingly.

It is interesting that a consequentialist view of ethical decisions is found precisely in the Wisdom literature, which tends to be grounded in a creation rather than a redemption theology. Much of the advice and guidance given in Proverbs is prudential. 'Think what will happen if ...' Behavioural cause and effect are repeatedly linked. Hard work produces wealth. Lending and borrowing will lose you friends. Careless words cost lives. And so it goes on.

Possibly the most interesting example concerns the Wisdom tradition's sexual ethic. It is in full accordance with the law, of course, but it is not explicitly sanctioned by law. Whereas the law simply says, 'Do not commit adultery, on penalty of death', the Wisdom teacher says, 'Do not commit adultery because of the appalling consequences that you will expose yourself and your whole family and property to. It isn't worth the risk' (*cf.* Pr. 5; 6:24–35; 7). Common sense itself warns against what the law prohibits. Moral rules and moral consequences actually reinforce one another in this way of thinking. We need to remember, however, that the Wisdom tradition's consequentialism is thoroughly personal and theistic. It is not impersonal fate, or karma. Behind all the prudential advice of the sages stands their own foundational axiom, 'the fear of the LORD is the beginning of wisdom'. Whatever results follow from our actions, they are not a matter of mechanical cause and effect, but the outworking of God's own order in his world. The consequentialism of Wisdom is thus based on what we would theologically call God's sovereign providence and justice.

In the narratives also we come across a kind of empirical

121

consequentialism when appeals to conscience are made on the grounds of likely outcomes. Abigail's warning to David takes this approach (1 Sa. 25:30f.). Conversely, the category of 'folly' is sometimes portrayed not merely as the absence of common sense (though it can be that, as Jonathan's reaction to his father's absurd prohibition on his soldiers eating on a day of battle shows, 1 Sa. 14:24–30), but a failure to look beyond the pressure or emotion of the moment (1 Sa. 14:29; 2 Sa. 13:12ff.)

c. A desacralized worldview

Another dimension of the creation ethic of the Hebrew Bible is the way it desacralizes certain areas of life which in polytheistic cultures tend to be shrouded in mystique, taboos and risk for mortal men and women. Death, for example, in the Old Testament is not some external power or independent deity, but a fact decreed and controlled by God, and given moral and spiritual rationale in relation to human sin. It remains a horror and an enemy, but has no personal power to direct or guide how one lives here and now. For that, you go to the living God alone and neither to death itself nor to the dead (Is. 8:19f.).

With greater practical and ethical relevance, Old Testament creation faith also desacralized sex. It played no part in the process of the creation of the world, but is simply one feature internal to creation. Human sexuality is part of the image of God, but not in itself part of God. It is a gift within creation, to be enjoyed with God's blessing, but not a means of manipulating either God or nature, as it is within the fertility cults that usually exist symbiotically with polytheism. Thus it is that in the Hebrew Bible strict laws on the proper context for the exercise of our sexuality coexist with the unrestrained freedom of the Song of Solomon's exaltation of the joy of sex under God's blessing. In this case, the Wisdom tradition adorns what the law protects.

This desacralizing of important areas of life in the Hebrew Bible actually increases the scope of personal freedom. Old Testament law can sound restrictive because of its negative tone. But on reflection it is actually the case that negatively framed law is much more liberating than positive or directive law. It is more liberating to be told you may do what you choose, with specified limits and exceptions, than to be told what you must choose or do in all circumstances. The park which allows you freedom to do what you like, but 'Do not pick the flowers', is a better place to be than the safari park where you must follow the prescribed route and stay in your car. Even in the garden of Eden it was thus. 'You are free to eat of any tree of the garden – except ...' This gave to humanity a range of freedoms in the world which so many 'religions' would have hedged much more restrictively.

Yet, having given to humanity such freedom to act within the created order, and having entrusted to us dominion over creation, one route to achieving mastery was prohibited – magic and the occult. The creation narratives themselves exclude any magic dimension to the way in which God created and ordered the world, and likewise the task of working out our appropriate ethical task in the world is not to be short-circuited or bypassed by magical mechanisms. Magic is intrinsically contrary to the personalist biblical worldview. It attempts to evade the responsibility of making personal choice and response to our personal God and instead yields up to other forces the mastery that God entrusted to us through our own moral choices.

d. The image of God

Perhaps the most familiar of all the implications of the creation material for biblical ethics is the affirmation that God made human beings in his own image. This has been explored in great depth by many scholars, biblical and ethical. I would want to pick out just two main results of it as regards ethical decision-making in the Old Testament.

1. *The sanctity of human life.* As early as the texts of the Noah covenant the principle was stated that human life was to be treated as inviolable, on the grounds of the image

of God. Even animals would be held to account by God for the killing of humans. The influence of this principle can be seen in Israel's law. Laws about domestic animals that injure or kill humans are common in ancient Near Eastern legal corpora. All of them prescribe various degrees of compensation and punishment of the owner. Only the Hebrew law prescribes also that the 'guilty' ox was to be stoned to death. It seems most likely that this was because of the religious influence on the law of the principle of the sanctity of human life, as crystalized in Genesis 9:5.[5]

Empirically, this high value shows itself in the narratives in several places where there is an abhorrence of the shedding of innocent blood. Sometimes this has a marked effect an ethical decision at the time (e.g. 1 Sa. 19:4–6; 25:26; 2 Sa. 2:22; 3:28, 37).

2. *The equality of human beings.* The Old Testament did not eliminate all social distinctions, such as, for example, the social and economic inferiority of the slave. It did, however, go a long way in mitigating the worst effects, by a theology of essential human equality based on our common createdness. In its law, the Old Testament knows nothing of the graded penalties for crimes against different ranks of victim, as is common in ancient Near Eastern law. There was equality before the law for native and alien. The slave was given human and legal rights unheard of in contemporary societies. This is reflected in Job's great ethical self-defence in which he bases his claim to have treated his slaves with justice in any case they brought against him upon an unambiguous statement of created human equality between master and slave: 'Did not he who made me in the womb also make them?' (Jb. 31:15). Once again it is in the Wisdom literature that we find the broadest outworking of this creation theology into the social ethos of Israel. There are several texts in Proverbs which affirm the equality before God of rich and poor (Pr. 22:2; 29:13), and others which so identify God with every human being, regardless of status, that what we do to them we do to God himself (Pr. 14:31; 17:5; 19:17). This is not the only place where we can hear distinct echoes of the

Wisdom tradition in the ethical teaching of Jesus.

e. Disordered creation

All the points above flow from Israel's understanding of the world as a place created and ordered by God. But of course it is also a place spoiled and disordered by humanity. Ethical decision-making, therefore, has to respond to the presence of evil and apparent chaos within human society and the world itself. It could be said that the whole Old Testament from Genesis 4 onwards is the deposit of that struggle. But as regards specific ethical behaviour, the main thrust of the Old Testament is that a person must persevere in his commitment to upright behaviour in the sight of God, even in the face of contradiction from fellow human beings or from adverse and inexplicable circumstances. I would point to two significant areas.

First, in the Psalms there is a remarkable reflection of Israel's ethical values, struggles and endeavour, scarcely matched at all in Christian hymnody. It is noticeable how often the psalmists affirm their intention to continue to pursue righteous behaviour in spite of a surrounding climate of evil, to speak and do the truth when engulfed in lies, to keep clean hands in a dirty world. The cost of this stance is considerable and is also reflected in the anguish of the Psalms. The person who keeps his word will sometimes find that it ends up hurting himself, but it is a qualification of acceptable worship that he still does so (Ps. 15:4). Surrounded by prosperous, complacent evildoers, the believer is tempted to think his own moral efforts are futile, and can find respite and perspective only in worship (Ps. 73). The world is a wicked place, but the only path to happiness in it, as the deliberately prefatory Psalm 1 makes unambiguously clear, is the committed, systematic, choice of the way of the Lord. Such a stance is wise and good and godly. That is to say, the ethics of the psalmists bind together in one inclusive worldview, the intellectual, the moral and the religious spheres. For, conversely, the opposite stance is foolish, evil and ungodly: the *fool* says in

125

his heart, 'There is no God', because he has chosen the way of *corruption* (Ps. 14). If the ethos of a people's worship is a good guide to the ethics of their society, then the strong ethical character of the Psalms is very revealing of the moral climate among devout Israelites.

Secondly, the Wisdom tradition, for all its commitment to a consequentialist view of the world in which moral causes and effects are broadly predictable, so that ethical decisions can be made with reasonable confidence, is nevertheless aware that it does not always work out like that in real life. Ecclesiastes is often regarded as in a sense Wisdom's own self-criticism, as a counterbalance to the broad optimism of Proverbs. It refuses to ignore the brutal realities of life in this world (some have said it is the Hebrew Bible's best commentary on Genesis 3)[6] – the absurdities, the injustices, the way the unexpected disaster can ruin our best endeavours, the unpredictability of life (how a tree will fall or the wind will blow) and, above all, the menacing enigma of death. Yet in the midst of all these, the writer of Ecclesiastes remains both a theistic believer (this is still God's world and we are accountable to him) and a committed subscriber to the essential moral stance of Yahwism – to fear Yahweh and keep his commandments (12:13), for that is what it means to 'remember your Creator' (12:1).

In conclusion to this first main section, then, we have seen that ethical decisions in the Old Testament were made first of all in response to Yahweh as creator. That includes:

1. A monotheistic stance which both excludes the moral degeneracy of polytheism and also simplifies ethics to a fundamentally single choice – to love and obey Yahweh, or not to;

2. Basic confidence in the world as a place created and ordered by God in such a way that moral choices matter and have predictable moral consequences that can be known and anticipated;

3. A high degree of 'secular' freedom in how we live in the earth, unfettered by the bondage of occultism, sacral

taboos and the fear or manipulation of magic;

4. A primary regard for the value of human life as made in the image of God, which both sets the shedding of innocent blood near the top of the list of ethical negatives and sets the equality of all human beings near the top of the list of ethical positives.

And we have seen that the ethical values that flow from these sources are to be preserved and lived out, even in the midst of a cursed earth and a fallen humanity which constantly undermine, deny or reverse them.

2. Responding to the God of covenant purpose

The God who created our world and then watched us spoil it chose to destroy neither it nor us, but instead to commit himself under covenant to a project of ultimate redemption and re-creation that would involve the whole of the rest of time and space. This is the scope of what God initiated through his dealings with Abraham, beginning in Genesis 12. It is the covenant of grace which stands behind all subsequent acts of God in history, for it represents God's commitment to the ultimate good of humanity. 'In you shall all the families of the earth be blessed.' The universal scope of this promise echoes throughout the patriarchal narratives (Gn. 18:18; 22:18; 26:4f.; 28:14) and then on through the rest of the Hebrew Bible.

a. Teleological ethics

A major effect for ethics of this commitment to a covenant purpose of redemption on God's part is the injection of hope. We live within history and all our ethical decisions and actions are subject to its apparent uncertainties. As Ecclesiastes observed so long ago, it is easy to succumb to the meaninglessness of life if we cannot see beyond even our own lives, let alone fathom a grand design to 'life, the universe and everything'. Ethics becomes little more than short-term expediency for a slightly more tolerable social existence in our short allotted span. From such nihilism we are rescued only by the teleological view of history which sees an ultimate goal declared by God's covenant promise to Abraham and amplified in the rest of the Hebrew Bible to include a whole new creation. There is a future. There is hope. There is purpose. With such foundations, ethics is worth the effort. The empirical impact on ancient Israel of this eschatological context for Old Testament ethics is rather indirect, but still discernible, and we shall take it up shortly.

b. The people of God

The second very significant dimension of the covenant with Abraham for biblical ethics was the promise of a people. God's answer to a world of nations scattered in arrogance and strife, which was the world portrayed through the story of the tower of Babel in Genesis 11, was to create a new community. It would be a people descended from Abraham and blessed as he was, but which would ultimately be the vehicle for blessing to the whole world of nations. And it would be a people whose contribution to that purpose would be by their ethical distinctiveness. Simply being Israel was an ethical agenda and mission in the midst of the world. To be an Israelite was to be called to respond to God's covenant purpose for the nations by living as the people of God in their midst.

This may not seem to fit with the common view that the covenant with Abraham was unconditional. But I question whether that view is correct. In a sense all God's covenant arrangements in the Bible are unconditional in that they do not depend for their initiation on any action or merit of ours and in that they will be fulfilled ultimately by God's grace and not by our power to sustain our response. Yet at the same time, all the covenants recorded in Scripture are also conditional in the sense that a response is required. In the case of the covenant with Abraham, this was not merely the personal requirement of faith and obedience on his part, but included also the intention that the people descended from him should be committed to the way of the Lord in full ethical obedience.

The clearest expression of this is Genesis 18:19.

128

> I have chosen him, so that he will direct his
> children and his household after him to keep the
> way of the LORD by doing what is right and just,
> so that the LORD will bring about for Abraham
> what he has promised him.

The context of this verse is God's imminent judgment upon Sodom and Gomorrah. It is, in fact, part of a conversation between God and Abraham while God, with his two angelic deputies, was on his way down, so to speak, to find out the truth about the cities and act accordingly. This makes the ethical heart of the verse even more notable. In the midst of a world characterized by Sodom – whose evil is causing an outcry (18:20f., twice: $s^e\,\bar{a}q\hat{a}$, the technical term for the crying out of those suffering from oppression and cruelty) that can be heard in heaven itself, God wants a community characterized by his own values and priorities – righteousness ($s^e\underline{d}\bar{a}q\hat{a}$: one wonders if the word-play is intentional here, as it certainly is in Is. 5:7) and justice. The presence here in the patriarchal narratives of these two phrases, 'the way of the LORD' and 'doing what is right right and just', both of which would come among the top five of the most used summaries of Old Testament ethical values, shows that Israel's identity as a distinct ethical community comes well before the Sinai covenant and Mosaic law. It was something written into their genetic code, so to speak, while they were as yet in the loins of Abraham. In fact, such ethical distinctiveness is put forward here by God himself as the very reason for the election of Abraham: 'I have chosen him … so that …' The sense of purpose is very strong in the verse. Election means election to an *ethical* agenda in the midst of a corrupt world of Sodoms.

But that ethical agenda is itself only part of a still wider purpose. The goal of the verse moves on into a third purpose clause: '… so that the LORD will bring about for Abraham what he has promised him'. That is a clear reference, in the light of the preceding verse, to God's ultimate intention to bring blessing to all nations through the descendants of Abraham. That is God's mission, God's universal agenda. That too was the reason for the election of Abraham. What is therefore highly significant in the structure of this verse, syntactically as well as theologically, is the way ethics stands as the middle term between election and mission. The distinctive quality of life of the people of God, committed to his way of righteousness and justice, stands as the purpose of election on the one hand and the means to mission on the other. It is the fulcrum of the verse.

c. Ethics and eschatology

What we have seen, then, is that Israel was called to specific forms of ethical life in order to facilitate God's purpose of bringing the blessing promised to Abraham to the nations. Old Testament ethics is set in a universal and eschatological framework, linked to the mission of being the nation for other nations. This was a dimension of their calling that Israel tended to forget and so it could not be called common or widespread. But there are echoes of it in some places in the rest of the Hebrew Bible.

1. *Psalm 72.* There are a number of connections between the Abrahamic covenant and the covenant with David.[7] Among them is an interest in the universal scope of what God was doing. In David's response to God's covenant promise, for example, there is the awareness that what God would do through the house of David would become a talking-point among the nations (2 Sa. 7:25f.). The prayer of Solomon at the dedication of the temple has the remarkable section asking God to fulfil the prayers of foreigners who will pray to him there having heard of his reputation (1 Ki. 8:41–43). The motive behind the prayer is that 'all the peoples of the earth may know your name and fear you'. God's ethical demands on the house of David were written into the covenant from the start in the sonship response of obedience (2 Sa. 7:14f.). They had in any case been spelt out in the law of the king in Deuteronomy 17:14–20, which unmistakably put the king under the covenant law of Sinai, with its demands for justice and protection of the weak.

This was precisely what so many kings failed to do. Towards the end of the monarchy, Jeremiah stood at the gate of the royal palace itself to declare the ethical requirement on the incumbents of David's throne – a declaration which clearly subordinated Zion to Sinai (Je. 22:1–3). Note that the nations are in view again, if only in bafflement (22:8f.).

The clearest link between the universal scope of the Davidic ideal and the ethical demand is found in Psalm 72. In the form of a prayer for the king, it concentrates strongly on the various forms of moral government that should flow from him, emphasizing yet again the socio-ethical combination of 'righteousness and justice' which he, as the embodiment of Israel, should manifest *par excellence*. And in verse 17b it looks beyond Israel to the rest of the world, with a clear echo of the Abrahamic covenant of blessing to the nations.

> All nations will be blessed through him [*i.e.*, in
>   this context, the royal son of David, ruling in
>   justice],
> and they will call him blessed.

The main thrust of this Psalm is that if the king would rule the nation in line with God's moral requirements then, first of all, the nation itself would enjoy peace and prosperity. But beyond that, by linking the king's rule to the Abrahamic covenant, the psalmist makes the point that God's purpose of blessing for the nations is inseparable from the ethical quality of life among his own people.

2. *Jeremiah 4:1-2.* The same thought exercised Jeremiah's mind as he called the people to repentance at a time, probably early in his ministry, when repentance was still felt to be a possibility. In 4:1–2, Jeremiah first urges the people to renounce idolatry and make their worship and general social life (which is probably what is meant by swearing 'as surely the LORD lives') compatible with truth, justice and righteousness. Only such a radical return to the covenant demands would be credible as a genuine 'return'

to Yahweh (1a, which follows the lengthy exposition of the 'return' sub-theme in ch. 3). But what if they do respond thus? The fact that judgment would thereby be averted from Israel herself is taken for granted, and Jeremiah's vision skips forward to a more universal vision, and another clear allusion to the Abrahamic covenant:

> Then the nations will be blessed by him
> and in him they will glory.
> (Je. 4:2b)

Clearly Jeremiah believed that the quality of Israel's ethical life was not just an end in itself, but was supposed to have far-reaching consequences for the nations as well. Much more was at stake in the matter of Israel's moral and spiritual repentance than just saving Israel's own skin from judgment.

3. *Isaiah 48:1, 17-19.* In the following generation, those who had failed to heed the warning of Jeremiah and the pre-exilic prophets heard the almost wistful voice of God ruefully pondering on what might have been the case if they had done so. In Isaiah 48:1, the prophet makes a similar point to that of Jeremiah above: the people were claiming the name of God's people and were using his name in worship and social life. But all this was contradicted in their practical life by the absence of 'truth' and 'righteousness'. Then, in verses 17ff., in a kind of 'unrealized eschatology', God indulges in a very human kind of 'if only ...' Verse 19 effectively says that if only Israel had been the community of obedience and righteousness that he desired and planned for them, then the promise to Abraham could have been fulfilled! The point is rhetorical and hypothetical, of course, and not to be pushed literally. But it does very strongly bind together again the link between God's redemptive purpose for humanity, as signalled in the Abrahamic covenant, and his ethical demand on Israel as the people of God.

3. Responding to the God of redemptive action

The God who declared his covenant purpose to Abraham went on to act in accordance with it in the historic deliverance of Israel from Egypt. The exodus is explicitly said to be motivated by God's faithfulness to his covenant with Abraham. And within three months of the event, God introduced Israel to the ethical implications of what had happened to them.

a. Priestly and holy

A crucial text in this connection is Exodus 19:3–6. It is a hinge between the redemptive history of the exodus and the law and covenant texts that follow. In these verses God gives to Israel an identity and a mission, which constitute the basis for the ethical demands of the law. And behind both stands the redemptive action of God himself. So by way of preface to all the detailed legislation to follow, the fundamental ethical principle is that God's requirements depend, first, on what God himself has done and, second, on who Israel is. We shall look at both of these.

1. *God's initiative and universal interest.* 'You yourselves have seen what I did …' Just as he would later do when introducing the Ten Commandments, so here God begins with a historical reminder of his own action. For those listening on this occasion it was a recent memory. Three months previously they had been slaves in Egypt. Now they were free. And God reminds them that it had been because of his own initiative of grace and promise-keeping. The importance of this cannot be overstated, for it is a principle running through the whole of biblical ethics. Whatever moral endeavours we may make can never be more than a response to what God has already done for us. The priority of grace over law was not a New Testament discovery or revolution, but built into the nature of divine–human encounter from the beginning and an explicit part of the covenant with Israel. We will note the theme of gratitude as a motivation for some Old Testament laws later.

133

But even as the historical reference homes in on God's special action for Israel, his 'treasured possession', two phrases make sure that the perspective stays broad – as broad as God's concern for 'all nations' and 'the whole earth'. Israel as God's special possession was not his exclusive possession, for he can say that 'the whole earth is mine'. Even while Israel had been in Egypt God had made this clear, in word and deed, to Pharaoh (Ex. 9:14, 16, 29). So, although at this point in the canonical story the focus is primarily on Israel and the unique redemptive and covenant relationship between them and God, the universal scope of the Abrahamic covenant has not been lost sight of. Whatever ethical demands follow must be set not only in the immediate historical context, but in the same broad context that we sketched above in section 2, 'Responding to the God of covenant purpose'.

2. *Israel's identity and moral obligation.* Having laid the foundation of his own redemptive action and universal concern, God goes on to spell out the role and mission of Israel in two phrases which echo elsewhere in the Old Testament and indeed are picked up and applied to the church in 1 Peter 2:9). 'You will be for me a priestly kingdom and a holy nation.' It is the qualifying terms, 'priestly' and 'holy', which are significant. That is the kind of kingdom and nation Israel was to be in the midst of the world of nations. Each term deserves some explication, for both are key words in Israel's ethical system.

Priestly. A priest in Old Testament Israel was someone who stood in between God and the rest of the people. He was a mediator in both directions. On the one hand he represented God to the people, in both his life and example, but especially through his responsibility for teaching the law (Lv. 10:9–11; Dt. 33:8–10; Je. 18:18; Ho. 4:6; Mal. 2:1–9). Through the priest, then, the people *could know God*. On the other hand, he represented the people before God, since it was his task to bring the sacrifices and to make atonement for the people at the altar. Through the priest, then, the people *could come to God*.

134

So it is with this double significance that God says to Israel *as a whole community*, 'You are to be my priesthood in the midst of the nations of the earth.' On the one hand, Israel would represent the true God to the nations – revealing his will, his moral demands, his saving purpose, *etc.* Through Israel, other nations *would know Yahweh.* But also, it would be through Israel that God would eventually bring the other nations to himself in redemptive, atoning, covenant relationship. Through Israel, other nations *would come to Yahweh.* Later prophets pick up both ideas: the law of God going out from Israel to the nations, and other nations coming up to God to or through Israel (or Jerusalem). The priesthood identity of Israel thus gives to Old Testament ethics yet another dimension of 'missionary' relevance. Right at the start of their historical journey, God sets their ethical agenda in the context of their mission in the midst of the nations.

Holy. The word does not mean that the people of Israel were to be extra-specially religious. Rather it has the sense of distinctiveness and difference. Israel would be a nation as other nations, but they were to be holy – different from the rest of the nations. The so-called Holiness Code expresses this very succinctly:

> You must not do as they do in Egypt, where you
> used to live, and you must not do as they do in
> the land of Canaan, where I am bringing you.
> (Lv. 18:3)

This is the practical implication of the priestly doctrine of Israel's election from among the nations:

> You shall be holy to me; for I Yahweh am holy,
> and have separated you from the peoples that
> you should be mine.
> (Lv. 20:26, my translation)

Even the foreigner Balaam recognized this conscious sense of distinctiveness about Israel (Nu. 23:9).

The outworking of this characteristic affected every dimension of national life, including their religion, but permeating social, economic, political and personal affairs also. This is most clearly seen in Leviticus 19, a chapter full of very practical laws for daily life, all under the heading, 'You shall be holy, as I, Yahweh your God, am holy.' Some of the laws in this chapter have to do with the cultic life of Israel, but the majority are social in nature. Holiness affected more than the ritual area of life. Holiness, in Leviticus 19, dictates: caring use of agricultural produce (9f.; *cf.* Dt. 24:19); fair treatment and payment of employees (13; *cf.* Dt. 24:14); practical compassion for the disabled and respect for the elderly (14, 32; *cf.* Dt. 27:18); the integrity of the judicial process (15; *cf.* Dt. 16:18–20); safety precautions (16b; *cf.* Dt. 22:8); ecological sensitivity (23ff.; *cf.* Dt. 20:19f.); equality before the law for ethnic minorities (33f.; *cf.* Dt. 24:17); and honesty in trade and business (35f.; *cf.* Dt. 25:13ff.).

In short, to love your neighbour (and even the stranger) as yourself (18, 34) is not a revolutionary love ethic initiated by Jesus but the fundamental ethical demand of Old Testament holiness.

John Gammie's recent book, *Holiness in Israel*, very helpfully distinguishes the different responses to the demand to be holy that are found in the priestly materials, the prophetic books, and the Wisdom tradition. For the priests, holiness required fundamental cleanness in every part of life. For the prophets, holiness must be demonstrated in societal justice. For the Wisdom schools, holiness must be seen in personal and practical morality. The categories are helpful, but not, of course, mutually exclusive. For example, Gammie appreciates that Leviticus 19 is a most important chapter in demonstrating that the priestly tradition was not concerned merely with the cultic expression of holiness. It not only contains most of the Decalogue in one way or another, but also echoes many of the concerns of the Deuteronomic and prophetic movements (not to mention its being a major source behind the ethical teaching of the epistle of James).

[For the authors of the Holiness Code] the meaning of the divine challenge to be 'holy (ones)' extends far beyond the idea of 'separation' from other peoples to include the deepest kind of ethical and humanitarian concerns ... Not only are proper attitudes and duties toward fellow human beings enumerated in this chapter as the requirements of holiness but also proper duties and attitudes toward God – among which reverence especially is emphasized (vv. 14, 32) ... Leviticus 19 must clearly be ranked as one of the high points of Old Testament ethics, along with Amos 5, Micah 6, Ezekiel 18, and Job 31 ... It is thus altogether misleading and a caricature of the priestly understanding of holiness to reduce it to a set of rules pertaining to purity ...[8]

b. Obeying the law

The first response, then, to God's redemptive action was for Israel to recognize their own identity and mission in the world, as God's priesthood, called to be holy – distinctive in every area of life. That having been grasped, they were then given detailed and specific content in the law itself. The logic of Exodus 19:5–6 is that *if* Israel will obey the law and keep the (Sinai) covenant, *then* they can function as God's priesthood in the midst of the nations. That is, obedience to the law is a condition of the fulfilment of their *mission*, not a prior condition of their *redemption*. Their redemption had already been accomplished, as God repeatedly insists. All else is response. But the response is essential to God's purpose for them. Once again we see the vital link between ethics and mission.

Setting the Old Testament law in this perspective (God's redemptive action and human response to it) is helpful in softening the otherwise starkly deontological flavour of the law. In the popular mind, 'Old Testament ethics' is used as a shorthand for absolute rules, mostly beginning 'Thou shalt not', and sanctioned by severe retributive punishments. Like all caricatures, this popular impression exaggerates a feature of the Old Testament which nevertheless does exist. The covenant relationship between Israel and God entailed obedience to 'laws, statutes and ordinances'. Ethics certainly involved rules, not just results. But the important thing is that the Old Testament's deontology was as theistic as its consequentialism. The authority of the law was not that of abstract ethical absolutes but the authority of the personal God whom they knew as creator and redeemer. Obedience to the law was thus not just conformity to the rules *per se* but personal loyalty to the God who gave them.

Making ethical decisions in the Old Testament, then, certainly took account of obeying God's law (to the extent that it was known – a point discussed further below). But the law itself contains a high degree of 'motive clauses' which clarify why and how the law was to be obeyed, and some of these can be illustrated empirically from other parts of the Old Testament.

1. *Love and gratitude.* The very juxtaposition of God's redemptive action with the moral demand of the law creates the impression that the latter is viewed as the appropriate response of those who have enjoyed the blessing of the former. This impression is confirmed by the heavy emphasis on this motivation for obedience in Deuteronomy 4 – 11. The God who loved Israel's fore-fathers enough to rescue their descendants from slavery is a God to be loved in return, with a covenant love expressed in obedience. Significantly, the area of law where this motive of gratitude for historical deliverance is most pressed is that which concerned the poor, the stranger, the debtor, the slave – the very conditions from which God had rescued Israel (*e.g.* Ex. 22:21; 23:9; Lv. 19:33–36; 25:38, 42f., 54f.; Dt. 15:15).

There are some examples in the narratives of decisions being taken in the light of God's historical example. These do not simply go back to the paradigmatic history of exodus to conquest, but sometimes set particular decisions in the light of an act of God in the immediate past. Saul's choice of mercy over revenge (1 Sa. 11:12f.) and David's choice of equal shares of the booty (1 Sa. 30:22–25) were both based on immediately prior acts of Yahweh. Likewise it is characteristic of psalms of individual thanksgiving (and some parts of psalms of lament) to make a renewed commitment to obedience and upright living out of gratitude for an experience of God's deliverance or blessing (*e.g.* Ps. 40:6–8).

2. Imitation of Yahweh. The way God had acted on behalf of Israel was not to provide merely the motive for ethical obedience but also the model for it. This is implied in the common expression for obedience to the law, 'walking in the way of the LORD'. In Deuteronomy 10:12–19 this motive of imitation (17b–19) is added to the motive of gratitude (15).[9]

The life of David again affords an example of this particular influence on conduct. His treatment of Mephibosheth in 2 Samuel 9 arises from a deliberate desire to show 'the kindness (*ḥeseḏ*) of Yahweh' to any survivor of the house of Saul, for the sake of his promise to Jonathan. The expression probably means not only the *ḥeseḏ* (faithfulness to a commitment) which Yahweh commands, but also that which he characteristically shows. Likewise again, the Psalms give evidence that this dimension of ethics featured in Israel's worship. The constant praising of Yahweh for his *ethical* attributes was bound to have a subconscious effect on the ethical conscience of the worshipper. But it was not always left at the subconscious level. Psalms 111 and 112 are parallel acrostic psalms clearly meant to be taken together. The first is a descriptive praise of Yahweh, the second a description of the man who fears Yahweh. In several places the cross-parallellism between the two is striking and must be deliberate. Note the following (the verse numbers are the same for both psalms):

3   their righteousness endures for ever

4   both are gracious and compassionate

5   God provides food; the righteous man is generous and just

139

7   God is trustworthy; the righteous man is
     trusting
9   God provided redemption; the righteous man
     scatters gifts to the poor (used by Paul to
     encourage Christian giving, 2 Cor. 9:9).

Again one marvels at the poverty of so much Christian
hymnody which rarely makes such direct links between
the ethical character of God and the specific ethical quality
of life required of the worshipper (*cf.* Pss. 15 and 24).

3. *For our own good*. Obedience to the law is not an
arbitrary or inexplicable duty, but is constantly buttressed
by the assurance that it is for our own good. This is the
thrust of the exhortations in Deuteronomy (*e.g.* 4:40; 5:33;
6:24f.; 30:15–20; *etc.*). Psalm 72 links the degree of obedience
to the law on the part of the king, as representative and
pace-setter for the whole community, with the degree of
blessing and prosperity enjoyed by the nation. Conversely,
the prophets can link economic or political disaster with
practical disobedience (*e.g.* Ho. 4). Nehemiah counteracts
the greedy kind of self-interest that had led to exploitation
and impoverishment among the post-exilic community
with a higher level of self-interest in his appeal to the
wealthier to walk in the fear of Yahweh, lest his judgment
fall on the whole nation (Ne. 5).

In these ways, the law is anchored in the covenant reality,
which was the personal relationship between Yahweh and
not just Israel collectively but also every Israelite. That is
why the language of Israel's worship which is richest in
praise of the law sees it as the prime way of maintaining,
expressing *and enjoying* that relationship which God had
made possible by his redemptive righteousness. The ethos
of Psalms 1, 19 and 119 is light years distant from the
bondage of legalism. True, day-to-day ethical decisions
must be made in obedience to God's law. Perhaps that
makes the 176 verses of Psalm 119 the lengthiest piece of
personalized deontological ethics in the Bible! But the
author could never be accused of rule-book morality. On
the contrary, it is in obedience that, paradoxically, he finds

the greatest peace, security and freedom.

> I will always obey your law,
>   for ever and ever.
> I will walk about in freedom,
>   for I have sought out your precepts.
>   (Ps. 119:44f.)

c. Knowing the law

Canonically, then, it is clear that ethical decisions in the Old Testament were related to the moral authority and explicit detail of the law. Empirically, however, we must ask how the law would have been known in Israel. There were two main mechanisms for dissemination of knowledge of the law and its moral demands.

1. *The family.* Much stress is laid on the teaching role of the family. This is not only seen in the hortatory chapters of Deuteronomy (*e.g.* 6:7; 11:19; 32:46f.), but is also reflected in the Wisdom tradition. The head of each household had a primary responsibility in this domestic education. Some scholars have also detected the evidence of ancient Israelite catechetical materials in the texts where a father is instructed how to respond to a son's questions concerning vital events in Israel's history and also about the meaning of the law itself (Ex. 12:26f.; 13:14f.; Dt. 6:20–24; Jos. 4:6f., 21–23).[10] I have discussed this familial dimension to Israel's ethical life elsewhere.[11] The expectation that the moral ethos of Israel should be handed on from father to children is thrown into relief by two notable occasions when it was not met: the failure of Eli's sons (1 Sa. 2:12–17), and even more poignantly, the failure of Samuel's (1 Sa. 8:1–5).

2. *The priests.* The teaching function of the priests is often forgotten because of their role in the sacrificial system, but as we saw above, it was of vital importance. It was virtually part of their ordination charge (Lv. 10:10f.). It is put before their sacrificial role in the blessing of Moses (Dt. 33:10), and is the sole, almost proverbial, function attributed to them in Jeremiah 18:18. A reforming king like Jehoshaphat turned to the levitical priests to assist in the dissemination and

administration of the law under his new judicial arrangements (2 Ch. 19:4–11). Similarly, Ezra employs Levites in his mass programme of 'theological education by extension' in the restored post-exilic community (Ne. 8). Thus, it was through the priests that the people should have known the moral will of God. The prophets' quarrel with the priests was precisely that they had failed in their teaching role, and thus the people, deprived of knowledge of the law, were understandably living in disobedience to it (Ho. 4:4–9; Mal. 2:1–9).

In spite of the failures in both mechanisms, there is evidence that apart from the periods of rampant paganism and moral decadence (such as the reign of Manasseh), average Israelites shared a common ethical ethos which was substantially informed by the major distinctives of the Mosaic law. That evidence is to be found in the ethical 'typologies' that are found here and there; that is, the portraits of typically righteous or unrighteous behaviour. These are very revealing precisely because they are not in a legal context, but reflect the extent to which the values of the law penetrated the commonly accepted and assumed values of society. Examples of such lists are found in the narratives (*e.g.* 1 Sa. 12:1–5), in the Psalms (15; 24), in the Wisdom tradition (*e.g.* Jb. 31), and in the prophets (*e.g.* Ezk. 18). Again, this is material which I have compared in more depth elsewhere.[12] The most notable feature of all these lists is the extent to which they combine what we would call private and public morality – everything from inward thoughts to social responsibility. The narratives also provide some evidence of decisions and actions being taken either explicitly or implicitly in relation to a particular law (*e.g.* 1 Sa. 28:3; 2 Sa. 11:4; 12:6; 2 Ki. 14:6).

Conclusion

It is clear from all our discussion that Old Testament ethics overflow any attempt to pour them into a single category. The superficial appearance of being exclusively deontological, because of the prominence and priority of the law in the canonical order of the Hebrew Bible, has to be balanced in several ways. We have seen that the Old Testament itself engages in several kinds of consequentialism and indeed urges the believer to look to the ends of any course of action and evaluate it thereby.

Furthermore, the narratives put before us, usually without much moralistic comment, cases where clashes of moral rules occur and the actors in a story have to make choices according to some implicit prioritizing even of the Ten Commandments. Saving life appears to justify telling lies (1 Sa. 19:14ff.). Sheer survival seems to demand it also (*e.g.* 1 Sa. 21:2ff.), though the narrator may be concealing an ethical critique behind the wonderfully ironic compliment that the pagan Achish pays to David who has repeatedly lied to him (1 Sa. 29:6–9; *cf.* 27:10–12). Another pagan, Abimelech, actually teaches the father of Israel a lesson on the priority of truth-telling over personal protection (Gn. 20).

The ambiguity of situations in themselves is also recognized. Had David slain Saul in the cave or the camp (1 Sa. 24 and 26), both he and even Saul acknowledged that he could have felt morally justified in taking the life of one intent on killing him. His men added to an instinctive situation ethics the theological argument that God himself had engineered the situation for that very purpose. But David (in a rare Old Testament reference to the conscience, 24:5) places a prior principle above the apparent demands of the situation, namely the sanctity of one anointed by God, and chooses the still higher principle of entrusting just retribution to God himself (12) almost as if he had just read Romans 12:17–21 (which is, of course, based on Old Testament texts). On that occasion his own moral reasoning triumphed over an instinctive and opportunist ethic. On another, it was the calm moral reasoning of a woman that prevented him carrying through an emotional and vengeful course of action against Nabal. Abigail's arguments (1 Sa. 25:26–31) included a mixture of deont-ology (the sanctity of human life, the wrongness of innocent bloodshed, and of taking personal vengeance) and consequentialism (the later effects on David's conscience as king of what he was now planning in hot blood). These kinds of examples of ethical argument and decision in the Old Testament are an illuminating sidelight on the more didactic material.

Finally, we have to face the question whether the ethical teaching of the Hebrew Bible is still authoritative for Christians, or relevant at all to the wider world of peoples and nations outside the covenant of grace. I cannot agree with either the theonomist view which advocates literal (but sometimes curiously selective) obedience to the Mosaic law, or the kind of dispensational millennialist view which demotes or postpones the importance of the Old Testament for Christians in a way that seems incompatible with the words of Jesus and Paul.[13] My own view, which I have tried to set out in more detail in *Living as the People of God = An Eye for an Eye,* is that there are scriptural grounds in both Testaments for regarding Israel as God's model, a paradigm for both the people of God throughout history and for the nations as well. This depends partly on the fact that Israel were never meant to be 'a law unto themselves', but were chosen precisely because of God's wider purposes for the rest of humanity. So although the ethics of the Old Testament are very particular, historical and specific, they intentionally had a universal relevance from the beginning. God's revelation and redemptive action in Israel were explicitly unique, as we have seen. But once we accept both the moral consistency of God and the fact that Israel was called for the sake of the nations, there is an essential continuity between what he required of Israel and what he requires of all human beings, including but not confined to Christians. Thus I would argue that the historical particularism and specificity of Old Testament ethics does not restrict but rather sharpens their universal relevance.[14]

What we must do, then, when seeking to apply the relevance of any Old Testament law, for example, is to question the text in order to discover the objective of the law and then seek to preserve that objective while changing the context from then to now, from there to here.

We need to ask questions such as: what state of affairs is this law aiming to produce? What kind of situation is it trying to prevent? What category of people is it trying to protect because of their vulnerability or to restore because of their loss? What kind of person is it trying to restrain because of their power or to punish because of their wickedness? What moral principles underly it? What values and priorities does it embody? What is the balance of creation ideals and fallen realities, of justice and compassion, in this law? Then, having thought deeply through all these dimensions of the law in its Israelite context, one has the challenging task of thinking about our own society and asking: what are comparable situations, persons, principles, values and objectives in our own context? What kind of action – legal, personal, collective, charitable or statutory – will be compatible with the paradigm of the Old Testament law? What existing laws or customs in our society should we critique as being out of line with the biblical paradigm? How can we fulfil its objectives in a very different (or sometimes not so different) human context?

That at least is the beginning of our task. From there we would have to go on to fill out the whole Old Testament picture, drawing on the riches of its narratives, prophets, worship and wisdom. And then, of course, we have to set all our reflections in the light of the New Testament, relating Old Testament moral teaching to our status of redemption in Christ, our freedom in the Holy Spirit, our fellowship in the church and our eschatological hope. But all that is another story!

Chapter Six

The ethical relevance of Israel as a society[1]

Introduction

The Old Testament is not merely a collection of literary documents for us to sift and assess for their ethical relevance. It is the story of a people who formed a living society with its own customs, institutions, laws and culture. Its social system lies before us as a legitimate subject for the attention of sociology. This essay is concerned to outline and evaluate, through a detailed review of one particular model, the contribution that sociological study of Israel can make to our Christian ethical understanding.

Possibly the most substantial sociological study of Israel, and certainly the one which has become a landmark for the discipline, is that by N. K. Gottwald, *The Tribes of Yahweh*.[2] Gottwald seeks to apply sociological method rigorously to Israel in what he considers its constitutive period (the two centuries preceding the monarchy). He aims to elaborate an overall, structural and systematic sociology of Israel and to analyse and describe Israel's religion as part of that social whole. He maintains that 'the question about the form and function of Israel's religion as a social complex is the sociological equivalent of the theological question: wherein lay the uniqueness of Israel's faith?' (p. 19; throughout this chapter, a page number at the end of a quotation refers to Gottwald, *Tribes of Yahweh*).

This massive work of Gottwald lies behind much of what follows here. Though I have used it extensively and derived great stimulation for ethical reflection within it, I must register strong disagreement, in this introductory section, with some aspects of his work. These include the following.

1. His literary-critical presupposition about the Old Testament documents, which is broadly the classical documentary hypothesis with the modifications introduced by M. Noth. Gottwald's dating of Old Testament texts assumes the validity of this hypothesis and rarely argues for the dates he assigns to texts (and therefore the use he makes of them in his historical reconstructions), or considers the variety of other scholarly opinions that exist in most areas of Old Testament textual study.

2. His dogmatic and *a priori* historical scepticism about the historical worth of the Old Testament literary documents, in which the very possibility of substantial accuracy is discounted (pp. 25–31). He uses the texts as historical evidence in relation to his own reconstructions, but not straightforwardly in regard to their reliability in terms of their own contents.

3. His rejection of a historical conquest of Palestine in favour of Mendenhall's 'internal revolt' hypotheses.[3] This is still an area of considerable controversy in Old Testament historical studies, and the issue is far from settled.

4. The sociological positivism and reductionism of the later sections, according to which the religion of Israel is said to be wholly explicable as the 'societal feedback' of Israel's social life and socio-political and economic aspirations. Theology is, for Gottwald, only a subsidiary function of sociology. I do not believe this is a necessary outcome of the relationship between them.

The task before us may be arranged in three ways.

1. *The descriptive task.* What kind of society was ancient Israel? What was the comprehensive 'shape' of their social, economic, political and cultic life; and in what way was it distinctive from comparable contemporary social systems?

2. *The theological task.* Was that social shape of Israel an integral part of Israel's theological significance? Or was it simply a historical 'accident'? Could their social shape have been different while their religious beliefs and

148

theological significance remained the same?

3. *The hermeneutical task.* If the social shape of Israel does turn out to be theologically significant, how do we assess the relevance of the plethora of individual laws, institutions, and narratives? How do we evaluate their relative importance? In what ways can they be legitimately applied to our own ethical work? Do they apply to the church, to the rest of society, or to both?

1. What kind of society was ancient Israel?

Gottwald concentrates on the Israel of the pre-monarchic period, though he draws material from later periods. While Israelite society changed over the centuries due to the advent of the monarchy, a basic infrastructure of characteristically Israelite arrangements of social, economic and political life remained which were sufficiently coherent and enduring to be worthy of systematic study. Indeed, it is often the later prophetic response to the changes in Israel's social system, many of which were associated with the monarchy and were perceived as a threat, which shows up most clearly the ideals that were inherent in their system, *i.e.* what they felt they *ought* to be, even when they failed to achieve it.

a. Social structure

Israel was a 'tribal' society. The term 'the tribes of Israel' is the nearest approximation to a technical term for the total Israelite social system, and this shows the organizational 'looseness' of the nation. There were three levels of this tribal structure: the tribes themselves, the intermediate sub-groupings of households, and the smallest units – the extended family households. These three levels have received considerable study and each is thoroughly analysed by Gottwald.[4]

1. *The tribe (šēḇeṭ/maṭṭeh).* The tribe was both the primary territorial and organizational unit of the nation. Israel's tribes were of unequal size and differing histories. Their major common feature was a consciousness of being part of the entity known as 'Israel', the 'people of Yahweh'.

Gottwald rejects M. Noth's amphictyony model but asserts that there must have been some form of deliberate, formal confederacy of the tribes in the pre-monarchic period. The most concrete expression of this Israel-consciousness was mutual aid, as illustrated in the stories of Deborah and Gideon. The z^e'aqâ, 'cry for help', was a technical term for this obligation. Although it was not always met in practice, the expectation of mutual aid was nevertheless an authentic feature of early Israelite society. The story of the Benjamite war in Judges 21 emphasizes both this ideal unity and also the concern that none should be lost. So, at this primary level of social structure, we see a combination of loose, non-centralized autonomy, with an ideal unity and a mutual obligation springing from a shared religious commitment.

2. *The mišpaḥâ*. This word is best left untranslated since there is no easy equivalent. It is frequently rendered as 'clan'. Gottwald prefers not to use this, since in common anthropological and sociological terminology the word 'clan' usually means 'exogamous clan' (*i.e.* marriage must be outside one's own clan), with communal land ownership and a strongly centralized hierarchical power. This kind of clan was definitely not part of Israel's social structure (Gottwald, pp. 301–305). Nevertheless, the *mišpaḥâ* was a very important secondary level of social organization between the tribe and the extended family household. It was both a kinship grouping, incorporating a number of related families, and a territorial entity, often based on a village or a locality of identical name. The *mišpaḥâ* names were those of sons or grandsons of the tribal ancestors – the sons of Jacob.

The primary function of the *mišpaḥâ* was economic; to protect and preserve the viability of its constituent families through mechanisms such as the redemption of land or persons in danger of passing out of the hands of the kinship group (*cf.* Lv. 25). Old Testament evidence shows that the *mišpaḥâ* did not own land collectively or have any coercive power over family units. It was a restorative and protective organism. Gottwald paraphrases the meaning of the word as 'a protective association of extended families'.

Its other main function was military. The word *'elep* is an alternative for *mišpāḥâ*, usually found in military contexts where it signifies the complement of fighting men provided by the *mišpāḥâ* for the tribal military levy. *'elep* also stands for the numeral 1,000, which was perhaps the ideal number of soldiers. But in practice the *mišpāḥâ*-at-arms would usually have been far fewer than the full 1,000 men. The military census lists of Numbers 1 and 26 show the *mišpāḥâ/elep* as the basic unit of the military levy,[5] while the Gideon narrative shows that Gideon's call to arms was first addressed to the men of his own *mišpāḥâ*, the Abiezrites, then to the rest of his tribe, and finally to the neighbouring tribes (Jdg. 6:34f.).

The *mišpāḥâ* was a very important social entity in Israel. It bonded, sustained and preserved the household units, yet did not suppress their autonomy economically or socially. It was superior to the extended family in a numerical, geographical and functional sense. But it apparently did not burden the smaller units with a hierarchial pyramid of power, social control, or economic exactions.

3. *The extended family (bêt 'āb*, lit. 'father's house'). The 'lowest' social unit was the extended family household. This comprised all the living generations within a single lineage from a living ancestor (the 'head of the father's house'), along with their families and servants. The 'head' could therefore be in a position of authority over several generations. A typical extended family, under average conditions of fertility and age of marriage, and even with monogamy, would comprise quite a number of smaller nuclear families in three or four generations. So it would have anything up to fifty or 100 persons who would live together in a cluster of dwelling units.

Socially, the *bêt 'āb* was the primary locus of the individual Israelite's sense of identity and status. This is seen by the inclusion of the *bêt 'āb* name in formal nomenclature. A full Israelite name began with the personal name, then the patronymic father's name, then the *bêt 'āb* name – that of the head, then the *mišpāḥâ* name, and finally the tribe; it was virtually a geographical address as well! Mendenhall makes the point: 'There is little doubt indeed that it was the smallest political unit, not the largest, that conferred status upon the individual by giving him its protection and educating him in his obligations to society.'[6] It was the mainstay of educational and cultic life for the Israelite family, and also a place of security and protection for the non-Israelite dependent labouring class (the *gērîm* and *tôšābîm*, 'resident aliens').

The most important social function of the *bêt 'āb* was probably its judicial role. Its judicial functions were both internal and external. Internally, the head of the household had authority to act judicially in many matters without reference to any outside legal authority, for example in the marriage of his children, in divorce, in making permanent a slave's relationship to himself, or in any parental discipline short of the execution of a death penalty – which had to be brought before the elders.[7] Externally, the heads of households functioned as elders in public judicial action which took place in the gate of the city or village. Job describes his exalted role in this sphere, before calamity removed him from it (Jb. 29:7–25). The internal judicial functions meant that the extended family household enjoyed considerable independence from interference in the exercise of their jurisdictional rights; the external functions ensured that when intervention by the wider community was necessary, it had a 'democratic' nature, for the judges were fellow elders and 'brothers' (*cf.* Dt. 1:16). It was no accident, therefore, that the spread of *judicial* corruption, so vigorously condemned by the prophets, was part of the evil consequences of the *economic* degeneration. Families were dispossessed because of debt, allowing the qualification for exercising judicial office and eldership to fall into the hands of a decreasing number of wealthier people, who could then manipulate judicial affairs to their own advantage.

Israelite society, then, as a fabric of such sturdy units enjoying considerable autonomy and social freedom, was socially decentralized and non-hierarchical. It was geared towards the social health and economic viability of the 'lowest' units, not to the wealth, privilege or power of the 'highest'. Gottwald notices this feature even in typical Old Testament genealogies. There is a contrast with comparable ancient Near Eastern genealogy, which is 'top-heavy' – *i.e.* replete with gods, heroes and royalty as the ancestry of the ruling establishment, whereas Old Testament genealogy is 'bottom-dense' – *i.e.* solidly popular in its listing of the kinship relations of the ordinary populace (p. 336).

b. Economic structure

The division of the land recorded in the book of Joshua clearly intends that the possession and use of the land should be distributed as widely as possible throughout the whole kinship system. The tribal areas were allotted 'according to their *mišpᵉḥôt*' (Jos. 15:1; *etc.*). But, as we have seen, the major function of the *mišpāḥâ* was to protect and maintain its constituent household units. So the land tenure system was one of multiple ownership by the smallest units – the extended family households. The *bêt 'āḇ*, therefore, was also the basic unit of the economic structure. It was largely self-sufficient in production, storage and consumption of agricultural and pastoral produce. In contrast to the replaced Canaanite society, there was no feudal arrangement by which households owed produce to higher human authorities. The material demands of the cult of Yahweh were also comparatively low. So the autonomy of the *bêt 'āḇ* was not crippled by built-in economic burdens.

There were other ways in which households could decline economically: infertility, childless deaths, war, famine, and inescapable climatic and geographical factors. Major efforts were made to protect the survival and viability of such threatened households. The primary protective measure, which was a governing principle of Israelite land law, was the inalienability of land – *i.e.* land could not be bought and sold as a commercial commodity. It was to be retained within the kinship group, primarily within the *bêṯ 'aḇ*, but failing that, within the *mišpāḥâ*. The key text prescribing this is Leviticus 25:23. Here the prohibition on the permanent sale of land is theologically based on the belief that God was the ultimate owner of the land and that the Israelites stood in a dependent relationship to him – in the same way as the *gērîm* and *tôšāḇîm* were 'tenants' in Israelite households.

> The land must not be sold permanently, because the land is mine and you are but aliens and my tenants.

The Israelites were not free to buy and sell Yahweh's land, any more than a resident alien could buy and sell the land of the household in which he lived and worked.

This principle is borne out by the absence of any evidence of legal and voluntary sale of land in Israel outside the kinship unit. The legally permitted way for disposing of, or obtaining, land was by family inheritance. The narratives of the Old Testament provide not a single case of an Israelite voluntarily selling land outside his kinship group. Land sales are either within kinship boundaries (*e.g.* Je. 32; Ru. 4), or by non-Israelites (*e.g.* 2 Sa. 24; 1 Ki. 16:24), or non-voluntary (*e.g.* for debt, Ne. 5:3). Nor is there any archaeological evidence of inscriptions recording Israelite sales and purchase of land, or of 'disguised sales', where the buyer is 'adopted' in order to give the transfer the appearance of inheritance. There is abundant evidence of such transactions from Canaanite and other surrounding societies. The *cause célèbre* of Naboth and Ahab (1 Ki. 21) shows the strength of this principle among the ordinary populace. It also shows the violent measures that royalty had to resort to in order to evade the principle and amass land for themselves or their favourites, and the vehement prophetic protest at such violation of fundamental Israelite principle regarding the land (*cf.* Is. 5:8; Mi. 2:1f.).

The rest of Leviticus 25 shows the socio-economic protective role of the *mišpāḥâ* in its various supportive functions. These included the redemption of the land of an impoverished kinsman (25ff.); economic assistance, including loans without interest (35ff.); employment of the totally impoverished, but not in a slave capacity (39ff.); and redemption of persons who have sold themselves for debt to an outsider (47ff.). Interwoven with these provisions was the jubilee institution.[8] This was designed to restore to its original property and independence a *bêt 'āb* which had fallen into debt or servitude, at the end of a fixed period of fifty years – *i.e.* not more than a maximum of about two generations for any family. Thus, while the redemption procedures protected the property and personnel of the *mišpāḥâ*, the jubilee was for the benefit of the *bêt 'āb*.

Elsewhere we find the institution of levirate marriage, by which a kinsman had the duty to seek to have a child by the widow of a fellow kinsman who had died childless. The child would then become the heir to the deceased brother's name and estate (see Dt. 25:5–10; and *cf.* Ru. 4). Another law allowed daughters to inherit in the absence of male heirs, provided they married within their own *mišpāḥâ*, so that family land would not pass out of the *mišpāḥâ* (Nu. 27:1–11; 36:1–12). A host of exhortations, found throughout the law codes, concerned those weakest members of society who lacked the natural protection of a land-owning family: widows, orphans, immigrants, slaves, hired workers and Levites.

So the economic system was geared institutionally and in principle towards the preservation of a broadly based equality and self-sufficiency of families on the land, and to the protection of the weakest, the poorest and the threatened – and not to the interests of a wealthy, land-owning élite minority. This prominent feature of Israelite law is a particularly important sociological indicator of the practical content of Israel's faith. Commenting on the law, Gottwald says:

> This practical content is of inestimable value for constructing a sociology of Israel's religion, for it gives an unmistakable skeletal structure to the

155

religion of Yahweh as the religion of a particular egalitarian social system. To worship Yahweh, to be an Israelite, meant above all else to practise a specific way of life in separation from and in overt opposition to time-honoured established ways of life regarded throughout the ancient Near East as inevitable if not totally desirable (p. 59).

The freedom and autonomy generated by such a system for the whole populace is thrown into relief by Samuel's negative contrast concerning what would happen if Israel persisted in demanding a monarchy – especially one modelled on surrounding cultures. Economic implications are prominent in Samuel's account and were only too grimly fulfilled in later years.

> This is what the king who will reign over you will do: He will take your sons and make them serve with his chariots and horses, and they will run in front of his chariots. Some he will assign to be commanders of thousands and commanders of fifties, and others to plough his ground and reap his harvest, and still others to make weapons of war and equipment for his chariots. He will take your daughters to be perfumers and cooks and bakers. He will take the best of your fields and vineyards and olive groves and give them to his attendants. He will take a tenth of your grain and of your vintage and give it to his officials and attendants. Your menservants and maidservants and the best of your cattle and donkeys he will take for his own use. He will take a tenth of your flocks, and you yourselves will become his slaves.
>
> (1 Sa. 8:11–17)

c. Political structure

The patterns of political activity and power in the Old

Testament followed the divisions of Israelite society. They were diffused and decentralized. Power in decision-making within the community, especially in judicial matters, resided in the network of elders. The elders were the mainstay of Israelite socio-political life at the broadest level throughout the whole Old Testament period. Although there is no clearly stated description of the qualifications for eldership, they were most probably the senior male members of each extended family – *i.e.* the 'heads of father's houses', although other adult males may have had elder status.[9]

In the pre-monarchic period, this plural and corporate leadership was supplemented in time of military need by individual 'charismatic' leaders. These 'judges' were considered as raised up by God and accepted by the people as mediating the rule of God. However, the stories of Gideon and Abimelech (Jdg. 8:22 – 9:57) indicate the difficulties facing any 'chief' who was offered or who sought a wider or more permanent, dynastic authority. Centralized power in Israel seems to have been strongly resisted until the external threat of the Philistines thrust it forcibly upon them. 'Obviously the chiefdom ran directly counter to the basic thrust of Israel towards locating power in equivalent and equal extended families.'

Even after the monarchy was established, the system of elders survived and proved resistant to hierarchical and centralized government. Jehoshaphat's judicial reforms established royally appointed judges, but they applied only to the fortified cities (2 Ch. 19:4–11). The administration of justice in town and village communities by their local elders presumably continued unaffected by royal appointment. They were not unaffected by the economic forces that precipitated judicial corruption – the very thing Jehoshaphat's reform tried to eradicate, but without success, to judge from the prophetic indictment of the judiciary in the following century. Even the panel of appeal judges in Jerusalem included a group of 'elders of the land'. This group were to play an important part in the legal defence of Jeremiah in the last days of the monarchy

157

(Je. 26:17). That such a group of non-royal, 'popular' elders should step forward in judicial defence of a prophet in a royal court shows the tenacity of the old, 'popular' judicial system even within the hierarchical court scene. But it is hardly surprising and is almost poetic justice. For a major role of the prophets for several centuries before this had been to speak up on behalf of the people of the land and against arrogant political authoritarianism, oppression and judicial corruption.

So there was resistance in Israel to centralized power and a preference for diverse and participatory politics, which tolerated – indeed sought – the voice of criticism and opposition from the prophets, even if some of them paid a heavy price. Such decentralized power stands in marked contrast to contemporary states especially in the formative pre-monarchic period. These had a highly stratified and pyramidical political and economic structure, both in the Canaanite city-state feudalism and in the Egyptian imperialism that interlocked with it in the international arena of the Amarna era. Certainly, Israel was a nation state, however loosely the tribal association may have cohered – before and indeed during the monarchy. But it was consciously a nation unlike those around. Balaam's oracle describes them as 'people who live apart and do not consider themselves one of the nations' (Nu. 23:9).

There may well be an ironic use of political vocabulary in Exodus 19:6. They were to be a 'kingdom' (mamlākâ), but a 'priestly' one; they were a 'nation' (gôy – the normal political term for a nation state), but a 'holy' one. Priestliness and holiness both denote separateness, but not an inward-looking, isolationist kind of existence. Rather, their distinctiveness was to be for the sake of the very nations they were different from – part of the meaning of priesthood (cf. also Dt. 26:18f.). This distinctiveness was far from being solely religious. It involved their whole system of socio-economic and political life and institutions.

d. Cultic structure

We are simply concerned here to see how the Israelite cultic

158

practice fitted in with the total social system. Three points may be made.

First, the Israelite cult as prescribed in the law (as distinct from some exceptional occasions laid on by the kings to mark a special event) excluded lavish and extravagant ceremonies that would have cast Yahweh as the beneficiary and guarantor of a pyramidical system of hierarchical politics or oppressive economics with an 'upward flow' towards the privileged top end of society. Those in power, whether judges or kings, could make no exclusive or favoured claim to Yahweh's favour through manipulation of the cult to their own advantage. They were subject to the same laws and the same covenant demand as the lowliest peasant. The sacrifices of a disobedient Saul or an adulterous David had no special virtue or efficacy just because the men who made them held the highest office (1 Sa. 13; Ps. 51:16f.). In fact, the sin of Jeroboam, immortalized as 'Jeroboam the son of Nebat who made Israel to sin', was precisely to manipulate the cult of Yahweh into a support system for his own political ends, with royally created shrines, royally appointed priests and all the trappings and the traps of 'established religion' (1 Ki. 12:26–33). Amaziah's indignant dismissal of Amos's exposure of the rotten social evils that lay beneath the façade of a thriving religious establishment summed up the situation in the northern kingdom neatly:

> Don't prophesy any more at Bethel, because this is the *king's* sanctuary and the temple of the *kingdom*.
>
> (Am. 7:13)

At the economic level, Yahweh's total ownership of the land lifted the land itself out of the reach of any exclusive human claim. So, for example, the royal accumulation of estates could not be sanctioned or celebrated in the cult.

Secondly, the cult consumed relatively little of the 'gross national product'. The occasional lavish royal occasions were financed by the king himself. But the demands of the cult on ordinary people were not over-burdensome, even allowing for the requirement that people offer the best of crop or herd. The sacrificial laws made generous allowance for the poorest and what little they could afford. Most important of all, there was no system of heavy taxation to support a powerful religious hierarchy. The Levites did not own land (in contrast to Egypt where the temples and their personnel were major land-owners). And they were widely distributed throughout the country, so that they could not command a powerful religious establishment. It was of course entirely fitting that a cult which had as its origin and its *raison d'être* the celebration and perpetuation of the traditions of historical deliverance from political and economic oppression, should not itself be the means of oppression or impoverishment for those who rejoiced in their deliverance through it.

Thirdly, while the worship of Yahweh in religious terms was more exclusive and strict than the religions of surrounding cultures, it actually produced greater social freedom and economic justice in practical life. Gottwald comments on this feature:

> Thus, while in explicitly cultic terms the demands of Yahwism were strict and excessive compared to the demands of official Canaanite religion, the actual social empirical situation was that the 'tolerant' Canaanite cult justified the centralised political rape of human and natural resources and energies by a small élite, whereas the 'strict' Israelite cult justified the development and enjoyment of human and natural resources and energies by the entire populace. Yahweh, in appearing to demand much more than the Canaanite gods, actually gave back to his worshippers the benefits and potentialities of productive human life which a small Canaanite minority had arrogated to itself under the symbolic approval of hierarchical polytheism (p. 616).

It is an interesting reflection that the stricter monotheistic religion produced greater social and economic benefits, whereas polytheism more easily adapted to conditions of injustice and oppression. It would not be hard to point to comparable links between religious and societal characteristics in the modern world, including that peculiarly Western polytheism (wherein Baal and Mammon are alive and well) which, while claiming to be very tolerant, yet coexists so congenially with appalling social and economic injustice and the 'rape of human and natural resources'. Further, the religious and ethical demands of the God of the Bible often appear strict, and run contrary to the natural inclinations of fallen human beings. But they are the benevolent will of the creator God who designed human society in the first place and knows how best to organize it to release the full 'benefits and potentialities of productive human life'.

Conclusion

This very brief sketch of Israelite society can be completed in detail from Gottwald and other similar sources. It is sufficient to show that Israel was self-consciously distinctive from surrounding nations, and especially the Canaanites, not just religiously but in their total social system. This distinctiveness was deliberate as part of what it was to be 'Israel'. Gottwald argues that this was the result of their origin as an internal Canaanite revolt movement, involving a joining together of 'Hebrews' with disaffected peasants, rising against feudal oppression, and marginal pastoral nomads. This mixed group 'withdrew' from Canaanite political society, sometimes violently, and then set about producing their own social system – a form of 'synthetic egalitarianism'. He thus develops and refines Mendenhall's 'revolt' thesis in this matter. However, even without that hypothetical model for the origins of Israel in Palestine (which is open to serious question and which I would not regard as historically probable), the substantive general fact remains of Israel's remarkable conceptual and actual difference. Gottwald sums up the results of his detailed study of Israel's social system in this way:

> The result has been the emerging cross-section of Israel as an egalitarian, extended-family, segmentary tribal society with an agricultural-pastoral economic base ... characterised by profound resistance and opposition to the forms of political domination and social stratification that had become normative in the chief cultural and political centres of the ancient Near East (p. 389).

Israel's determined assertion of religious 'otherness' (holiness) was indeed linked to aspirations and a degree of achievement in the social, economic and political spheres. The shape of their social system was a conscious and deliberate part of their holiness, as they understood it.

2. Is the social shape of Israel an essential part of its biblical theological significance?

Whether the social shape of Israel has theological significance is not just a question about the theological motivation for its social laws. The extent to which such theological motivation is interwoven with the social laws of the Old Testament can be seen, for example, in Leviticus 19 and 25. There, many laws and provisions for economic support, respect for persons and protection of the family are sanctioned by a strong, historical Yahwistic faith. But the question we should ask is more significant than this. Was the shape of Israel's social system an essential part of its being Israel – the people chosen and called by God as the vehicle of redemption for the world? Is the theological importance of Israel found not only in its message but also in the social system which it embodied?

An important part of Gottwald's work bears on this question. Gottwald first focuses on the weaknesses of those commentators who, though they have recognized Israel's unique historical social system, have failed to show its relationship to Israel's religious beliefs satisfactorily. He singles out Bright, Mendenhall and Fohrer for criticism, accusing them of succumbing to 'idealism' in their attempts to account for Israel's social system in

162

religious and theological terms ('idealism', for Gottwald, is a highly negative term).

He then describes 'structural-functional modelling', which is designed to display the 'mutual reinforcement of mono-Yahwism and social egalitarianism'. A 'functional' relationship, in sociological terminology, is 'a relation of dependence or interdependence between two or more variable factors in a field of social action' (p. 609). The two factors in this case are the nature of Israel's social system, and the nature of Israel's mono-Yahwistic faith. He gives an outline of the constituent features of these two factors in the functional model.

1. *'Socio-political egalitarianism'*. After describing briefly Israel's society in terms of territory, language, means of production, socio-economic organization, policy-making, norms and rules, and military organization, he sums up the meaning of this term as designating, in Israel's case,

> a self-governing association of economically self-sufficient free farmers and herdsmen constituting a single class of people with common ownership of the means of production vested in large families ... [with a] paradoxical combination of political decentralization, on the one hand, and of socio-cultural cohesiveness, on the other (pp. 613f.).

2. *'Mono-Yahwism'*. This obviously included the worship of a single God, conceived primarily with reference to his rule over a people in history, but who was also a God who, as shown in Israel's creation beliefs, subordinated nature to the social needs of human beings. As a religious system it included a limited priesthood and sanctions for political equality. 'The ultimate symbolic attribution of sovereignty and leadership was reserved to the deity, with the result that all communal leadership roles were conceived either as temporary task assignments, or, if hereditary, as sharply limited in function and scope.' There were also sanctions for economic equality. Yahweh's ownership of the land ensured equal rights of access and use of it for all members

of his people. There were sanctions for collective self-defence ('the Yahweh wars'); and sanctions against 'religious mystification' such as sacralized sex, ancestor worship and speculation about life after death. In every vital area of life, Yahweh, as the sole Lord, upheld the goals of the community. He was sole patron of the cult, the ultimate judge, the commander-in-chief of the army, the theocratic king.

> All the symbols of Yahweh in his various guises refer with positive reinforcement to socio-economic desiderata in the community and the assurance that power will be used in ways that preserve the system externally and internally (pp. 614f.).

Gottwald shows that each side of his model facilitates and reinforces the other. This means that socio-economic equality facilitated religious equality, and *vice versa*, and that socio-economic unity facilitated religious exclusiveness, and *vice versa*, in such a way that neither would have been the same if the other had been different. He concludes:

> The rise and maintenance of a viable Israelite egalitarian social system with its structural features of extended-family ownership of the means of production, mutual aid measures for keeping the extended families on an approximate par in production and consumption, and the dispersal of social, military, political and religious power among the structural sub-units, *was dependably related* to the innovative conceptual-institutional projection of Yahweh as the sole God of Israel, who motivates and sanctions the desired system of social relations by means of a cult with minimal command of political power and minimal consumption of communal wealth (pp. 618f., Gottwald's italics).

In other words, Israel was what it was as a society because Yahweh was what he was as God.[10] This is precisely the relationship envisaged in Deuteronomy 10:12ff. between the character of Yahweh and the social nature of Israel. There, to 'walk in his ways' means to imitate Yahweh as the God who 'shows no partiality and accepts no bribes ... defends the cause of the fatherless ...' (17–18). The kind of society Yahweh desires and commands is based explicitly on the kind of God Yahweh is. This is supported extensively by the legal, prophetic and Wisdom literature, and is here reinforced by detailed sociological study. We may conclude that, far from the social life of Israel being immaterial or incidental to their theological significance, it is actually through observant study of that social life that a major part of God's self-revelation is to be discerned. This gives critical importance to our getting the social study of Israel right, for the more carefully we understand Israel, the more 'coloured-in' will be our understanding of God. Gottwald makes the point that, 'Since the primary manifestation of Yahweh is Israel itself, any misconstruction of Israel entails a misconstruction of Yahweh' (p. 688).

Theologically, the purpose of Israel's existence was as a vehicle both for God's revelation and for the redemption of humanity. This is clear in the covenant with Abraham, through whose descendants blessing would come to all the nations. As previously mentioned, it was also implied in the description of Israel as a 'priesthood'. The priests were mediators between God and the rest of the people by their lives and examples, by their sacrificial offices, and by their teaching. Israel as a whole was to have a comparable role in relation to other nations. In that way they were to be a light to the nations (cf. Is. 42:6; 49:6). They were not only the bearers of redemption, but a model of what a redeemed community would be like, living in obedience to God's will. Their social structure, aspirations, principles and policies, so organically related to their religious faith, were also part of the content of that revelation, part of the pattern of redemption.

The social facts of Israel's life cannot, then, be treated as merely interesting antiquities for the legal or social historian. Nor can they be regarded as the material husk of Old Testament theology, to be quickly discarded once a spiritual kernel has been extracted. It is insufficient for us to pick out some of the more remarkable social laws or prophecies of the Old Testament and then present them out of context as a showcase of charitable duties or economic justice. God's passionate concern for the weak, the poor and the oppressed in society, which the Old Testament shows so emphatically, must not be separated from the whole of the social system which his law sanctioned. It was because God was the God of the whole people, and because he made demands on them as a whole, that he was particularly concerned when that society failed to care for its weaker members.

> Indeed, it was precisely the will of Yahweh that there should be a social system in which such suffering and disempowerment would be hastily alleviated and rectified, not so much by charitable deeds to individuals, as by assuring the ongoing stability of a functionally effective egalitarian social system (Gottwald, p. 689).

It is Deuteronomy which expresses this aspect of God's purpose. Deuteronomy 15 is concerned to alleviate poverty and commands unstinting generosity. The ultimate will of God is not that the poor should continue to receive charity indefinitely through generosity from the better off. It is for a society in which *there will be no poor*, because there will be no hindrance to the outpouring of God's blessing caused by the disobedience of his people (verses 4f.). This obvious tension between verse 4 ('there should be no poor among you') and verse 11 ('There will always be poor people in the land') is not just accidental. It must be seen in the context of the sabbatical institutions with which this chapter is concerned, and in the light of the sabbatical eschatology which is also found in the jubilee tradition – in the tension

166

between what now is and what God will one day bring to pass along with the restoration of his people to perfect obedience and an unbroken relationship with himself. This sabbatical eschatology surfaces again in Isaiah 58 and 61, feeds into the ministry of Jesus (Lk. 4:16ff.), and was probably regarded by Luke as partially fulfilled in the early, Spirit-filled socio-economic life of the church in Acts (see the virtual quotation of Dt. 15:4 in Acts 4:34).

Where, then, does this lead us as regards a biblical theological understanding? The New Testament regards the Christian church as organically related to Old Testament Israel, through the Messiah, Jesus (*cf.*, *e.g.*, Lk. 22:29f.; Rom. 4:16f; Gal. 3:14, 26–29; Eph. 2:11–22; 3:6; 1 Pet. 2:4–10; Hebrews *passim*).[11] If the New Testament church saw itself as the spiritual heir of Israel, is there evidence that it regarded the social patterns and principles of Israel as part of its inheritance as well? I believe there is.

a. The 'reversal of values' theme in the gospels

Jesus insists that the community life of his disciples is to be radically different from the standards and practices of the rest of society. 'You are not to be like that' (Lk. 22:26) is almost a motto and is Jesus' own echo of the familiar Old Testament theme of the distinctiveness of God's people, who were called not to be 'like those round about'. This difference is to be seen in social relationships (*cf.* Mt. 5:43–47), in attitudes to economic needs (*cf.* Mt. 6:32), and in the 'political' sphere of authority and leadership within the new messianic community (Lk. 22:25–27).

b. The influence of jubilary concepts on the teaching of Jesus

The influence of jubilary concepts on Jesus has been examined by R. B. Sloane, Jr, among others.[12] He takes into account not only the 'Nazareth Manifesto' of Luke 4:16ff., based on Isaiah 61, but also the Lukan beatitudes (Lk. 6:20ff.). He shows how the word *aphesis*, taken from the jubilee language of 'release', is used by Jesus in both the

material sense which it had in the Old Testament
(remission of actual debts) and the spiritual sense
(forgiveness of sins). He also examines other eschatological
themes which were part of the jubilary circle of ideas which
moulded Jesus' preaching of the kingdom of God. He
concludes that the social and economic dimensions of the
original institutions were by no means ignored, or simply
spiritualized in Jesus' preaching, but were part of the total
response demanded from those who entered into the life of
the kingdom of God.

c. The initial communality of the early church in Acts

Much has been written on the early communality of the
church, seeing it as either a timeless blueprint mandatory
on all Christians, or dismissing it altogether as merely a
dispensable by-product of Pentecost possessing no
normative ethical force. Neither extreme is valid. Yet it
cannot be merely accidental that Luke emphasizes it
by double reference in contexts which seem designed
to convey to the reader the essence and ethos of this
new, Spirit-filled, eschatological community (Acts 2:44f;
4:32–35). What the sabbatical eschatology of Deuteronomy
15 had hoped for was now being realized: there was no
poor person among them. It seems almost certain that Luke
intended this allusion, by the similarity of language: *ouk
estai en soi endeēs* (Dt. 15:4, LXX); *oude gar endeēs tis ēn en autois*
(Acts 4:34). Without compulsion or even any apparent
command from the apostles (*cf.* Acts 4:34), they desired to
give their exuberant spiritual unity (4:32) the manifestation
of economic equality. This is the same pattern as the socio-
economic thrust of the Old Testament. The messianic
community embodied the social and spiritual fulfilment of
the Old Testament in its day-to-day life.

d. The economic dimension of koinōnia

The above principle, combining spiritual unity and
economic equality, was not confined geographically to the
Jerusalem church, or canonically to the book of Acts. It
features in Paul's teaching on the true nature of Christian

fellowship – our all-too-weak English translation of *koinōnia*. The root meaning of that word has to do with sharing (as is well known), both intransitively (sharing *in* something *with* another) and transitively (giving a share *of* something *to* another). In its Christian usage it involves the believers' sharing Christ and sharing in the Holy Spirit. But it also involves the sharing of material goods. Indeed, for Paul, the spiritual and the material were very closely intertwined here. Spiritual blessings demanded a material response (*cf.* Rom. 15:26f.; 1 Cor. 9:11; Gal. 6:6). But on the other hand also, material giving, like an investment, produces spiritual returns (*cf.* Phil. 4:17f.; 1 Tim. 6:18f.; 2 Cor. 9:6–12). Spiritual unity demanded economic equality. The clearest exposition of this principle is in 2 Corinthians 8:13–15, in the context of the collection Paul was administering among the Gentile Christians for the benefit of the then impoverished Judean church. Paul envisages the plenty of one group of Christians meeting the need of another group, 'that there might be equality' (verse 13, repeated in verse 14).

On the same matter, Paul turns the issue into one of obedience to the gospel, in 2 Corinthians 9:13. By their economic sacrifice and sharing (which Paul terms their *koinōnia*), the Gentiles were giving tangible proof of their oneness with the Jewish Christians and evidence of the transforming power of the gospel they professed. In this way they would cause thanksgiving for the grace of God which made such unity and generosity possible. A concordance study of Paul's use of the *koinōn-* root and its compounds shows that about half of the occasions he uses it refer to material or financial or practical sharing. This dimension of Christian experience clearly has deep roots in the socio-economic soil of the Old Testament – particularly the theology and ethics of the land.

e. The plurality of the church's leadership

Like Israel, the New Testament church appears to have resisted a centralized, hierarchical form of leadership, though this is not to say that there was no authority structure within the church. The authority of the apostles was very clearly recognized – but even that was a plural authority. In local congregations, the leadership was modelled on the local Israelite communities, the authority being vested in a group of elders. They were treated with respect, but there is a far greater emphasis in the New Testament on their responsibilities than on their privileges – if indeed they can be said to have held any. Just as in the Old Testament the supreme sovereignty of Yahweh and his ultimate ownership of the land stood out against the oppressive usurping of power by individuals and small groups, so in the New Testament the sole lordship of Christ and his 'ownership' of the church ('my church', 'my sheep'), produced resistance to any kind of élite leader caste and to any kind of domineering human autocracy within the church (*cf.* Tit. 1:7; 2 Cor. 4:5; 1 Pet. 5:2). Only Christ is the Head; all Christians are equally necessary parts of his body. Only Christ is the foundation and cornerstone; all Christians are living stones built on him. Only Christ is the Shepherd; all Christians, even his 'under-shepherd' elders, are part of his flock (*cf.* 1 Pet. 5:1–4). All share in his kingship. All, together, form a priesthood (*cf.* Rev. 1:6). All are saints, all are brothers, all are heirs. These are all motifs drawn from the social nature of Israel.

f. The social power of the gospel

The most remarkable visible manifestation of the Christian gospel in the New Testament era was arguably its ability not only to transcend ethnic, religious, social and sexual barriers in its rapid spread, but also to dissolve them, so that they no longer existed for those united in Christ (Gal. 3; Eph. 2; Philemon). Spiritual equality in Christ was seen in this social equality – yet the functional structures of human relationships, sexual, familial, economic and political, were not abandoned. Some subtle moral argument was required from Paul to cope with the tension produced by this new redemptive freedom and equality while living within the structural constraints of a society tainted and distorted by the effects of the fall (1 Corinthians; Rom. 13; Eph. 5 – 6; Col. 3; and *cf.* 1 Pet. 2:9 – 3:8). There is in the New Testament an indictment of hierarchical privilege and social deference, not only in the preaching of Jesus but especially in James 2:1–7; 5:1–6; and *cf.* 1 Cor. 1:26–29. This matches the Old Testament prophets.

Conclusion

It is clear that in the New Testament the social nature of the church is a vital and integral part of the work of God in the world. It is not just a neutral bearer of a message; not just a collection of people who happen to have a common experience. It is in itself a part of the message, a witness to that experience by its very nature and existence. The church in Paul's thinking was God's 'showcase', demonstrating his wisdom and power at the highest cosmic levels. This is the church in which Gentiles and Jews were 'heirs together … members together of one body … and sharers together' in the promises of God through the gospel. The miracle of spiritual reconciliation and social harmony was at the very heart of Paul's 'insight into the mystery of Christ'. It was his gospel (Eph. 3:4, 6).

Our New Testament theology is incomplete unless it includes this understanding of the social shape of the church, just as our Old Testament theology will be deficient if it lacks an understanding of the social shape of Israel. There is an organic theological continuity between the Testaments in this matter which encourages us to believe that the hermeneutical, ethical task is relevant and worthwhile. To this we turn.

3. How is the ethical relevance of Israel as a society to be applied?

a. Bridging the 'culture gap'

Some scholars make great issue of the differences of civilization, culture and ways of life that separate the world of Old Testament Israel from the modern world of the twentieth century.[13] The argument is that all the laws and institutions of ancient Israel were obviously entirely 'culture relative' to their day, and for that reason they can be only marginally relevant to the major ethical concerns of our day, if at all. In its extreme form, this view effectively gags and paralyses the Bible as an authoritative source of normative ethics.

Gottwald's study illuminates the different features of the socio-cultural world of the Old Testament, from the smallest social units to the huge international empires. The picture he lays before us shows that Israel faced issues which have many points of similarity with our modern social and political tensions. It was a world of unceasing international power struggles, of oppressive forms of political economic and religious control, of state absolutism, of massive exploitation of certain groups, of gross social inequalities and of a powerless majority. In the midst of this world, and in conscious dissent from it, Israel articulated a response in the form of a total social, economic and political system, theologically rationalized and undergirded. The system did not survive intact in its entirety, and the monarchy certainly introduced some irreconcilable conflicts into the social order. Nevertheless, Gottwald has shown how much was achieved in the pre-monarchic centuries, and the legacy of the ideals and objectives is still recognizable in the Torah and the prophets.

Israel's example, its struggle, its failures and achievements in this sphere must surely be a highly relevant model when formulating our social ethical task in today's world – whatever the cultural differences. These differences are often a matter of form and degree rather than essence. This is the conclusion at which Gottwald arrives:

> A social understanding of early Yahwism might encourage us to see what forms of oppression are inhibiting and frustrating the full development of human life today, what has to be done to

change those conditions in specific terms, and
what praxis and ideology are needed if we are to
develop in the needed direction (p. 705).[14]

It is also the conclusion, of course, from which theologians
of liberation have already been working for some time. We
may have questions to ask of their methods in using the
Old Testament, but we cannot deny their right to use it, or
its manifest relevance to the issues they are addressing.[15]

b. Text and context

A comprehensive understanding of the total Israelite social
system helps us interpret any single feature of it. To take
random social, economic or political features of Israel,
individually and in isolation, and to try to squeeze some
ethical relevance out of them, is often implausible because
of the cultural strangeness of the isolated institution when
examined out of its own context. The result founders in the
hermeneutical despair of cultural relativity, or takes refuge
in an allegorical, spiritualized interpretation which tends to
remove the relevance of the text from the social field
altogether.

The vital importance of taking texts in their context
includes not only the immediate textual context of the
passage itself, but also the wider literary context ('What
kind of literature is this? Who is the author? What are his
literary and theological purposes?'), as well as the historical background in which it is set, if known. In our socio-
ethical interpretation of the Old Testament we must seek
to relate each individual law, institution, custom or
principle to the whole social system – that is, to interpret
the text within its proper *social context*, as well as its
literary and historical contexts. We must ask what was the
function of any particular feature within the overall aim
and effort of Israel towards the kind of social system they
desired. We should approach the text from various angles.
How does it fit into the social dimension of Israel's kinship
structure with its emphasis on the smaller units of the
extended family households and its diffusion and

173

decentralization of power throughout the community? How does it relate to the economic angle: Israel's desire for a broadly based system of multiple ownership of the land, with provisions for preserving and restoring the balance of economic equality and justice? How does it relate to the theological angle: the gifts and demands that the character and acts of Yahweh made upon his people in the social realm?

The value of working with a text using this method is that we can ascertain and evaluate its function and relative importance within its own social environment before we attempt to assess its ethical relevance and its application to our own world. It enables us to be comprehensive and to take account of all the material, yet at the same time we are able to give due proportion to its significance, seeing some aspects as having a central importance to the overall social thrust of Israel (for example, the system of land-tenure and the centrality of the family), while others have a lesser but contributory function (for example, levirate marriage, the variety of civil laws, *etc.*). Other aspects we would have to regard as peripheral to Israel's social goals, even though they were tolerated as part of their empirical social life – features such as polygamy and slavery. Though they were tolerated, there were legal controls and social protection for those involved, as well as theological criticism which undermined the validity of the institutions themselves.

Some features of Israelite social life we might have to treat negatively in one respect but positively in others. This is certainly true of the monarchy. As Samuel feared, it did introduce some socially disastrous processes into Israel's history, economically and politically. It was deeply resisted in some quarters, and, in terms of the total span of the history of Israel as a nation, was comparatively transient. Yet it contrived to generate a theology and an eschatology of its own, which absorbed many of the socio-ethical ideals of earlier Israel. The deuteronomic law of the king (Dt. 17:14–20) sets an ideal for kingship in Israel which would have rendered it utterly different from any form of contemporary monarchy in surrounding countries, if it had

174

been adhered to. Likewise, some of the royal psalms (*e.g.* Ps. 72) attach to the king responsibility for the cardinal Israelite social virtues. The ambivalence of Israel towards its monarchy is a fascinating theme; especially so for Gottwald, since in his view, Israel came into existence by means of an effective cancellation of the power of the Canaanite kingship.

Such a method requires extensive and detailed work within the Old Testament. We cannot jump straight from the text to modern application without analysis and assessment. This does not mean that we cannot apply lessons drawn from the social system of Israel in a valid ethical way; it simply asks that we thoroughly understand the totality of what we are seeking to apply. For this reason, the studies of Gottwald are of immense value, though we may profoundly disagree with the philosophical, anti-supernaturalist and positivist presuppositions and conclusions of his work.

c. Israel as God's paradigm

Holding the infant Jesus in his arms, and seeing in him 'the Lord's Christ', the promised Messiah and fulfilment of all the Old Testament hope of salvation, Simeon rejoices in the double blessing heralded by his arrival:

> A light for revelation to the Gentiles
> and for glory to your people Israel.
> (Lk. 2:32)

This couplet sums up the dual relevance of the Old Testament as it is focused through the Messiah – namely, for the world and for the church. The Messiah was the embodiment of Israel and of God's purpose for Israel in the world. This purpose was both revelatory and redemptive. Jesus inherited and passed on to the new messianic community which he founded (*i.e.* the church) the social role of Israel in its relation to the world. A messianic interpretation of Old Testament social ethics requires, therefore, that we seek to apply the Hebrew Scriptures with

175

ethical authority both in the world and in the church.

1. *In the world*. The paradigm approach saves us from limiting the relevance of the Old Testament to the Christian church, and saying that it has no valid application to the unregenerate world of fallen human society. Israel was brought into existence for the sake of all nations, as an example and a light, and was God's redemptive response to human failure to live by the values and ordinances of creation. Many of its social and economic laws can be seen to enshrine those creation values. Though we cannot address secular society in the terms God addressed Israel, or presuppose a covenant relationship, it is nevertheless valid to argue that what God required of Israel as a fully human society is *morally consistent* with what God requires of all human societies. It is therefore possible to use Israel as a paradigm for social ethical objectives in our own society. It could be argued that such an assumption was made by Israel's prophets, in their day, in their indictment of other nations. If we pursue social objectives based on the paradigm of Israel's social system, we cannot avoid applying its theological rationale and sanction. This means working in the light of, and making known, the sovereignty of God and his historical acts of redemption. This was the motivation behind Israelite ethics. The relevance of Israel as a society will feed and shape our evangelism and our social action. Both together are the means of extending the redemptive sphere of the kingdom of God in the world.[16]

2. *In the church*. It is here that the social relevance of Israel must surely have its primary application, for it is the church, as the redeemed community of the Messiah, which is the organic spiritual heir of Old Testament Israel. The church, as Israel redefined in the Messiah Jesus and extended to include the nations as always intended, is meant, like Old Testament Israel, to show a radical discontinuity with the world and its surrounding culture, while at the same time being called to live within it: 'in the world but not of it'. There are many extremes advocated by those who view the church as 'the alternative society', but

theologically they are on the right lines. 'Alternative society' has overtones of separatism, exclusiveness and 'opting out', whereas the biblical picture is of God's redeemed society functioning in the midst of the nations, as an eschatological prototype, witnessing to the manifest new society of God.

Gottwald may exaggerate the extent to which Israel's distinctiveness was the result of a socio-political revolution within Canaanite society, but he does make good his case for the ways in which these differences were exhibited. These differences could not have gone unnoticed by their neighbours, for they were not just a religious difference tacked on to an otherwise identical social lifestyle.

> Had these contemporaries of Israel in Canaan been asked what they noticed about Israel, it would certainly not have elicited this kind of reply: 'We notice that Israel has a very unusual belief in God and a strange set of cultic practices. Some of us are convinced by those beliefs and practices and have adopted them. Others of us just can't accept them as true, or at least as right for us. The rest of us are thinking the matter over but haven't decided yet. Except for their strange religion, the Israelites are like us in every way. When we become Israelites, we just change religions; otherwise, we remain the same.' It is difficult to formulate such a reply without caricaturing it (p. 596).

Indeed it is, and yet is this not a caricature which fits much of the Christian church which has succumbed with complete acquiescence into the surrounding culture and its standards and as a result has lost its effectiveness? Gottwald formulates the sort of social challenge Israel presented:

> A socially conscious version of what her contemporaries 'noticed' about Israel would go something like this: 'We notice that Israel is a

total community that confronts and challenges us to join its way of living. To do this we have to relinquish voluntarily or involuntarily the old forms of socio-political domination, including the old religious ideologies. Israel calls us to a new form of social relations which destroys class privileges ...' (*ibid.*).

Does this not remind us of the impact and challenge of the early Christian church which 'turned the world upside down', overcoming social and class barriers?

At the heart of Christian social ethics is the necessity that the society of the church should be obedient, as God created it to be. This is where Israel so often failed. The 'Christian lifestyle' debate cannot be allowed to remain the preserve of the so-called 'fanatic'. Christianity is more than a spiritual experience or a set of spiritual beliefs that can be added congenially to any kind of lifestyle or social system. God went to great pains to create and mould Israel as a society into a form that was central and integral to its theological significance. Israel's social relevance for us is that to be 'Israel', old or new, obligates certain social forms and relationships, while rejecting and undermining others. Our ethical task is to distinguish between the two and to work out our mission accordingly.

To paraphrase Gottwald (p. 59) in Christian terms:

To worship Christ, to be a Christian, means to practise a specific way of life in separation from and in overt opposition to time-honoured established ways of life regarded throughout our contemporary culture as inevitable if not totally desirable.

178

Part Three

A selection of
issues

Chapter Seven

The theology and ethics of the land[1]

Presented as it originally was at a conference devoted to a Christian response to contemporary environmental issues, this chapter reflects that concern and is not aiming to provide a full account of the rich depths of biblical resources on the earth in general or the land of Israel in particular. An attempt to provide such a comprehensive synthesis can be found in my *God's People in God's Land*, which also gives wide bibliographical access to the work of other scholars in this field.[2]

1. God's earth: reflections from creation

Reflections on land obviously have to begin with the biblical theme of creation as it is found in the familiar texts of Genesis 1 – 11, and also poetic texts such as Psalms 33, 104, *etc.* Considering the material with an ecological-ethical focus in mind, the following points seem significant.

a. The goodness of creation

This is one of the most obvious points of Genesis 1 and 2, in view of its repetition.[3] It sets the Hebrew account of creation in contrast to other ancient Near Eastern accounts where powers and gods of the natural world are portrayed in various degrees of malevolence. Part of the meaning of the goodness of creation in the Bible is that it witnesses to the God who made it, reflecting something of his character. (*e.g.* Pss. 19; 29; 50:6; 65; 104; 148; Jb. 12:7–9; Acts 14:17; 17:27; Rom. 1:20). That being the case, it is not going too far to make an analogy to the text, 'He who oppresses the poor shows contempt for their Maker' (Pr. 14:31; *cf.* 17:5), along the lines of 'He who destroys or degrades the earth dirties its reflection of its Maker.'

b. Creation, distinct and dependent

The affirmation that God created the heavens and the earth implies a fundamental ontological distinction between God as creator and everything created. This *duality* is essential to all biblical thought and to a Christian world-view. It should not be confused with other kinds of unbiblical *dualism* (*e.g.* between body and soul). It stands against both monism and pantheism and thus is a major biblical point of contrast and polemic with New Age spirituality which adopts a broadly monistic worldview.

The Bible not only denies the idea of ontological identity between the world and God, it also denies the idea that the world is a self-sustaining bio-system. The 'Gaia hypothesis' as originally proposed by James E. Lovelock is a hypothesis about the interconnectedness of the whole biosphere.[4] Lovelock himself, while he suggested that the earth seems to behave like a single organism, a huge living creature, did not 'personalize' nature in the sense of regarding the whole biosphere as a divine being and indeed has rejected such religious metamorphoses of his work. But Gaia has certainly been taken that way in popular presentations of New Age thinking. The earth itself is regarded as god. The Bible, however, portrays the whole universe as separate from God and dependent on him for its existence and its sustenance. This is not to deny that God has built into the earth an incredible capacity for renewal, recovery, balance and adaptation. But the way in which all these systems work and interrelate is itself planned and sustained by God.[5]

The combination of these two points means that Christian ecological ethics need not be tarnished with some of the implicit or explicit pantheism of certain brands of 'deep green' ecology.[6] Evangelicals are easily repelled by the radical politics of some green advocates or the New Age links of others, and then fall into ecological indifference or conspiracy-hunting paranoia.[7] We need to oppose distortions not with negative apathy or hostility, but with the proper presentation of biblical truth.

c. Creation desacralized

The distinctness of creation from God not only rules out monism, it also ruled out nature polytheism, which was much more prevalent in the cultural and religious environment of Israel. Nature itself and natural forces were desacralized in the faith of Israel. That is, they had no intrinsic divine power. Thus, on the one hand, the fertility cults of Canaan were rejected, because the people of Israel were taught that Yahweh himself provided the abundance of nature for them (e.g. Ho. 2:8ff.), and on the other hand, the immensely powerful and influential astral deities of Babylon were unmasked as nothing more than created objects under Yahweh's authority (Is. 40:26). In both cases, fertility and astrology, Israel's distinctive belief about creation brought them into severe cultural and political conflict with surrounding worldviews. The Hebrew Bible, therefore, while it can certainly be seen to inculcate respect and care for non-human creation, resists and reverses the human tendency to sacralize or personalize it, or to imbue it with any power independent of its personal creator.[8]

d. Creation and humanity

It is not quite true to say that human beings were the climax of God's creation in Genesis 1 – 2. The real climax comes with God's own sabbath rest, as he entered into the enjoyment of his 'very good' creation. Yet even 'the sabbath was made for man', said Jesus. The sabbath day, as a recurrent reminder of the deeper 'rest' that was and remains God's purpose for creation as a whole, is for human benefit, and in that respect mirrors the rest of creation.

It is important to note that the creation is not *solely* for human benefit. The Old Testament gives it value in relation to God directly, to glorify him and to bring him delight. Creation is good and beautiful independently of our presence within it and our ability to observe it. This is at least part of the thrust of the speech of God in Job 38 – 39 with its majestic descriptions of created glories and curiosities, some of which are not even observed by humans, let alone created for their benefit, at least directly (*cf.* 38:25ff.). It is also significant that in Genesis 1 the affirmation 'It is good' was made not by Adam and Eve in the creation narratives but by God himself. That is, the goodness of creation (which includes its beauty) is theologically and chronologically prior to human observation. It is something that God 'saw' before humanity was around to see it. So the goodness of creation is not merely a human reflexive response to a pleasant view on a sunny day. It is rather the seal of divine approval on the whole universe.

Missiologically there is an important point here too. If creation were exclusively for human benefit rather than being primarily for God's glory and pleasure, then active caring for creation could be accused of being just another form of human self-serving. Now of course it *is* true that in caring for creation we ultimately also do what is best for humanity, but the task has a legitimacy of its own as well. In serving the non-human created order we are also serving God and fulfilling a mandate never revoked.

However, it is clear that the Bible does recognize the uniqueness of human beings, both in the fact that they alone of all creatures have been made by God in his own image, and in the fact that God explicitly gives human beings a position of priority within creation (Gn. 1:29; 2:9ff.; Pss. 65:9; 104:15; *etc.*). Indeed, there is a view in science known as 'the anthropic principle', which suggests that in some sense the initial conditions at the very origin of the universe, on a Big Bang understanding of it, had to be very precisely set in order to produce the relatively recent conditions in which human life on planet Earth has been possible, with its incredible potential for discovering what those initial conditions actually were.[9]

This principle need not be derided as the kind of anthropocentrism which gives us licence to abuse, neglect, rape or destroy the natural environment. The accusations

184

of Lynn White[10] and others may be justified to some extent as regards the arrogance of westernized Christian cultures towards creation, but they are not justified biblically.

On the other hand, it is a principle which does give biblical legitimacy to the priority of human beings within the created order. Rejected as 'speciesism' by some deep ecologists, this has to be maintained by Christian ethics, in relation both to environmental issues and the emotive question of animal rights. The uniqueness of human beings by virtue of their definitive nature as created in the image of God means that wherever a conflict exists between human needs and those of other animate or inanimate parts of creation – *a conflict which cannot be satisfactorily resolved by meeting the needs of both simultaneously* – then human beings take priority. This of course raises enormous issues of justice as well as environmental ethics, as the Earth Summit in Rio de Janeiro (1992) highlighted. From a Christian point of view, it is this principle which makes the conflict, in some contexts, between developmental and environmental objectives so sharp.

e. Servanthood

The word *stewardship* stood as the heading of this section in the original draft, but has been changed in the light of points made at the conference. 'Stewardship' is commonly used in Christian circles as a term implying appeals for money ('stewardship campaigns'), and is sometimes used in non-Christian circles to give a moral aura to what may be unscrupulous exploitation of resources. The term 'servanthood', on the other hand, reflects two biblical truths: first, that Christ, as Lord of creation, exercised his lordship historically through becoming a servant, so dominion through servanthood is both biblical and Christlike; second, that God's instruction to the man he placed in the garden in Eden was literally 'to serve it and keep it' (Gn. 2:15). We humans have been given dominion over the rest of creation, but it is to be exercised by serving creation on God's behalf.

God entrusted the earth to human management (Gn. 1:28,

2:15) and has not revoked the trust deed, in spite of the mess we have made of it. The concept of 'dominion' has been misunderstood (as mentioned above), but biblically includes both responsibility for the earth itself and its non-human resources (*cf.* the concern for trees and animals in Old Testament law, *e.g.* Dt. 20:19f.; 22:1-4; 6; 25:4) and the exercise of justice in human economic relationships. Elsewhere, I have suggested four basic principles that are threaded through the economic understanding of steward-ship (in its proper sense) in the Old Testament: (1) shared access to natural resources, in view of the fact that the earth was given to humanity as a whole; (2) the right and responsibility of productive work; (3) the expectation of growth and the naturalness of exchange and trade; (4) justice in the sharing and use of the products of human effort.[11]

f. Earth under curse: the fall

The biblical description of the entrance of sin and evil into human life significantly includes its effect in the realm of the human relation to the earth, and particularly the soil. I do not enter here into the debate as to whether the fall of humanity can be said to be responsible for all the phenomena in nature which we regard as threatening or catastrophic from our human point of view.[12] But the event described in Genesis 3 is certainly portrayed as having radically distorted and fractured our relationship with the earth itself, and also, as Paul points out (Rom.8:20f., echoing probably Ecclesiastes), as having frustrated the creation's function in relation to God. In my view, much Christian thinking about the earth does not take sufficient account of the biblical reality of God's curse upon it. Perhaps it is a sentimental discomfort with God being associated with anything 'not nice'. It is easier to lay all the blame on the devil. Perhaps it is lack of familiarity with Ecclesiastes ...

g. Earth under covenant: Noah

Equally, however, much other Christian thinking about the

earth far too readily jumps on the bandwagon of doom and gloom, as if the fate of the entire cosmos depended on which deodorant spray we use. That is to ignore the tremendous significance of the covenant with Noah. God has entered into a covenant commitment with all life on earth (explicitly not just human life, Gn. 8:21f.; 9:8-17), to preserve the necessary conditions of life on the planet. How long he will continue to do so is not stated, except that it will be 'as long as the earth endures'. The point is that the future of the planet rests finally in God's hands, not ours. This is of course not meant to induce complacency or indifference to urgent environmental issues. I am not saying that as human beings we could not contrive to destroy much of the planet or to render it virtually uninhabitable. But such a catastrophe, if it ever takes place, will not be outside the sovereign will and power of God and his purpose in history. We live not only in a cursed earth, but also in a covenanted earth, and have to cope with the tension. It is tragic that the rainbow has been hijacked as a New Age symbol when it could and should be the symbol of positive, hope-filled Christian affirmation about our world.

2. Israel's land: reflections from redemption

a. Noah: prototype of new creation

Noah got his name (echoes of 'comfort' and 'rest') because of his father Lamech's longing for God to lift the curse from the earth (Gn. 5:29). This is a clue to the earliest biblical understanding of what salvation should mean. If the effect of sin was to blight and belabour human existence in the earth by laying it under curse, then this antediluvian longing points to the answer: let God remove his curse from the earth. Not, one notes, let us human beings escape to heaven somewhere, leaving the earth behind. The consistent biblical hope from Genesis to Revelation is that God should do something with the earth so that we can once again dwell upon it in 'rest', with him. The Bible speaks predominantly of God coming here, not of us going somewhere else.

Lamech did not see the answer to the wish he made on Noah's birthday. On the biblical reckoning of the years, he missed it by five years and should have been glad to have done so. For when it came, it was an act of simultaneous judgment and salvation which in *both* dimensions included the natural creation along with human beings. Theologically, the flood is a prototype of both sides of God's response to the cursed earth: destruction and renewal. An old sinful world perished. A new world began as Noah's family and his animal menagerie stepped out on to Mount Ararat. The echoes of the creation narrative are strong in Genesis 8:15–17. It was, of course, still the old world not yet washed clean of its sin, as the narrative quickly shows. But the whole story becomes the sign not only of God's commitment to life on earth while it lasts (in the covenant tied up with its rainbow ribbon), but also of the coming final judgment and renewal – the new creation (*cf.* 2 Pet. 3).

b. The covenant with Abraham: land as an integral part of redemptive blessing

It is not surprising, therefore, that the covenant promise which actually launched the work of redemption in history included land in its terms. In fact in purely statistical terms, land is clearly the dominant note in the ancestral promise. Of forty-six references to the promise in Genesis to Judges, only seven do not mention the land, while twenty-nine refer solely to it (*e.g.* in Gn. 28:4, the 'blessing given to Abraham' is simply possession of the land).[13]

There is thus a continuity and consistency in the total biblical story. Genesis 1 – 11 shows humanity in God's earth, but living in a state of alienation from it and longing for restoration and the removal of the curse from the land. The concluding vision of Scripture looks to a new creation in which God will once again dwell with redeemed humanity. The foundational redemptive covenant of grace with Abraham, therefore, includes land in order to make particular and local what will ultimately be universal – blessing not only to all nations but also to the whole earth itself.

c. Israel's land as microcosm of the earth

It follows from the above point that Canaan, as the land of Israel, has to be viewed in the light of the universality of the Abraham covenant as well as its particularity. That is, while the historical gift of the land to the tribes of Israel is certainly described in the Old Testament as the direct action of God in faithfulness to his promise to Abraham, that promise had as its ultimate scope the blessing of all nations. Its other two main ingredients have that in view: posterity (the fact that Abraham would become a nation, which would be the vehicle of God's blessing to the nations), and relationship (the special covenant relationship between God and Israel, which the Old Testament envisages being ultimately extended to the nations). The land element has to be viewed consistently in the same universal context. Israel possessed its land as part of its mission in relation to the rest of the nations and as part of God's redemptive intention for the whole earth. That is a vitally important point concerning the concept of election.

Now this link between the land of Israel and the whole earth can be viewed eschatologically (as we shall note below, and *cf.* ch. 1)). But as we have already seen, it is also vitally important as the basis for a *paradigmatic* understanding of the relevance of Old Testament Israel to other cultures and societies separated by history and geography. Israel was created and commissioned to be 'a light to the nations'. There was, therefore, a sense in which everything connected with them was exemplary in principle. The gifts of land to live in and law to live by were intrinsic to the way God shaped Israel to be a 'model' people. All the time one studies the particulars of Israel's social, economic and political structures one must keep in mind the universal goal of their existence in the first place. This important hermeneutical principle helps to unlock the relevance of the Old Testament for our own ethical construction – in many areas, including especially ecological concern.[14]

Among the clearest parallels between creation teaching about the whole earth and Israel's theology of their land are the twin themes of divine ownership and divine gift. The creation basis of Old Testament teaching gives us two complementary truths about the earth: on the one hand, it belongs to God who made it (Ps. 24:1; 89:11; 95:4f.; Je. 27:4ff.; 1 Ch. 29:11); on the other hand, it has been given and entrusted to human beings (Pss. 115:16; 8:6; Gn. 1:28–30). God, as ultimate owner, thus retains the right of moral control over how the earth is used. As we saw above, human beings, as stewards and 'servant-managers', are accountable to God for the care and use of the earth and all its resources.

Israel's system of land tenure embodied the same two principles. On the one hand, the land was God's gift to Israel, an essential part of the promise to Abraham and a tangible proof of his faithfulness. As their 'inheritance', it was at the heart of their covenant relationship to Yahweh. On the other hand, the land was still owned by God (Lv. 25:23), so that as divine landlord he retained authority over how it should be used. Hence Israel's whole economic system was subject to God's moral critique. The paradigmatic connection between Israel as a society and the rest of humanity means that we can make positive use of Israel's comprehensive and detailed laws and institutions concerning the distribution and use of land in our own efforts to think biblically about economic and environmental ethics in our day. This gives us a broader and richer set of resources, with a greater degree of practical specificity and sharpness, than the application of the creation principle of stewardship alone. While fundamental and challenging, that principle is higher up the 'ladder of abstraction', whereas the specific land economics of Israel are at ground level.

d. Creation values in redeemed economics

When we turn to examine the details of Israel's economic legislation, it is possible to see how so much of it was geared to restoring the creation values referred to above in the section on 'Servanthood'. In a fallen world, such a restoration cannot be total, so one finds the same kind of tension in Old Testament economics between the ideal and the given reality that is also there in other aspects of Old Testament law and ethics (*e.g.* on divorce, slavery, *etc.*). Thus, taking up each of the four principles there referred to (p. 186):[15]

1. Shared access to and use of the land and its resources were built into the initial distribution of the land among the tribes at the time of the settlement. The purpose was made very clear – that each tribe, clan and family should have sufficient according to its size and needs (Nu. 26:52–56, Jos. 13 – 19).

2. The right and responsibility to work productively are reflected in the sizeable number of laws concerning working humans and animals, slaves, hired labour, conditions of work, treatment by employers, payment, sabbath and festival rest, *etc.* (*e.g.* Ex. 21:1–6, 20f., 26f.; Jb. 31:14; Lv. 25:39f., 43; Lv. 19:13; Dt. 24:14f.; Je. 22:13; Ex. 20:11; 23:12; Is. 58:3–14; Dt. 25:4).

3. Economic growth in material goods and provisions is both validated and put under careful control and critique, from the tenth commandment ('You shall not covet') onwards. The same chapter of Deuteronomy points to the God-given goal of abundance and sufficiency (8:7–10), and the dangers of excessive surplus (8:11–18). Most interestingly, and of great practical effect in Israel throughout its whole biblical history as far as the evidence shows, was the principle of inalienability of family land. Land itself was not to be treated as a commercial commodity, for private speculation and profit. It could not be bought or sold, apart from within the kinship groups (Lv. 25:23ff.). The story of Naboth (1 Ki. 21) and its context shows that the violation of this principle involved a capitulation to a foreign religious worldview on the one hand and the invasion of gross rural injustice on the other.

4. Justice in the use and distribution of the product of economic activity is also a major concern of Old Testament law. There can be all kinds of 'neutral' reasons why some people become wealthier and others poorer.[16] The Old Testament law seeks to redress the economic balance by

structural measures aimed at the control of debt especially (Ex. 22:25; Lv. 25:36f.; Dt. 23:19f; 24:6, 10), and other tactics to relieve poverty and to restore the poor to dignified participation in the community – gleaning rights (Lv. 19:9f.; Dt. 24:19–22), storage and distribution of the triennial tithe (Dt. 14:22–27; 26:12ff.), the sabbatical year (Ex. 23:11; Lv. 25:6f.; Dt. 15:1–3), jubilee year (Lv. 25:8ff.), *etc.* All of this was part of the structures of Israel's economic system, to encourage justice and compassion in the ordinary vicissitudes of a functioning economy.[17] This is not yet even to mention the reaction of the Old Testament to poverty and injustice caused by direct oppression and greed – *i.e.* the economic message of the prophets.

e. The link between human morality and ecological health

The land functioned like a moral and spiritual barometer in the Old Testament. So much of the prophetic anger is directed at economic injustice and oppression, in which the abuse and misuse of the land is dominant. On the one hand, Israel fell into the kind of nature polytheism that characterized the Canaanite view of the land, and thus compromised their unique covenant relationship with Yahweh. On the other hand, they allowed economic practices in the use of land, mostly associated with the monarchy, which eventually polarized the nation into a wealthy land-owning élite and an oppressed peasant population. In other words, the land stood at the junction of the vertical and the horizontal of covenant relationships. The combination of idolatry and injustice is still much in evidence in our own world, provided we are careful and comprehensive in our evaluation of what constitutes each.

Sometimes the specifically ecological aspect is brought into focus. Psalm 72, for example, positively looks for environmental and economic well-being as a by-product of just and benevolent government. Conversely, Hosea 4:1–3 climaxes the list of social evils with the observation that nature itself is suffering the consequences (I think the text is going further than a mere personification of nature in response to a broken covenant). Habakkuk 2, in the midst of a series of woes against the Babylonian excesses, includes gross environmental damage along with the normal victims of war.

> The violence you have done to Lebanon will
>   overwhelm you,
>   and your destruction of animals will terrify you.
> For you have shed man's blood;
>   you have destroyed lands and cities and
>   everyone in them.
> (Hab. 2:17; 'Lebanon' almost certainly is a figure for
> forests, as the parallel with 'animals' suggests.)

The American deforestation of vast areas of Vietnam in the course of that war, and the Iraqi ecological atrocities in the Gulf War, give the ancient prophetic text a chilling relevance.[18]

f. Jesus affirmed the goodness of creation and demonstrated his lordship over it

Turning all too briefly to the New Testament,[19] we have to begin with the tremendous fact that the incarnation itself affirmed and vindicated the goodness of creation. From there we could take note of the highly positive attitude of Jesus to nature, both in his direct teaching and in his parables (*e.g.* Mt. 6:26ff.; 10:29; *etc.*). And as scholars have often pointed out, his miracles of calming the storm and walking on the sea demonstrate not merely the power of the creator, but specifically that power in relation to the element of creation normally associated in Old Testament thought with the chaotic, uncontrollable forces of nature – the sea. Hence the astonished question of his disciples (Mt. 8:27).

g. The atonement and resurrection include creation in their effects

Paul affirms that through the atoning death of Jesus on the cross, 'all things' in creation have been reconciled to God

(Col. 1:20). The scope of Christ's redeeming work is thus as universal as the scope of his creating and sustaining work already referred to (Col. 1:16f.). Likewise, the resurrection is not only the vindication of the whole created order,[20] but is also the firstfruits of a new creation.

3. New creation : reflections from eschatology

a. Return to land symbolic of restored relationship

Having jumped ahead to New Testament eschatology, we must pause to step back to the Old Testament. As the prophets spoke about the devastating loss of land that came upon Israel in the early sixth century BC, and then enabled Israel to see beyond it to a restored relationship with God, it was the land itself that stood at the fulcrum of their message.[21] Thus, in Jeremiah 30 – 34, Isaiah 40 – 55, and Ezekiel 36 – 48, to name just the major text blocks, the promised restoration of Israel after the time of judgment is expressed in terms of return to the land. There are many new dimensions to this fresh promise, but it never 'evaporates' into the spiritual stratosphere. Land was still part of God's redemptive package for Israel in the centuries before Christ.

b. Future blessing portrayed as a super-abundance of nature

However, one feature of these and other texts (*e.g.* Am 9:13– 15) is the vision not merely of a return to the land as it was (that in fact turned out to be a tough new assignment for the tiny post-exilic restoration community, fraught with many disappointments), but of a renewed nature, echoing Eden itself in abundance and beauty. In other words, as Israel's eschatology sought to express its conception of God's ultimate purposes, it found its most natural resource in God's original purpose – namely a good and perfect earth available for human enjoyment and blessing.

c. The final vision: a new creation

The climax of Old Testament eschatological vision regarding creation is found in Isaiah 65 – 66. The words, 'See, I am creating new heavens and a new earth!' (Is. 65:17, REB), introduce a wonderful section which portrays God's new world as a place which is joyful, life-fulfilling, with guaranteed work-satisfaction, and environmentally safe! It is a vision that puts most New Age dreams in the shade. This and related passages are the scriptural (Old Testament) foundation for the New Testament hope, which, far from rejecting or denying the earth as such or envisaging us floating off to some place else, looks forward likewise to a new, redeemed creation (Rom. 8:18ff.), in which righteousness will dwell after purging judgment (2 Pet. 3:10–13)[22] because God himself will dwell there with his people (Rev. 21:1–4).

d. The ecological relevance of biblical eschatology

Finally, as Francis Bridger points out, the eschatological orientation of all biblical ethics has the important consequence of protecting our ecological concern from becoming either purely anthropocentric, or pantheistically earth-centred.

> The primary argument for ecological responsibility lies in the connection between old and new creation ... We are called to be stewards of the earth by virtue not simply of our orientation to the Edenic command of the Creator but also because of our orientation to the future. In acting to preserve and enhance the created order we are pointing to the coming rule of God in Christ ... Ecological ethics are not, therefore, anthropocentric: they testify to the vindicating acts of God in creation and redemption ... Paradoxically, the fact that it is God who will bring about a new order of creation at the End and that we are merely erecting signposts to that future need not

act as a disincentive. Rather it frees us from the burden of ethical and technological autonomy and makes it clear that human claims to sovereignty are relative. The knowledge that it is God's world, that our efforts are not directed toward the construction of an ideal utopia but that we are, under God, building bridgeheads of the kingdom serves to humble us and to bring us to the place of ethical obedience.[23]

We might finish, however, with a poem more in the genre of the prophets and psalmists.

> The time of rest, the promised Sabbath comes! ...
> Rivers of gladness water all the earth,
> And clothe all climes with beauty. The reproach
> Of barrenness is past. The fruitful field
> Laughs with abundance; and the land, once lean
> Or fertile only in its own disgrace,
> Exults to see its thistly curse repeal'd.
> The various seasons woven into one,
> And that one season an eternal spring,
> The garden fears no blight, and needs no fence,
> For there is none to covet, all are full.
> The lion, and the lizzard, and the bear
> Graze with the fearless flocks ...
> One song employs all nations, and all cry,
> 'Worthy the Lamb, for He was slain for us!'
> The dwellers in the vales and on the rocks
> Shout to each other, and the mountain tops
> From distant mountains catch the flying joy,
> Till, nation after nation taught the strain,
> Earth rolls the rapturous Hosanna round.[24]

Chapter Eight

The jubilee year[1]

The jubilee (*yôḇēl* or *šᵉnaṭ hayyôḇēl*, Lv. 25:13, 'the year of jubilee') came at the end of the cycle of seven sabbatical years. Leviticus 25:8–10 specifies it as the fiftieth year, though some scholars believe it may have been actually the forty-ninth – *i.e.* the seventh sabbatical year. In this year there was a proclamation of liberty to Israelites who had become enslaved for debt, and a restoration of land to families who had been compelled to sell it out of economic need in the previous fifty years. Instructions concerning the jubilee, and its relation to the procedures of land and slave redemption are found entirely in Leviticus 25. But it is referred to also in Leviticus 26 and 27 in other contexts.

It is an institution which has inspired much curiosity, in ancient and modern times, and in recent years it has come to prominence in the writings of those committed to radical Christian social ethics.[2] A text with liberty at its heart must have something to say to a theology and ethic of liberation! This essay aims to come to whatever applied relevance the institution may be accorded only after a detailed study of its background and practical details.[3]

1. Socio-economic background

The jubilee was in essence an economic institution. It had two main points of concern: the family and the land. It was rooted, therefore, in the kinship structure of Israelite society and the system of land-tenure that was based upon it.

a. Israelite kinship structure[4]

Israel had a three-tier pattern of kinship, comprising the

tribe, the clan, and the household. Gideon's modest reply to his angelic visitor shows us all three: 'Look at my clan – it is the weakest in the tribe of Manasseh; and I am the least in my father's house' (*cf.* Jdg. 6:15). The last two smaller units (household and clan) had greater social and economic importance than the tribe in terms of benefits and responsibilities relating to individual Israelites. The father's house was a place of authority, even for married adults like Gideon (*cf.* Jdg. 6:27; 8:20). It was also the place of security and protection (Jdg. 6:30ff.). The clan was a larger grouping of a number of father's houses and an important sub-unit of the tribe. The clans were named after the grandsons of Jacob, or other members of the patriarchal family tree (see Nu. 26 and 1 Ch. 4 – 8), thereby acknowledging that they were units of recognizable kinship. But sometimes the clan name was attached to the territorial area of their settlement, such as a village or group of villages. The clan had important responsibility in the preservation of the land allotted to its constituent households. The jubilee was primarily for the economic protection of the smallest of these units – the father's house, or the extended family. However, in Leviticus 25, it is interwoven with the economic practice of the redemption of land and persons, and those redemption procedures were primarily for the protection of, and the responsibility of, the clan. The two sets of provision were complementary, as we shall see.

b. Israelite land-tenure

Whatever may have been the process by which Israel emerged in Canaan, once they were able to establish control over the land (which was not everywhere, of course, for quite a long time – especially in areas of Canaanite city domination), they operated a system of land-tenure which was based on these kinship units. Thus the territory was allotted to tribes, 'according to their clans', and within the clans each household had its portion or 'heritage'. Judges 21:24 describes the Israelite soldiers returning each to his tribe, his clan, and to his (household) inheritance. This system had two features that stand in complete contrast to the preceding pattern of Canaanite economic structure.

1. *Equitable distribution.* In Canaan the land was owned by kings and their nobles, with the bulk of the population as tax-paying tenant farmers. In Israel the initial division of the land was explicitly among the clans and households within the tribes, under the general rubric that each receive land according to size and need. The documentary evidence for this is to be found in the tribal lists of Numbers 26 (especially note verses 52–56) and in the detailed territorial division of land recorded in Joshua 13 – 21, where the repetition of the phrase 'according to their clans' indicates the intention that the land should be distributed throughout the whole kinship system as widely as possible.

2. *Inalienability.* In order to protect this system of kinship distribution, family land was made inalienable. That is, it was not to be bought and sold as a commercial asset, but was to remain as far as possible within the extended family, or at least within the circle of families in the clan. It was this principle which lay behind Naboth's refusal to sell his patrimony to Ahab (1 Ki. 21), and it is most explicit in the economic regulations of Leviticus 25.

2. Theological basis

> The land must not be sold permanently, because the land is mine and you are aliens and my tenants.
>
> (Lv. 25:23)

This statement, at the heart of the chapter containing the jubilee, provides the hinge between the social and economic system described above and its theological rationale. Having stated the inalienability rule, it goes on to present the two basic factors in the theological context of the jubilee and related laws: the theology of the land and the status of the Israelites.

a. The theology of land

One of the central pillars of the faith of Israel was that the land they inhabited was Yahweh's land. It had been his even before Israel entered it (Ex. 15:13, 17). This theme is found often in the prophets and Psalms, as part of Israel's cultic tradition. At the same time, although ultimately owned by Yahweh, the land had been promised and then given to Israel in the course of the redemptive history. It was their 'inheritance' (Deuteronomy *passim*), a term which points to the relationship of sonship between Israel and Yahweh.

This dual tradition of the land – divine ownership and divine gift – was associated in some way with every major thread in Israel's theology. The promise of land was an essential part of the patriarchal *election* tradition. The land was the goal of the exodus *redemption* tradition. The maintenance of the *covenant* relationship and the security of life in the land were bound together. Divine *judgment* eventually meant expulsion from the land, until the *restored relationship* was symbolized in the return to the land.

The land, then, stood like a fulcrum in the relationship between God and Israel (*cf.* its position in Lv. 26:40–45). It was a monumental, tangible witness both to that divine control of history within which the relationship had been established, and also to the moral and practical demands which that relationship entailed. For the Israelite, living with his family on his allotted share of Yahweh's land, it was the proof of his membership of God's people and the focus of his practical response to God's grace. Nothing that concerned the land was free from theological and ethical dimensions – as every harvest reminded him (Dt. 26).

b. The theological status of the Israelites

The Israelites are described in two ways in Leviticus 25.

1. 'You are aliens and my tenants' (NIV), 'strangers and sojourners' (RSV) (verse 23). These terms, *gērîm wᵉtôšābîm*, describe a class of people who resided among the Israelites in Canaan, but were not ethnic Israelites. They may have

been descendants of the dispossessed Canaanites, or immigrants. They had no stake in the tenure of the land, but survived by hiring out their services as residential employees (labourers, craftsmen, *etc.*) for Israelite land-owning households. Provided the household remained economically viable, its resident alien employees enjoyed both protection and security. But otherwise, their position could be perilous. Hence they are frequently mentioned in Israel's law as the objects of particular concern for justice because of their vulnerability.

The Israelites were to regard their status before God as analogous to that of their own residential dependants to themselves. Thus, they had no ultimate title to the land – it was owned by God. Nevertheless, they could enjoy secure benefits of it under his protection and in dependence on him. So the terms are not (as they might sound in English) a denial of rights, but rather an affirmation of a relationship of protected dependency.

The practical effect of this model for Israel's relationship with God is seen in verses 35, 40 and 53. If all Israelites share this same status before God, then the impoverished or indebted brother is to be regarded and treated in the same way as God regards and treats all Israel.

2. 'They are my slaves whom I brought forth out of Egypt' (verse 42, REB, *cf.* 55). Three times in this chapter the exodus is mentioned, and twice more in the following chapter (26:13, 45). It was regarded as an act of redemption in which God had 'bought' Israel for himself. Freed from slavery to Egypt, they were now slaves of God himself. Therefore, nobody could now claim as his own private property a fellow Israelite who belonged by right of purchase to God alone. The exodus redemption thus provided the historical and theological model for the social and economic practice of redemption and jubilee. Those who are God's freed slaves are not to make slaves of one another (25:39, 42).

This weight of theological tradition concentrated into 25:23 gives a seriousness to the economic measures outlined in the rest of the chapter.

201

3. Exegetical outline

Leviticus 25 is a complex chapter in which several different economic practices have been thrown closely together, along with parenthetical sections and exceptive clauses. Source critics have come to no kind of consensus over alleged documentary division of the material, and the multiplicity of theories is little help in understanding the chapter. However, in its present form, the text has some definable paragraphs (as can be seen in the RSV and NIV), which guide us through its provisions.

a. Verses 1–7

The chapter opens with the law of the sabbatical year on the land. This is an expansion of the fallow-year law of Exodus 23:10f. which was also further developed in Deuteronomy 15:1–2 into a year in which debts (or more probably the pledges given for loans) were to be released.

b. Verses 8–12

The jubilee is then introduced as the fiftieth year to follow the seventh sabbatical year. Verse 10 presents the twin concepts that are fundamental to the whole institution, namely liberty and return: *liberty* from the burden of debt and the bondage it may have entailed; *return* both to the ancestral property if it had been mortgaged to a creditor, and to the family which may have been split up through debt-servitude. It was these two components of the jubilee, freedom and restoration, that entered into the metaphorical and eschatological use of the jubilee in prophetic and later New Testament thought.

c. Verses 13–17

The financial implications of a recurring jubilee are then spelt out. The apparent sale of a piece of land really amounted only to a sale of the use of the land. So an approaching jubilee diminished the cost for the purchaser, inasmuch as he was buying the number of harvests until the jubilee restored the land to its original owner.

d. Verses 18–22

At this point some exhortation is inserted to encourage the observance of the sabbatical regulations, by promising special blessing in the preceding year. The theological principle was that obedience to the economic legislation of Israel would require, not prudential calculations, but faith in the ability of Yahweh to provide through his control of nature as well as history.

e. Verses 23–24

These central verses in the chapter constitute a heading to the remaining paragraphs which are primarily concerned with the economic redemption of land and persons, interwoven with the jubilee. We have already noted the major theological traditions embodied in them.

f. Verses 25–55

We come now to the practical details of redemption and jubilee. In these verses there are three descending stages of poverty with required responses, interrupted by parenthetical sections dealing with houses in cities and Levite properties (29–34) and non-Israelite slaves (44–46). The stages are marked off by the introductory phrase, 'If your brother becomes poor' (25, 35, 39 and 47, RSV). Probably this phrase introduced an original series of redemption procedures, unconnected with the jubilee. The addition of jubilee regulations complicates matters in places, but, as we shall see, functions as a necessary complement to the effects of redemption.

Stage 1 (25–28). Initially, having fallen on hard times (for any reason: none is specified), the Israelite land-owner sells, or offers to sell, some of his land. To keep it within the family, in line with the inalienability principle, it was first of all the duty of the nearest kinsman (the gō 'ēl) either to pre-empt it (if it was still on offer), or to redeem it (if it had been sold). Secondly, the seller himself retains the right to redeem it for himself, if he later recovers the means to do so. Thirdly and in any case, the property, whether sold or redeemed by a kinsman, reverts to the original family in the year of jubilee.

> *Exception 1* (29–31). The above rules did not apply to dwelling-places in the walled cities. This was probably because the primary intention of the redemption and jubilee provisions was to preserve the economic viability of families through the secure possesion of their inherited land. City houses were not part of that productive economic base, and so need not be subject to indefinite redemption rights or jubilee return to seller. However, village dwellings were treated as part of the rural scene, and therefore were included.

> *Exception 2* (32–34). This is a rider to exception 1. Since the Levites as a tribe had no inherited share in the land but were allotted certain towns, their dwellings in them were to be subject to normal redemption and jubilee provisions.

Stage 2 (35–38). If the poorer brother's plight worsens and he still cannot stay solvent, presumably even after several such sales, it then becomes the duty of the kinsman to maintain him as a dependent labourer, by means of interest-free loans.

Stage 3a (39–43). In the event of a total economic collapse, such that the poorer kinsman has no more land left to sell or pledge for loans, he and his whole family sell themselves to, *i.e.* enter the bonded service of, the wealthier kinsman. The latter, however, is commanded in strong and repeated terms not to treat the debtor Israelite like a slave, but rather as a resident employee. This undesirable state of affairs is to continue only until the next jubilee – *i.e.* not more than one more generation. Then the debtor and/or his children (the original debtor may have died, but the next generation were to benefit from the jubilee, verses 41, 54) were to recover their original patrimony of land and be enabled to make a fresh start.

> *Exception 3* (44–46). This is a reminder that the redemption and jubilee provisions applied to

Israelites and not to foreign slaves or resident aliens. This reinforces the point that they were primarily concerned with the distribution of land and the viability of Israelite families, neither of which applied to the non-landowning population.

Stage 3b (47–55). If a man had entered this debt-bondage *outside* the clan, then an obligation lay on the whole clan to prevent this loss of a whole family by exercising their duty to redeem him. The list of potential kinsman-redeemers in verses 48f. shows how the responsibility moved outwards from the nearest kinsman to the extent of the clan itself ('family' in verse 49, RSV, is misleading; the Hebrew is *mišpāḥâ,* clan). The whole clan had the duty of preserving its constituent families and their inherited land. It also had the duty to see that a non-Israelite creditor behaved as an Israelite should towards an Israelite debtor, and that the jubilee provision was adhered to eventually.

From this analysis of the chapter, it can be seen that there were two main differences between the redemption and jubilee provisions. First, *timing*. Redemption was a duty that could be exercised at any time, locally, as circumstances required, whereas jubilee took place twice a century as a national event. Secondly, *purpose*. The main aim of redemption was the preservation of the land and persons of the clan, whereas the main beneficiary of the jubilee was the extended family, or 'father's house'. The jubilee therefore functioned as a necessary override to the practice of redemption. The regular operation of redemption over a period could result in the whole territory of a clan coming into the hands of a few wealthier families, with the rest of the families in the clan in a kind of debt-servitude, living as dependent tenants of the wealthy – *i.e.* precisely the kind of land-tenure system that Israel had overturned. The jubilee was thus a mechanism to prevent this and to preserve the socio-economic fabric of multiple-household land-tenure with the comparative equality and independent viability of the smallest family-plus-land units.

Now these household units held a central place in the

experience and expression of Israel's covenant relationship with God, as can be seen from their role in social, military, judicial, cultic and educational spheres.[5] In the light of this centrality of the family, the jubilee can be seen as more than merely an economic regulator (and certainly more than the utopian measure of social justice it is sometimes portrayed as). In attempting to maintain or restore the viability of such households it was in fact aimed at preserving a fundamental dimension of Israel's relationship with Yahweh. We noticed this already in considering the weight of theological tradition packed into verse 23. It is also underlined three times in the reminders of the exodus and its implications (38, 42, 55). This in turn explains why the neglect of these institutions, bemoaned in the following chapter, Leviticus 26, led not merely to economic distress but also to a broken relationship and eventual exile – a connection also very clearly perceived by the prophets.

4. Historical questions

But did it ever happen? Were the jubilee regulations real and practicable legislation, or were they academic and utopian? The fact is that, while there is evidence that kinship-redemption was practised (*e.g.* Je. 32; Ruth 4), there is simply no evidence of a national jubilee in the extant historical documents of Israel (though some would discern an allusion to a jubilee year in Is. 37:30, where a double year of fallow seems to be envisaged; but it may refer merely to the disastrous effect of invasion). This silence does not, of course, prove that it never did happen. There is similarly no mention of the observance of the Day of Atonement in the historical documents. Nor can we say that it was economically impossible and so *could not* have happened, because there is evidence from other ancient Near Eastern civilizations of periodic nationwide remissions of debt in connection with the accession of a new king. And this ancient Near Eastern evidence comes from centuries earlier than the origins of Old Testament Israel.[6]

Nevertheless, scholars are divided: some see the law as a late, idealistic, formulation from the same period as the

Holiness Code within the priestly compilation to which this part of Leviticus is usually assigned.[7] Others regard the jubilee as part of Israel's earliest, pre-monarchic, laws, which fell into disuse. This latter position is more commonly held by those scholars who have done most research into the ancient Near Eastern parallels and the sociological background.[8] Gottwald regards the redemption provisions, but not the jubilee, as reflecting 'old conditions'.[9]

We have seen that the aim of the jubilee was to maintain or restore the socio-economic basis of the nation's covenant relationship with God. This would reduce the likelihood of its being an exilic invention in view of evidence that there developed in the later period a loosening of the ancient family-land basis in the future vision of an expanded people of God that would include foreigners and eunuchs (cf. Is. 54:1, 56:3–7). Israel's identity and relationship with God would no longer be so closely tied to a social system in which kinship and land ownership were determinative of one's standing within the religious community. It is hard to see what purpose would have been served by framing new idealistic legislation designed to preserve those very things. Conversely, it makes sense to see the jubilee as a very ancient law which fell into neglect during Israel's history in the land, not so much because it was economically impossible, as because it became irrelevant to the scale of social disruption. The jubilee presupposes a situation where a man, though in severe debt, still technically holds the title to his family's land and could be restored to full ownership of it. But from the time of Solomon on this must have become meaningless for growing numbers of families as they fell victim to the acids of debt, slavery, royal intrusion and confiscation, and total dispossession. Many were uprooted and pushed off their ancestral land altogether. After a few generations they had nothing to be restored to in any practicable sense (cf. Mi. 2:2, 9; Is. 5:8). This would explain why the jubilee is never appealed to by any of the prophets as an economic proposal (though its ideals are reflected metaphorically). On the only occasion when a slave release is mentioned by a prophet, in Jeremiah 34, the law appealed to was the sabbatical-year release of Hebrew slaves (Ex. 21:1–7; Dt. 15:12ff.) – not the jubilee. The people in question were fellow Judeans, but they were effectively landless (a definitive feature of the 'Hebrew' class), not mortgaged debtors who could be restored to their property. The story shows how fragile and transient their actual release was.[10]

5. Ethical development

a. In the Old Testament

We have seen that the jubilee had two major thrusts: release/liberty, and return/restoration. Both of these lent themselves readily to the process of transfer from the strictly economic provision of the jubilee itself to a wider metaphorical application. There are allusive echoes of the jubilee particularly in later Isaiah. The mission of the Servant of Yahweh has strong elements of the restorative plan of God for his people, aimed specifically at the weak and oppressed (Is. 42:1–7). Isaiah 58 is an attack on cultic observance without social justice, and calls for liberation of the oppressed (6), specifically focusing on one's own kinship obligations (7). Most clearly of all, Isaiah 61 uses jubilee images to portray the one anointed as the herald of Yahweh to 'evangelize' the poor, to proclaim liberty to the captives (using the word $d^e r\hat{o}r$, which is the explicitly jubilary word for release), and to announce the year of Yahweh's favour (almost certainly an allusion to a jubilee year). The ideas of redemption and return are combined in the future vision of Isaiah 35, and put alongside a transformation of nature. Thus, within the Old Testament itself, the jubilee attracted an eschatological imagery, which, however, went along with an ethical application in the present. That is, it could be used to portray God's final intervention for messianic redemption and restoration; but it could also support ethical challenge for justice to the oppressed in contemporary history.

b. In the New Testament

Jesus announced the inbreaking of the eschatological reign of God. He claimed that the hopes of restoration and messianic reversal were being fulfilled in his own ministry. The 'Nazareth manifesto' (Lk. 4:16–30) is the clearest programmatic statement of this, and quotes directly from Isaiah 61, which is strongly influenced by jubilee concepts. Scholars are mostly agreed that Jesus made use of jubilary imagery, though there is some division over exactly what he meant by it. Trocmé argued that Jesus' ministry co-incided with a year when the jubilee should have happened (AD 26), and that his teaching drew inspiration and challenge from that fact.[11] Others, noting that Jesus used the prophetic texts and not the levitical law, argue that he was merely using jubilary language as a way of showing the kind of response required by the arrival of the kingdom of God, without intending an actual national jubilee. Yoder, who first brought Trocmé's work to an English-speaking readership in the first edition of his book, argues in the second edition that it is a misunderstanding of Trocmé and himself to think that Jesus or the New Testament authors envisaged a literal re-enactment of the levitical laws every seven or forty-nine years. Rather, 'the fundamental notion of periodic leveling ... would have become in Jesus' teaching a permanently defining trait of the new order'.[12] Sloan notes that Jesus' use of *aphēsis* carries both the sense of spiritual forgiveness of sin and also literal and financial remission of actual debts. Thus, the original background of economic $d^e r \hat{o} r$ has been preserved in Jesus' challenge concerning ethical response to the kingdom of God.[13] Ringe traces the interweaving of major jubilee images into various parts of the gospel narratives and the teaching of Jesus; *e.g.* the beatitudes, the response to John the Baptist (Mt. 11:2–6), the parable of the banquet (Lk. 14:12–24), various episodes of forgiveness, teaching on debts (Mt. 18:21–35), *etc.*). The evidence is broad, and conforms to the pattern already set in the Old Testament – namely, the jubilee as a model or image for the kingdom of God embodies both eschatological affirmation and ethical demand.[14] Likewise, in Acts, the jubilary concept of eschatological restoration is found in the otherwise unique idea of *apokatastasis*. It occurs in Acts 1:6 and 3:21, related to God's final restoration of Israel and all things. Significantly, the early church responded to this hope at the level of economic mutual help – thus fulfilling the sabbatical hopes of Deuteronomy 15 (Acts 4:34 is virtually a quotation of Dt. 15:4).

c. *Contemporary application*

Without envisaging any literal enactment of its provisions, the jubilee still remains a powerful model in formulating Christian biblical ethics. Its primary assumptions and objectives can be distilled and used as a guide and critique for our own ethical agenda in the modern world.

Economically, the jubilee existed to protect a form of land-tenure that was based on an equitable and widespread distribution of the land, and to prevent the accumulation of ownership in the hands of a wealthy few. This echoes the creation principle that the whole earth is given by God to all humanity, who act as co-stewards of its resources. There is a parallel between the affirmation of Leviticus 25:23, in respect of Israel, that 'the land is mine', and the affirmation of Psalm 24, in respect of humanity as a whole, that 'the earth is the LORD's, and everything in it, the world, and all who live in it'. The moral principles of the jubilee are therefore universalizable on the basis of the moral consistency of God. What he required of Israel reflects what in principle he desires for humanity – namely broadly equitable distribution of the resources of the earth, especially land, and a curb on the tendency to accumulation with its inevitable oppression and alienation. The jubilee thus stands as a critique not only of massive private accumulation of land and related wealth, but also of large-scale forms of collectivism or nationalization which destroy any meaningful sense of personal or family ownership. It still has a point to make in modern Christian approaches to economics.

210

Socially, the jubilee embodied a practical concern for the family unit. In Israel's case, this meant the extended family, the 'father's house', which was a sizeable group of related nuclear families descended in the male line from a living progenitor, including up to three or four generations. This was the smallest unit in Israel's kinship structure, and it was the focus of identity, status, responsibility and security for the individual Israelite. It was this that the jubilee aimed to protect and periodically to restore if necessary. Notably, it did so not by merely 'moral' means – *i.e.* appealing for greater family cohesion or admonishing parents and children – but by legislating for specific structural mechanisms to regulate the economic effects of debt. Family morality was meaningless if families were being split up and dispossessed by economic forces that rendered them powerless (*cf.* Ne. 5:1-5). The jubilee aimed to restore social dignity and participation to families through maintaining or restoring their economic viability. The economic collapse of a family in one generation was not to condemn all future generations to the bondage of perpetual indebtedness. Such principles and objectives are certainly not irrelevant to welfare legislation or indeed any legislation with socio-economic implications.[15]

Theologically, the jubilee was based upon several central affirmations of Israel's faith, and the importance of these should not be overlooked when assessing its relevance to Christian ethic and mission. Like the rest of the sabbatical provisions, the jubilee proclaimed the sovereignty of God over time and nature, and obedience to it would require submission to that sovereignty, hence the year is dubbed 'holy' (Lv. 25:12), 'a sabbath to Yahweh' (*cf.* verse 2), to be observed out of the fear of Yahweh (*cf.* verse 17). Furthermore, observing the fallow-year dimension would also require faith in God's providence as the one who could command blessing in the natural order. Additional motivation for the law is provided by repeated appeals to the knowledge of God's historical act of redemption, the exodus and all it had meant for Israel. And to this historical dimension was added the cultic and 'present' experience of forgiveness in the fact that the jubilee was proclaimed on the Day of Atonement. To know yourself forgiven by God was to issue in practical remission of debts and bondages for fellow Israelites. And, as we have seen, the inbuilt future hope of the literal jubilee, blended with an eschatological hope of God's final restoration of humanity and nature to his original purpose. To apply the jubilee model, then, requires that people face the sovereignty of God, trust his providence, know his redemptive action, experience his atonement, practise his justice and hope in his promise. The wholeness of the model embraces the church's evangelistic mission, its personal and social ethics and its future hope.

Chapter Nine

The people of God and the state[1]

Introduction

My main purpose in this study is to trace the changing concept of the people of God in relation to the state in the period covered by the history of Israel in the Hebrew Bible. So I am taking for granted several assumptions that would fall within the range of creation-based theology, since I have briefly discussed them elsewhere,[2] and they are fairly commonplace in discussions of the topic of the Bible and the state. First, I assume that ethnic diversity and the multiplicity of nations are part of God's creative intention for humanity and not in themselves the result of sin. This seems to be evident from texts such as Deuteronomy 32:8, echoed in Acts 17:26, and the eschatological vision that the redeemed humanity will include, but not obliterate, the distinctions between every tribe, language and nation. Second, I assume that there is a social dimension to human life which is also part of God's creative intention, so that the proper and harmonious ordering of relationships between individuals and communities, locally and internationally, is part of human accountability to God as creator of all. The political task of maintaining a morally acceptable social order is a human duty under God.

Does the fulfilment of that duty require the existence of the state? Some would argue that the existence of states as such and their power of coercion are among the conditions of human life rendered necessary by the fall, and therefore not part of the original creative purpose of God, in the way that ethnicity in itself is. This may or may not be so. I would find it hard to think of biblical evidence that would carry the point either way. However, the hypothetical argument that states would have been unnecessary apart from the fall cannot legitimately be used to support non-involvement in the political process or rejection of the authority of the state here and now. We live in the world as it is, and must work out our obedience to God's authority in an inescapable context of states and politics.[3]

If we ask what was Israel's view of the state, we must also ask, which Israel and when? Do we take our theology of the state from the young revolutionary federation of tribes in the years after the settlement in Canaan? From the institutional and imperial state of Solomon and his successors? From the persecuted remnant preserving religious distinctives in a hostile environment of giant empires? To focus too narrowly on any one of these will produce distortions of what the Hebrew Bible as a whole has to contribute to Christian political ethics. We have to be comprehensive and draw our raw material for reflection from all the major periods of the story of Israel. This will undoubtedly throw up some apparently contradictory viewpoints on the nature of the people of God and their relationship with the state. But on the other hand, by seeing all of them together within the framework of canonical authority, we shall avoid elevating one only to a place of exclusive relevance. This in turn should help us to see if and where particular applications of the Old Testament are imbalanced or extreme. John Goldingay's book, *Theological Diversity and the Authority of the Old Testament*, takes precisely the question of the nature of the people of God as a case study when discussing a contextual or historical approach to the theological diversity in the Old Testament.[4] The following study is deeply indebted to his helpful outline of the matter.

Our procedure will be to look at Israel as the people of God in five different phases of their Old Testament history. In each context we shall discuss the nature of the people of God themselves at that time; the nature of the state as portrayed in that context; and the role or concept of God that dominates the consciousness of God's people.

1. The pilgrim family: the patriarchal period

Though Israel as a nation had its historical origin at the time of the exodus and settlement in Canaan, it is right to begin our survey with the patriarchs, since Israel's sense of national unity is always related to them. Though the Old Testament does acknowledge the diverse elements that were included in the formation of Israel, there was a strong sense of genetic oneness stemming from the belief that they were all the seed of Abraham. Accordingly, the reality of 'Israel', in essence or potential at least, could be seen to be there in the wandering patriarchal families.

a. The people of God

In the patriarchal context the people of God is primarily a community called out of the socio-political environment and given a new identity and future by the promise of God. They are a people only by this act of God's election. It was not that God elevated an existing people to a chosen status, but that God called Israel into existence as his people, as an entity distinct from the surrounding nation states from their very beginning. This went along with a form of life which included maximum independence from the socio-political and economic structures of their day. They did not own land, and regarded themselves (and were regarded) as resident aliens, sojourners, in the land of their movements. Not that they were socially isolated. Genesis records plenty of occasions of social and economic intercourse between the patriarchs and their contemporaries. But they remained a pilgrim people, called out and called onward.

Corresponding to this given status, there was the requirement of faith in the promise of God and obedience to God's command. Here again a distinctiveness emerges with the surrounding peoples. The most illuminating text on the ethical character of Israel from the patriarchal tradition is Genesis 18:19.

215

> For I have chosen him, so that he will direct his
> children and his household after him to keep the
> way of the LORD by doing what is right and just,
> so that the LORD will bring about for Abraham
> what he has promised him.

The context of this declaration is God's imminent act of judgment on Sodom and Gomorrah, whose wickedness had caused such an outcry that God must intervene. In contrast to that kind of society, the world in which Abraham lived, God required that the community now emerging from Abraham himself was to be characterized by totally different values. They were to be a people who would imitate the character of Yahweh himself ('the way of the LORD') by their commitment to righteousness and justice. These are unquestionably social-ethical values, with economic and political implications. It is clear, therefore, that while God's intention for God's people was to be called out from the surrounding environment, that did not mean an abdication from the socio-political process itself. Rather that sphere, as all spheres of their corporate life, was to be governed by justice, because that is precisely God's own way.

So then, the people of God in this context: (1) are called into existence by God's act of sovereign election, (2) live in the light of God's promise, which enables them to (3) sit loose to the surrounding socio-political power centres while not losing contact with the communities among which they live, and (4) are committed to an ethical obedience specifically characterized by God-imitating justice.

b. The state

The portrayal of the state in the patriarchal context, as it is represented by the various political power centres and cities of the ancient Near Eastern world, varies from neutral to negative. They are not portrayed as excessively oppressive, in anything like the same way as the Egypt of Moses or the Babylon of the exile. Yet when Abraham first appears, in Genesis 12, it is in the context of a society already marked by the story of the tower of Babel in chapter 11. Indeed, it is the land of Babel out of which he is called. As the story indicates, it was a culture of immense self-confidence and pride. At the very least, Abraham's God-required departure relativized it. Human salvation was not to be found in the state *per se*. The ultimate redemptive purpose of God lay elsewhere, invested in the typically tenuous human vessel of the ageing husband of a barren wife. The calling of Abraham out of his country and his people (Gn. 12:1) was 'the first Exodus by which the imperial civilizations of the Near East in general receive their stigma as environments of lesser meaning'.[5]

On the other hand, as well as being portrayed in this relativized fashion, the external city state can be seen as a place of moral rebellion against God and thereby a source of threat to the pilgrim people of God. Sodom and Gomorrah are obvious cases. God was aware of an 'outcry' against them (Gn. 18:20f., twice). The word, z^e'$āqâ$, is virtually a technical term in the Old Testament for the cries of those who are suffering from oppression, cruelty and injustice, prominently, for example, in the story of Israel's groaning in bondage in Egypt. Genesis 19 catalogues the violence and perversion found in Sodom and Gomorrah. Isaiah 1:9f., seen in the light of the rest of the chapter, links them with innocent bloodshed. Ezekiel 16:49 lists the sins of the cities of the plain as arrogance, surplus affluence, callousness and failure to help the poor and needy (a very modern-sounding list, which helps to explain why Sodom and Gomorrah stand as proverbial prototypes of universal human wickedness). For these reasons, they stood in the blast path of God's judgment. The response of the people of God, as represented by Abraham, was intercession.

c. The portrayal of God

The portrayal of God in these narratives is of one who is in sovereign control, as much in Mesopotamia as in Canaan and as in Egypt. Alongside that is the dominant fact that Yahweh is a God of redemptive purpose, whose ultimate goal is the blessing of all nations. In initiating a special relationship with a people of his own creation and possession, God actually has in mind the best interests of the very nations out of whom they are called but among whom they continue to live. The promise of blessing for the seed of Abraham is a promise of blessing for the nations.

This means that although we understand from Scripture as a whole that the entire world stands under God's judgment, and from books such as Daniel and Revelation that that judgment is especially directed at human states in their 'beastly', rebellious condition, nevertheless the very existence of the people of God in the midst of those states is a sign of God's wider and final purpose of redemption of humanity, and the transformation of the kingdoms of the earth into the kingdom of God. The interesting thing in the story referred to above, from Genesis 18 – 19, is that it was precisely on his way to deliver the fires of judgment on a particular human community, Sodom and Gomorrah, that God reminded himself of that universal purpose of redemption for all nations, and saw it embodied in Abraham, Sarah and their as yet unconceived (and inconceivable) son.

d. Influence of the material

The influence of the patriarchal material on Christian views of church–state relationships has been strong, particularly *via* the use that is made of it in Hebrews 11. Negatively, it can result in a world-denying attitude, in which believers are discouraged from *any* participation in the affairs of this world, since, like Abraham, we are to be seeking a city not made with hands. On the other hand, the pilgrim nature of the patriarchs should make us remember that however much we believe, from the rest of the Scriptures, that the people of God have a mission of earthing the love-justice of God in human society, we do so still as a people called out, looking for the fulfilment of God's promise of redemption, but not expecting our hope of salvation to be found in the state itself.

2. The liberated nation: the exodus to Judges period

The designated period here may seem enormous, but it hangs together as the period during which Israel was a theocracy in reality, not just in theory. Some scholars regard it as the time when Israel was most markedly herself, as a liberated and liberating people, different from the world around them. It is the period slung between the poles of what Brueggemann called the 'alternative and energizing consciousness of Moses' and the 'royal consciousness of Solomon' which 'countered the counter-culture'.[6]

a. The people of God

God's people begin this period as an oppressed ethnic minority within a very powerful imperial state. The demand of Yahweh confronts Pharaoh: 'Let my people go, so that they may worship/serve me' (cf. Ex. 8:1). A state which denies freedom to those who wish to worship Yahweh finds itself Yahweh's enemy. The God who, in the patriarchal narratives, has shown himself to be transcendant in the sense that he is neither bound to, nor very impressed by, the greatest of human imperial civilization, upholds the right of his people to freedom of worship in the midst of a state with other gods, including the pharaoh himself.

Yahweh's demands on Pharaoh's state go much further than the spiritual right of freedom of worship. Egypt was engaged in civil discrimination against Israel as an ethnic minority, on the grounds of political expediency, playing on public fears dressed up as in the public interest. They were engaged in economic exploitation of this pool of captive labour. And they were guilty of gross violation of normal family life through a policy of state-sponsored genocide. On all these fronts Yahweh demands and then achieves the liberation of his people. In the course of events, the state, which had professed ignorance of who Yahweh is (Ex. 5:2), learns his identity and his power in no uncertain terms. Indeed the process of Egypt's move from

219

ignorance to acknowledgment of Yahweh is undoubtedly one of the sub-plots of the narrative. (Notice the train of ideas through the following texts: Ex. 5:2; 7:5, 17; 8:10, 22; 9:15, 29; 14:18, 25.) The claims of Pharaoh and the other gods of the state must bow to the fact that Yahweh is God as much over Egypt as over Israel, his own people. Indeed, the claim is lodged that Yahweh is God over the whole earth. The climax of the song of Moses, after the sea has sealed the reality of Israel's deliverance, is that Yahweh is king for ever; and not, as a *sotto voce* implication, Pharaoh (Ex. 15:18).

Moving from the exodus of the people of God out of an imperial state, we come to their arrival in the midst of a city-state culture in Canaan. At this point it could be said that the people of God have become not merely a liberated people, but also a liberating people, though it might well be thought invidious, in view of twentieth-century history, to describe invaders as liberators. Nevertheless, the arrival or the emergence of Israel in Canaan[7] produced a most remarkable social, political, economic and religious transformation there. Israel, the people of Yahweh, not only thought of themselves as different – they *were* different. Gottwald's work, with all its ideological flaws, has demonstrated this at the factual level, I think, beyond doubt.[8]

The main feature of the people of God at this stage is that they were a theocracy in reality. And the rule of Yahweh was bound up with a commitment to certain societal objectives embodied in the Sinai covenant and law – objectives that were characterized by equality, justice and kinship obligation. Furthermore, these objectives were applied through the whole of Israel's corporate life, including the cult. Being the people of God at this stage was a task to be worked out. It was an alternative vision, requiring 'detailed obedience in the ethical, social and cultic spheres ... [which] ... establishes the notion of the people of God as an ethical principle. In their behavior the people of God are bound to one another. Yahweh being their overlord, they have no human overlords. Theocracy and socio-political equality (radical theology and radical sociology) go together.'[9]

This point underlines the importance of Sinai, which we might be in danger of overlooking, having jumped straight from Egypt to Canaan. Israel's route was less direct. Sinai stands significantly midway between liberation from Egypt and settlement in Canaan. Liberation was not an end in itself. The newly free people constantly fell prey to the disintegrating forces of licence, rebellion, dissent and failure of nerve. At Sinai God provided the bonding and moulding institutions and laws by which they were to progress from a mass of freed slaves to an ordered and functioning society. It is there, in the Torah, that we find the bulk of those features of Israel's polity that made them so distinctive: the kinship rationale of land-tenure; the jubilee and sabbatical institutions; the ban on interest; the equality of native and 'stranger' before the law; the civil rights of slaves; the diffusion of political leadership and authority among the elders; the limitation on the economic power of cultic officials. Israel at this period, though not strictly speaking a state, did not lack social institutions as such, with consistent goals and a coherent rationale.

b. The state

The state at this period is represented by Egypt on the one hand and Canaan on the other. The former was a large empire, exercising its power in blatant oppression of the people of God, in its own interests. The latter was a patchwork of small city-state kingdoms with pyramidal forms of political and economic power, which were oppressive and exploitative of the peasant population. Both are presented in the text also as idolatrous in nature and stand as enemies of Yahweh and a threat to his people. In both cases the stance of the people of God towards the state, with such a character, is one of confrontation, challenge and conflict.

The exit and entry of the people of God respectively, out of Egypt and into Canaan, spells judgment on both opposing human states, the one primarily because of its oppression, the other primarily because of its idolatry and 'abominable practices', which are catalogued in Leviticus and Deuteronomy. The state, then, in this particular context, stands over against the people of God as something to be opposed, defeated, dismantled, and finally replaced by a wholly distinctive kind of human society under the direct rule of God.

c. The portrayal of God

The portrayal of God in this context is exclusively the portrayal of Yahweh, the name which bursts on the scene to herald the exodus itself, and goes on to become the primary identity of the people of Israel. Thereafter, they are the 'tribes of Yahweh'. And Yahweh is a God who sets himself against injustice and oppression, initiating the exodus expressly to put it right. In so doing, God as Yahweh enters into history, and specifically political history, in a way not so apparent in the patriarchal narratives. Yahweh's transcendence injects itself into Pharaoh's empire and blows it open. Brueggemann comments forcefully on the double significance of the Mosaic 'alternative':

> The radical break of Moses and Israel from imperial reality is a two-dimensional break from both the religion of static triumphalism and the politics of oppression and exploitation. Moses dismantled the religion of static triumphalism by exposing the gods and showing that in fact they had no power and were not gods. Thus, the mythical legitimacy of Pharaoh's social world is destroyed, for it is shown that in fact such a regime appeals to sanctions that do not exist. The mythic claims of the empire are ended by the disclosure of *the alternative religion of the freedom of God*. In place of the gods of Egypt, creatures of the imperial consciousness, Moses discloses Yahweh the sovereign one who acts in his lordly freedom, is extrapolated from no social reality,

and is captive to no social perception but acts
from his own person toward his own purposes.
At the same time, Moses dismantles the
politics of oppression and exploitation by
countering it with *a politics of justice and
compassion* ... his work came precisely at the
engagement of the *religion of God's freedom* with
the *politics of human justice* ... Yahweh makes
possible and requires an alternative theology and
an alternative sociology. Prophecy begins in
discerning how genuinely alternative he is.[10]

Yahweh, the liberating God of justice, is next perceived as
king. The heart of theocracy lies here – that Israel initially
acknowledged no king but Yahweh. That Israel regarded
Yahweh as king from the earliest period of their settlement
(and not just from the time of her own monarchy) is clear
in several very ancient texts (*e.g.* Ex. 15:18; 19:6; Nu.23:21;
Dt. 33:5). Belief in the kingship of a deity is not at all unique
to Israel, and existed in the ancient Near Eastern world
long before Israel emerged.[11] But if theocracy in the general
sense of a nation regarding its god as a king was not
unique, Israel's particular manifestation and experience of
it certainly was. For in Israel theocracy excluded, for
several centuries, a human king. Lind comments:

While the kingship of Yahweh as such is
paralleled ... in the ancient mythologies of the
Near East, this exclusion and polemic against the
human institution is unparalleled, and gives to
Yahweh's kingship a new dimension ... the
remarkable point is that the kingship of Yahweh
excluded human kingship.[12]

The reason Yahweh's kingship was incompatible at this
time with human kingship is that Yahweh took to himself
entirely the two major functions and duties of kings in the
ancient world, namely the conduct of war and the
administration of law and justice. Indeed, in the exercise of

223

these two functions, human kings in the ancient Near East were at their most sacral – *i.e.* acting on behalf of the god they represented (or embodied). But in Israel, Yahweh himself took over these roles, and human political leadership was thus decisively demoted and relativized. Instead, Israel was a covenant nation, with Yahweh, as lord of the covenant, responsible both for their protection, by war if necessary, and for the just ordering of their social life in every aspect.

In this period of Israel's history, then, a truly radical and alternative political option was being launched on the stage of human history. And this radical political option was effected in the name of Yahweh, in such a way that the religion of Yahweh was inseparable from the social objectives of Israel. For Israel was not just the people of *God* (many nations would claim that in one form or another), but specifically the people of *Yahweh*, and that in itself meant a covenant commitment to a certain kind of society that reflected Yahweh's character, values, priorities and goals.

What this amounts to is that 'theocracy' in itself is not an ideal aim for the people of God in their political dreams. It all depends on who or what is the *theos*. Only the vision of Yahweh as the God he truly was revealed to be initiated and sustained Israel's theocracy. But sadly the state, like humans, tends to make its god in its own image. As Israel itself moved from the radical, alternative, surprising theocracy of Yahweh to the institutional state of the monarchy, they did just that, in spite of being reminded by the prophets of their true identity and calling.

d. Influence of the material

The influence of the exodus paradigm and the story of the conquest on social and political history has been simply incalculable. In Israel itself it became a model and a point of appeal at all times of suffering and oppression in biblical and post-biblical history. Through Christian history it has fired hopes and imagination, sometimes fruitfully, some-times disastrously. The confrontational stance of the people of God *vis-à-vis* the state, perceived as evil, satanic, godless, *etc.*, has fuelled many varieties of Christian utopianism, millenarianism and radical nonconformity. Such movements often end up in 'unreal expectations, fanatical devotion, irrational behaviour, dictatorial regimes and ruthless repression or elimination of the enemy'.[13] They were usually also fuelled by apocalyptic beliefs which set their whole agenda in a kind of trans-historical mode. By contrast, the exodus itself and the events which followed it were very much within the boundaries of historical reality, and, astounding though they were, they were limited by the possiblilities of history. Things were not perfect for Israel after the exodus, either in the wilderness, or in the land of promise. But within the limitations of history, an unparalleled act of justice and liberation *did* take place and a radically different kind of society *was* brought to birth. This reading of the exodus paradigm has been explored by Michael Walzer, and lays much greater emphasis on the achievement of attainable goals within history, goals which fit the objectives and values of the exodus paradigm.[14]

It is this latter use of the exodus paradigm which has been so much the backbone of liberation theology, in ways too many to document. It is also a major factor in black and feminist theologies, as well as the less sophisticated biblical encouragement that many groups of suffering believers have clung to in hope.

3. The institutional state: the monarchy period

a. People of God and political state

By the time of Samuel, the strain of living as a theocracy was proving more than the people felt able to bear in the face of external pressures. They opted for monarchy, survived Saul, served David, suffered Solomon, split in two and finally sank respectively into oblivion and exile. During this period (from Saul, or at least David, to the exile) the people of Yahweh were unmistakably an institutional state, with central leadership, boundaries, organized military defences, *etc.* Yet the identification of people of God with political state was never wholly comfortable. Within the Old Testament itself there are hints of conscious distinction between the two realities, even while there is formal and apparent identity. So there is the problem of the relationship of people of God and state *internally* to Israel itself. This is further complicated by there being two markedly different evaluations of the monarchy, even within closely related texts: pro and anti. Then, if we see the monarchical states of Judah and Israel as at least notionally the people of God, we should look at their relationship and attitude to the *external* states of their day – especially the dominant empires.

The origins of monarchy in Israel are laid before us in a narrative which subtly and intentionally interweaves two understandings of the process (1 Sa. 8 – 12). On the one hand, the demand for it arises from a retrograde desire of the people to be like the other nations by having a king. Their reasons at first sight seem unexceptionable: leadership against their enemies and the protection of justice (8:3–5, 19f.). Samuel (and Yahweh) interpret the request as a rejection of direct theocracy. But their explicit objection to monarchy is not so much theological as practical, and fundamentally economic. Samuel predicts that if monarchy is adopted, it will result in the characteristic forms of royal slavery: confiscation, taxation, military and agricultural conscription (8:10–18). The portrayal of Solomon's later reign is an unmistakable 'I told you so'. All very negative. So much so that Brueggemann can speak of the whole spirit, ethos and accomplishment of Solomon as a reversal of the Mosaic alternative, a return to the values and management mentality of the empire, a countering of the counter-culture of Sinai.[15]

On the other hand, according to the same texts, it was Yahweh himself who gave Israel a king, choosing, anointing and (for a while) blessing him. It is Yahweh who goes on to exalt David, embarrassing him with the multiplicity of victories, the gift of a city, rest from his enemies, and a covenant for his posterity. 'Solomon in all his glory' suffered no embarrassment, but his greatness is still attributed to Yahweh's generosity. In other words, Yahweh takes the human desire and resultant institution and makes them fit in with his own purpose. Indeed, he goes further, and tries to mould the monarchy, for all its origins as a *rejection* of theocracy, into a *vehicle* for theocracy by subsuming the reign of the king under his own reign.

And so the royal theology of Jerusalem is absorbed into the transcendent rule of Yahweh and given a covenant framework which harks back to Sinai in its call for loyalty and obedience.

If the monarchy, then, stood in a position of ambiguous legitimacy before God – neither totally rejected nor unconditionally sanctioned, it likewise had to struggle for legitimacy at a human level. This is how South African scholar Gunther Wittenberg interprets the texts of the Davidic-Solomonic era, seeing in them both attempts at theological legitimizing and also theological resistance to the claimed legitimacy of the Davidic house.[16] The legitimizing texts, of course, are those which related to the Davidic covenant, the temple, Zion and the relationship of the king to God.

Resistance to the legitimacy of the Davidic state was crystallized in the secession of the northern tribes under the leadership of Jeroboam. The presenting cause of this was the social and economic oppression which had developed during Solomon's reign, and which Rehoboam, though offered the chance of a change of policy, deliberately chose to continue and intensify. But there are hints also of a theological refusal in principle to accept the legitimacy of the glorious Davidic 'new thing'. The prophet Ahijah, who accosted Jeroboam to launch him on his secession from Judah, came from Shiloh. Now Shiloh was an ancient cultic centre of the pre-monarchic tribal federation, and former resting-place of the ark of the (Sinai) covenant and all its links with Israel's historical, exodus traditions. Above all it was closely associated with Samuel, whose denunciation of monarchy must have echoed loudly among northern Israelites in the later years of Solomon.

227

Furthermore, in the plea of the northerners to have their burdens lifted, there are echoes of the cry of the Israelites in their Egyptian bondage (1 Ki. 12:4). Had Solomon become a pharaoh? Noticeably, in setting up the religious foundations of his own state, Jeroboam recalls the exodus liberation: 'Here is your God, O Israel, who brought you up out of Egypt' (aside, 'not to mention, out of Jerusalem'; 1 Ki. 12:28, my translation). The irony of the text, of course, is that such a surface-level appeal to the God of the exodus echoed precisely the idolatrous words of Aaron at the great golden-calf apostasy, and heralds the idolatrous nature of the northern kingdom's religious establishment (discussed below).

What we have seen, then, is that the transformation of the people of God into an institutional state generated both approval and rejection, both in the heat of the historical process itself, and also in theological and canonical assessment. Nevertheless, it happened, and hypothetical reconstructions of what might have happened if they had listened to Samuel in the first place are as fruitless here as elsewhere. There was, as Goldingay puts it, 'a historical inevitability about the transition from (nominally) theocratic nation to monarchic state. The alternative to such a development was to cease to exist.'[17]

Goldingay goes further and sees God's acceptance of the monarchy, in spite of its dubious origins, as a case of God making allowance for human inability to live by God's ideal standards – even in his own redeemed and liberated people.

> Being an institutional state means that God starts with his people where they are; if they cannot cope with his highest way, he carves out a lower one. When they do not respond to the spirit of Yahweh or when all sorts of spirits lead them into anarchy, he provides them with the institutional safeguard of earthly rulers.[18]

One might take from this the view that the institutional

state, like certain other human conditions which the law permits, is a concession to human 'hardness of heart': permitted but transient.

b. The portrayal of God

The perception of God at this period has to be sought primarily in the voice of the prophets. From them we discover the conditional and qualified nature of God's acceptance of the monarchy as the political form of his people. One could summarize the view of the prophets towards the monarchic state of Israel (in both northern and southern forms) by saying that they accepted its God-givenness, but refused its God-surrogacy. It is significant, for example, that at the point of the secession of the northern tribes away from Judah, one and the same prophet, Ahijah, both encouraged Jeroboam before the event with a word from Yahweh that his secession was divinely willed as judgment on the house of Solomon, and also later severely criticized him for the idolatry into which he had led the Israelites (1 Ki. 11:29–39; 14:1–16).

That idolatry of the northern kingdom was focused on the golden calves at Bethel and Dan. But we need to see carefully what they meant. From 1 Kings 12:26ff., we see that Jeroboam did not apparently intend the worship of false gods as such. The calves represented the presence of Yahweh, who brought Israel up out of Egypt. In that sense it was a breaking of the second commandment more than the first. But the real thrust of Jeroboam's idolatry lies in the motives of his action, and the additional cultic action which he initiated. His intention was clearly the political protection of his own nascent kingdom from any hankering after the splendour of Jerusalem (verses 26f.). To make completely sure, he elaborated an alternative cultic system for the northern kingdom, designed, appointed and run by himself, to serve the interests of his state (verses 31–33). In effect, 'Yahweh' had become a figurehead for his state. The state in itself was idolatrous.

That this was in fact the case is shown with ironic clarity in the angry words of Amaziah, the high priest at Bethel under Jeroboam II (nearly two centuries later), against Amos: 'Get out, you seer! ... Don't prophesy any more at Bethel, because *this is the king's sanctuary and the temple of the kingdom'* (Am. 7:12f.). Amos, however, like Ahijah at the very start of the northern kingdom, and also like his anonymous fellow Judean who came to speak for God at Bethel (1 Ki. 13:1–6), refused to be silenced by the surrogate divine authority of the new political regime. God may have permitted it to come into existence, but that did not bind him to serve its self-interests. The prophets refused to allow the authority of God or his prophetic word to be hijacked to legitimize human political ambitions – a sometimes costly opposition.

One prophet who certainly could not be hijacked was Elijah. His ministry took place in the ninth century in the northern kingdom during the reign of Ahab and Jezebel, when the whole state became virtually apostate. Nevertheless, there were a faithful seven thousand who had not capitulated to the palace-imposed worship of Baal (1 Ki. 19:14, 18). The origins of the idea of a faithful remnant probably go back as far as this. It was not the state of Israel itself that constituted the true people of God, but a minority of 'true believers' within it.

In the view of the Old Testament narrative, the northern kingdom, of course, was lacking in legitimacy from the start. But in the southern kingdom of Judah, in spite of all the theological legitimation of the state and its monarchy, the prophetic voice of Yahweh could still stand out in conflict with it and challenge the moral validity of any given incumbent of the throne of David. And the criterion of assessment was the covenant law. Unequivocally the prophets subordinated Zion to Sinai.

The law in Deuteronomy which permitted (note, not commanded) monarchy, laid down strict conditions for it, including the requirement that the king should know, read and obey the law. He was to be, not a super-Israelite, but a model Israelite among his brothers and equals (Dt. 17:14–20). As one entrusted with the law, the king was committed to the maintenance of justice in a spirit of compassion (*e.g.*

especially Ps. 72). Jeremiah could proclaim this strong tradition of the legal, covenantal requirement on the king at the very gates of the palace in Jerusalem. His words are really a statement of the conditions of legitimacy and indeed for survival of the Davidic monarchy. Zion must conform to Sinai, or face ruin.

> Hear the word of the LORD, O king of Judah, you who sit on David's throne – you, your officials and your people who come through these gates. This is what the LORD says: Do what is just and right. Rescue from the hand of his oppressor the one who has been robbed. Do no wrong or violence to the alien, the fatherless or the widow, and do not shed innocent blood in this place. For if you are careful to carry out these commands, then kings who sit on David's throne will come through the gates of this palace ... But if you do not obey these commands, declares the LORD, I swear by myself that this palace will become a ruin.
>
> (Je. 22:2–5)

On this basis, Jeremiah then goes on, on the one hand, to commend with approval the reign of Josiah, who lived by the standards of covenant law, which is what it means to know Yahweh (22:15f.), and on the other, utterly to reject Jehoiakim, whose actions and policies included forced labour without pay, personal aggrandizement, dishonesty, violence and oppression. The legitimacy or illegitmacy of the two kings is evaluated respectively on the grounds of their treatment of the poor and needy, the workers, the 'innocent' – i.e. precisely the dominant concerns of the Sinai law.

Thus, even when the socio-political contours of the people of God had changed radically from the early theocracy to the institutional, royal state, the controlling paradigm was still that of the law and the covenant. This meant that royal theocracy could never be rightly regarded as 'the divine right of kings' *per se*. Being 'the LORD's anointed' was not an unconditional guarantee. The king was subject to, and correctable by, the covenant law.

The same moral criterion applies in the prophetic perspective on *the authority of external, secular rulers*. For they too rule by Yahweh's authority. As early as the ninth century Israelite prophets claimed to anoint the kings of outside nations in Yahweh's name (1 Ki. 19:15). In the eighth, Isaiah regarded Assyria and its tyrannical sovereigns as no more than a stick in the hand of Yahweh (Is. 10:5ff.). Most explicitly of all, Jeremiah could announce, in a seventh-century international diplomatic conference hosted by Zedekiah in Jerusalem, that Yahweh had delegated to Nebuchadnezzar supreme, worldwide authority and power – for the foreseeable future (Je. 27:1–11; note especially 5–7).

Now if Israelite kings as Yahweh's anointed were subject to evaluation by the moral standards of Yahweh and his law, so too were the pagan ones. The clearest example of this is Nebuchadnezzar again. Daniel had clearly absorbed the point of Jeremiah's assertion about Nebuchadnezzar, for he repeats it, almost verbatim, to his face (Dn. 2:37f.). Nevertheless, on another occasion, Daniel the civil servant dons the authentic prophetic mantle, when he goes beyond the requested interpretation of a dream to give Nebuchadnezzar some 'advice'. And that advice is really a warning that unless he pays attention to the injustice on which his boasted city had been built, by lifting the oppression of the poor and needy in his realm, he would face inevitable judgment. The boldness of Daniel's prophetic word in Daniel 4:27 should not escape us, hidden as it is in the midst of an otherwise somewhat weird story. The one to whom Yahweh had given all authority and power, far beyond what any Israelite king had every wielded, is here weighed in the balance of the standards of justice and found wanting (to anticipate a metaphor drawn from the next chapter, Dn. 5).

This must have some bearing on interpretations of Paul's view of state authority in Romans 13. The Hebrew Bible would wholly endorse the view that all human authorities exist *within the framework of God's will*. It would wholly reject the view that that gives them a legitimacy regardless of their *conformity to God's justice*, as revealed in the covenant law.

So then, the historical experience of the people of God in actually *being* a state generated enormous tensions. There was never complete ease with the monarchy, even in Davidic Judah, as the continuing existence of a group like the Rechabites in the late monarchy showed (Je. 35). There was always the feeling that Israel was really meant to be something different. Nevertheless, it is from the prophetic critique of the kings and institutions of this period (in both narrative and prophetic books) that we learn most in the Old Testament concerning God's radical demand on political authorities.

> [Israel] had discovered what it meant to be a Yahwistic theocracy, though they had not succeeded in realizing the ideal. Now they were challenged to discover what it meant to be a Yahwistic institution. They failed here, too, and ultimately the institutional state is put under the judgment of Yahweh, which the prophets declared.[19]

c. Influence of the material

The influence of the model of Israel as an institutional royal state can probably be seen most comprehensively in the 'Christendom' idea, in the centuries during which Christians seem to have collectively considered that the best way to save the world was to run it. The Constantinian transformation of Christianity and its dubious effects have often been compared to Israel's adoption of monarchy and statehood.[20]

4. The suffering remnant: the exile

In 587 BC the institutional, monarchic state of Judah vanished under the rubble of Jerusalem, devastated by the armies of Nebuchadnezzar. The northern kingdom of Israel had long since disappeared, scattered by the Assyrians in 721 BC. The people of God were not only no longer a state; they were scarcely even a nation. As a tiny remnant, they learned once again to live like their forefathers, as strangers in a strange land, in the very land indeed from which their ancestors had departed in obedience to God's call. Now they were back there under God's judgment.

But Babylon was not just strange. It was also an enormous, hostile and threatening environment, in which the people of God were now a small, uprooted, endangered species – exiles. At this point in their history, then, the people of God constitute a persecuted remnant, with the state as an ambient, hostile power within which they have to survive and somehow continue to live as the people of God. The danger at such a time was twofold: first, they might lose their identity by compromise and assimilation into their new environment, and thus cease to be distinctive; or secondly, they might stand out as so intractably different that they would bring destructive fires of persecution on themselves that might finally consume them. The same dilemma has faced the people of God at many times in history when they have been a suffering minority in a hostile environment. And in this case also we have a variety of responses from the Hebrew Bible to such a situation. We shall quickly look at four – two positive and two negative.

a. Prayer

First, there was the advice to *pray* for Babylon. This was the astonishing message sent by Jeremiah in a letter to the first group of exiles, recorded in Jeremiah 29. Contrary to those who were predicting a short exile, or a quick rebellion to end their exile, Jeremiah forecasts a long stay of two generations, and therefore counsels a policy of settling down to that. The exiles must realize that Babylon had done what it had done by God's permission, and in that sense, to pray for Babylon would put them in line with the purposes of God again. The shalom of the people of God was bound up with the shalom of the pagan nation among whom they now resided. Jeremiah here anticipates the New Testament command to pray for those in secular authority out of obedience to God who rules over them. Prayer puts all things in perspective. It seeks the good of the state, while refusing to absolutize it, since the very act of prayer appeals to a higher authority than any human power.

b. Service

Second, there was the response of Daniel and his friends, who went beyond praying for Babylon and were willing to *serve* the young imperial state of Nebuchadnezzar. The book of Daniel is a fascinating analysis of the extreme dangers, as well as the unique opportunities, of such a decision. There are parallels with the story of Joseph. Both were able to witness to the living God in the midst of a pagan and idolatrous state; both were able to influence the state's policies; both were able to benefit the people of God by their 'secular' career positions. The stories of Daniel 1 – 6 are a powerful study of the challenging possibilities of living as a believer at the highest levels of pagan political authority, and remaining faithful and uncompromised in doing so. [21]

c. Judgment

Third, coming again from the pen of Jeremiah, is the response of wholesale declaration of judgment on Babylon. It is this which underlines the astonishing paradox of Jeremiah's advice to the exiles to pray for Babylon. Virtually in the next diplomatic postbag as the letter of chapter 29, he also sent the massive tirade against Babylon recorded in Jeremiah 50 – 51. The scroll was to be read, and then dropped with a stone in the Euphrates, there to sink as mighty Babylon was destined to do. This shows clearly that the letter in chapter 29 was not a piece of rosy-eyed quietism based on a naïve faith in Babylon's benevolence. Jeremiah told the exiles to pray for the shalom of Babylon with his eyes wide open to the realities of Babylon, and especially to the fact that all it stood for was destined to be destroyed in the blast-path of God's judgment. One is reminded of Abraham's intercession for Sodom and Gomorrah, much closer to the brink of their annihilation.[22]

d. Mockery

Fourth, there was the response of deliberate *mockery* and unmasking of Babylon's imperial pantheon and sophisticated, 'scientific' civilization. The importance of Isaiah 46 and 47 can be missed if we fail to see their links with each other and the context. Here is a prophet seeking to energize his depressed people to believe that Yahweh can again do something great; that their present condition is not final; that they can actually get up and get out of Babylon. The people of God must again claim their identity in the world – an identity of servanthood, but now universalized to be of saving significance for all nations. But a paralysing awe of Babylon stands in the way of Israel's making such a response. So even before the armies of Cyrus dismantled Babylon's empire militarily, the poetry of Isaiah was already dismantling it psychologically and spiritually in the perception of the exiles. There is therefore a profoundly political, and contextually pointed, significance to the mockery of idolatry and the deflating of cultural arrogance in these chapters. Brueggemann captures this point with his usual pithiness.

> The poet engages in the kind of guerrilla warfare that is always necessary on behalf of oppressed people. First, the hated one must be ridiculed and made reachable, then she may be disobeyed and seen as a nobody who claims no allegiance and keeps no promises. The big house yields no real life, need not be feared, cannot be trusted, and must not be honoured.
>
> When the Babylonian gods have been mocked, when the Babylonian culture has been ridiculed, then history is inverted. Funeral becomes festival, grief becomes doxology, and despair turns

to amazement. Perhaps it is no more than a cultic event, but don't sell it short, because cult kept close to historical experience can indeed energize people. For example, witness the black churches and civil rights movements or the liberation resistance in Latin America. The cult may be a staging for the inversion that the kings think is not possible ... We ought not to underestimate the power of the poet. Inversions may begin in a change of language, a redefined perceptual field, or an altered consciousness.[23]

Yet, having said all this, the future of the people of God still depended on Cyrus, who was as much a pagan king of a pagan empire as Nebuchadnezzar and the Babylonians had been. The state Isaiah was mocking was the one once described as God's servant, executing his judgment on Israel (Je. 25:9, 27:6). He avoids the term 'servant' for Cyrus, since it has special significance in his prophecy as applied to Israel and the one who will fulfil Israel's mission. But he does describe Cyrus as Yahweh's 'shepherd' and his 'anointed' (Is. 44:28; 45:1), terms normally applied to Israel's own kings. So, while the prophet certainly declares that the deliverance of Israel from exile will be a triumphant work of Yahweh, he looks to the newly rising external state to accomplish it. *The new exodus will have a pagan for its Moses!*

Once again we see how fully the Old Testament puts all human political authority and military power under the sovereign will of Yahweh. The external empire-state may be oppressive and enslaving, as an agent of his judgment; or it may be more enlightened and liberating, as an agent of his redemption. Either way it is the arm of the LORD at work.

5. The distinctive community: the post-exilic period

a. The people of God

After the return from Babylon to Judea, the people of God were not an institutional state again. But neither were they the tiny dislocated group of captive exiles. They were scarcely a nation, in any sense of national independence. But they were a community with a clear sense of distinct ethnic and religious identity. As a sub-province within the vast Persian empire, they remained politically insignificant. Yet at the same time they had a much enhanced view of their own significance as the people of God in the world with a continuing role as his servant and a mixture of hopes as to how God's purpose for them and through them would ultimately be accomplished. So they were a restored community, a community of faith and a community of promise.

Goldingay identifies four main features of the post-exilic community. (1) They were *a worshipping community*, going back to the original conception of the Israelite *'ēḏâ*, the assembly gathered for worship. Ezra laid the foundations of this, and the Chronicler provided its validation in his narrative history. (2) They were *a waiting community*, looking forward with varieties of apocalyptic expectation to a new future from God. (3) They were *an obeying community*, with a new devotion to the law, fired by the realization that it was neglect of the law which had led to the catastrophe of exile. Thus the law, even more than the covenant of which it had originally been the responsive part, becomes the heart of the new community of faith to be known as Judaism. And (4) they were *a questioning community*. The tensions of faith posed by their own history produced doubts and uncertainties which some strands of the Wisdom literature wrestle with. Not all the questions found answers within the limits of the old faith.

b. The state

As to the state during this period, there were enormous fluctuations in the extent to which it impinged upon the life of God's people. Under Persia, they experienced a comparatively benevolent policy of religious freedom and considerable local autonomy, without independence, of course. But this could be used against them by unscrupulous enemies within the system. The stories of Nehemiah and Ezra repay study from the angle of how they made use of state sponsorship, protection and authority both in building up the infrastructure of the community, and in resisting its enemies. In the later years of the Greek control of Palestine, under the Antiochene rulers, however, the community came in for extreme pressures. Some of these pressures threatened to split the community between those who could accept and accommodate to Greek culture and ways, and those who would preserve the faith and its distinctives at all costs. If it was for people facing such dilemmas that the book of Daniel was written or preserved, then the response therein was one of patience, fortified by apocalyptic hopes, and the assurance that all was still in God's control. Neither an exodus nor a Cyrus was expected. Only endurance is called for.

Conclusion

a. Exploiting the diversity

Having observed the great range of material available to us for reflection on the relationship between the people of God and the state, what are we to do with it?

First, we need to make careful correlations between the facts of any given situation in which a community of God's people may find itself in relation to a modern secular state, and the features of specific periods of Israel's history. This needs careful thought and the avoidance of blanket assertions which may be more romantic than real. Not all Christians, for example, are living under oppression. Nor are all Christians who do live under oppression necessarily living in circumstances parallel to the Israelites in Egypt. Babylon may have closer parallels and more important challenges. Some Christians may be living in a time of nation-building after great political changes in their country, in which they have the real potential to affect the contours of the nascent state according to values drawn from the Sinai and theocracy paradigm. Others may be living as a tiny minority in a moderately benevolent state, but with little chance of any actual influence upon it. So we need to think through the diversity of Israel's experience to see when and where it matches our own and what lessons it has to teach. As Baum argues:

> Exodus politics [for example] demands that one does *not* designate every situation of injustice as Egypt ... In the biblical account, a sober analysis justifies the use of the categories, 'oppressor' and 'oppressed'. It seems imperative to me that in every single situation, in every existing social conflict in history, a rational investigation must decide whether the *oppressor/oppressed category is analytically appropriate* or whether it is necessary to look for another sociological paradigm.[24]

Secondly, we need to avoid making an arbitrary selection which may entice us to have a twisted view of the response of the people of God to the state, by merely conforming to the image of Israel in a given period and falling prey to the same temptations as they did in that period. Even if we find that a particular period has most to say to our situation, we need the corrective and balance of an awareness of the other periods also. For the great thing is that Israel 'found' God in all of them, and learned and coped within them. To quote Goldingay:

> It is a genuine encouragement to find within the Scripture itself the people of God coping with different modes of being with the ambiguities

that we ourselves experience. God has said yes to each of these. The monarchy was part of God's will, even though it had its earthly origin in an act of human rebellion. The community has to find ways of living with the experience of God's promises not being fulfilled. [But] ... The danger is that our choice of a perspective from the various ones the Old Testament offers us may be an arbitrary one. A predetermined under-standing of what it means to be God's people may be bolstered exegetically by appeal to biblical warrants which support a stance chosen before coming to the Bible.[25]

If we ask whether any particular period or event has prime significance as setting a paradigm for the rest, then I think we have to come back to the normative significance of the covenant and law at Sinai, and the attempts of the early theocracy to initiate a community that embodied those social objectives. We have already seen in detail that the prophets exercised a critical function during the monarchy on precisely that basis.

Another good example of the normative stature of the covenant law even in a pagan situation would be Daniel again. Living in the midst of period 4, above, when his people were an oppressed minority in a pagan state, he had visions of the empire as essentially 'beastly' in character. In other words, like Jeremiah, he was fully aware of the state as ultimately an enemy of God, indeed a kind of God-surrogate, destined for God's final destruction. Never-theless, he not only chose to serve the state at the civil-political level, but also took the opportunity to challenge that state in the name of the 'God of heaven' to mend its ways in line with a paradigm of justice derived from Sinai (4:27).

The subtlety and mature balance of Daniel's stance are remarkable. Knowing that it was God himself who had given Nebuchadnezzar all authority and dominion, he nevertheless did not feel bound to obey him in every particular, but set limits on the extent of his submission to the state. *Daniel's doctrine of the divine appointment of human authority did not make him a passive pawn giving uncritical obedience to the particular authority under which he lived.* But on the other hand, knowing that Babylon was one of the 'beasts' of his visions, an agent of evil and destruction with spiritual dimensions, he nevertheless continued his daily political duty at the office desk, maintaining his integrity and his witness at the top level of national life. *Daniel's doctrine of the satanic influence on human powers did not make him withdraw as an escapist from political involvement.*

b. The question of authority

This is obviously a key issue in any discussion of politics. I would make three points here from my reading of the Hebrew Bible.

1. *All authority is Yahweh's.* The Old Testament affirms this as strongly as the New affirms that all authority is Christ's. And this applies to the totality of human existence on earth. Therefore, any human authority is secondary and derived. The human tendency to absolutize our own human authorities has to be constantly unmasked and decisively relativized. This, of course, ought to be as true of human authority exercised within the people of God as in the sphere of political authority in the state. All human, relative, authority is accountable to, and addressable by, God. Hence the importance of the prophetic gift and ministry.

2. *Political authority comes from God and not only from the people.* This is affirmed in different periods. The people want a king, but it is God who gives one. Nevertheless, the role of the people is important, and legitimacy in the eyes of the people is important. Even in the history of the divinely appointed Davidic kings, it is interesting how often the people play a decisive part in the making or breaking of kings (*e.g.* 2 Ki. 11:17ff.; 14:19–21). But since the authority comes in reality from God, this sets a limit on the exercise of power by the appointed or elected authority, and indeed on the choices and behaviour of the people

also. A majority has no more divine right than a monarch, in Old Testament terms.

3. *The model of political authority is servanthood.* 'Moses was faithful as a servant in all God's house' is not an Old Testament text (Heb. 3:5), but the Israelites would have agreed with it (*cf.* Ex. 14:31). Though an outstanding leader, among the greatest in human history, he could be soberly described as 'more humble than anyone else on the face of the earth' (Nu. 12:3). Not surprisingly, then, the deutero-nomic law of kingship strictly forbids a king to exalt himself above his brothers, but rather to set an example in embodying the demands and values of the law (Dt. 17:14–20). In fact this remarkable text more or less says that whatever a king in Israel is to be, he is not to be like any king known on earth: enjoying neither weapons (military prestige), wealth, nor wives (harem). In the context of the day it might have been wondered whether it was worth being king at all on such terms. It was a very different model indeed, a model which David scarcely adhered to, and Solomon forgot altogether.

The pattern of true political leadership in Israel is nowhere more succinctly expressed than in the advice given to Rehoboam by his older advisors in 1 Kings 12:7:

> If today you will be a servant to these people and
> serve them ... they will always be your servants.

Kingship meant mutual servanthood. The same thought is inherent in the common metaphor of shepherd applied to political leadership. A shepherd had a responsible job, but a fairly lowly status. He existed for the sake of the sheep, who were not his own, but for which he was accountable to their owner. So when Jesus not only claimed to be the model shepherd but also affirmed that true greatness is a matter of servanthood, not status, he was recovering an authentically Old Testament perspective on leadership and authority.

Chapter Ten

Human rights[1]

The United Nations Declaration of the Rights of the Child includes the phrase, 'The right to free education'. When I first read that, I remember asking, 'Is that a "right"?' Only recently has free education become part of advanced welfare states. Even in such countries, it would certainly not have been regarded as a 'right' a few generations ago. And is it ever really 'free'?

Without pausing to address those specific questions, they do raise the bigger one – what constitutes a right? How can you tell whether something is merely desirable, or an 'inalienable right'? And what of the qualifier 'human'? Do we interpret it in minimal or maximal terms? That is to say, do we lay down a basic minimum requirement below which life seems to be less than human, and make that the criterion of fundamental human rights (a criterion which might exclude education itself as a right, let alone free education)? Or do we establish a utopian maximal model of a fully satisfying human life and then label everything and anything that anyone thinks contributes to such a model as a 'right'? The minimalist way can lead to tyranny and hypocrisy – when states claim to honour and allow human rights so long as people appear to be given minimal freedom to carry on life within a strict controlling framework. The second, however, can lead to such a proliferation and confusion of alleged rights that conflicts are inevitable. One person's right becomes another one's grievance. The resulting conflict of claims is made all the more intractable by the self-righteousness, self-pity, and appeals to justice that fill the air. Thus the whole language of human rights is debased and the matter becomes easy prey for cynics. I actually met a person who was sure that the International Year of the Child, and the UN Declaration of the Rights of the Child, were all a Communist plot to set children against their parents and destroy the family.

Christians, armed with their creation doctrines, believe they have a good idea of what it is to be 'human', and furthermore, they believe that God has revealed what is 'right'. Should there not then be a clear Christian consensus on the matter of human rights? Alas, there is not. Some fear that assertion of human rights is derogatory to the sovereignty of God. To them, the whole debate smacks of human arrogance and rebellion. Sinners don't have rights, they say. Others contend that the Bible has little or nothing to say about rights but a lot about responsibilities. Concern for rights is therefore misplaced, and in fact only an outworking of the fall. Something must be said on these viewpoints in what follows. Others smell only the political odour of current human-rights debates, and stay out of the arena on the grounds that Christianity has nothing to do with politics. Still others, asserting that Christianity has everything to do with politics, throw themselves body and soul into the struggle – often at the risk of isolation and misunderstanding from their fellow Christians.

In such a diverse situation, an essay on the subject has to have clear limitations. My purpose is to focus the matter from a biblical and theological perspective only. I do not intend to indulge in philosophical argument concerning the nature of justice, or to address any current political issue in the human-rights field, or to discuss the merits or otherwise of the various internationally agreed documents and conventions on human rights.

1. Perspectives from creation

a. Definitions

1. *Human*. The Christian faith has a distinctive doctrine of humanity which permeates almost every ethical issue it is

faced with. With profound simplicity, the Bible asserts that God created human persons in his own image (Gn. 1:27), thereby presenting us with the fundamental duality of human nature: that on the one hand, as creatures, we are an integral part of the created cosmos, formed out of the dust of the earth, animals among animals; and on the other hand, we stand unique within creation as bearing the image of God. In both respects the Christian speaks distinctively in any discussion of humanity. For although he may accept the researches of those who explore the similarities between human beings and the rest of the animal world, he will want to affirm his faith that these very similarities originate in the integrated coherence of God's creative act. And his doctrine of the image of God in human beings will repel any reductionist view that a man or woman is 'nothing but' a highly developed animal – whether expressed in biological, psychological or behaviourist terms. To be human is to be something different, for God made us so. Therefore, a Christian definition of what is human has to involve God in respect both of the *fact* of human existence, and of the *nature* of human existence. It is the second of these that we must probe to arrive at an understanding of humanness in relation to human rights. *Is there something in what it is to be human that entails rights?*

It is not enough, in defining what is human, simply to list those qualities and achievements of humankind that distinguish us from the beasts: rationality, culture, civilization, humour, science, art, *etc.* Such things are what our humanity makes possible; they are not in themselves the essence of our humanity. That lies in the combination of the *fact* of our origin in the creative Word of God, and the fact of our *awareness* of that origin. The human being alone is the creature who knows where, and knows who, he has come from, and is able to reflect and act upon the implications of this origin.

Thus the author of Psalm 139 can distinguish between his 'beginning' in the historico-physical process of animal reproduction (which he shares with the rest of the animal creation), and his 'origin' in the thought, will and creative act of God.[2] And it is the latter which gives rise to the psalmist's ethical response to God. What he may say, think or do, where he may go, are all determined by his origin in and present relation to the omnipresent, omniscient creator. The essence of his humanity lies not in the process of his human birth, or even in the mere fact of having been created by God, but in his *awareness* of the claim – the searching, knowing, testing claim – of God upon him, and of the inescapable demand for a response to that claim.

The psalmist, of course, writes on a basis of revelation and faith. It might be objected that fallen human beings without such a basis are not 'God-conscious' in this way. How then can this theocentric approach apply to them? Obviously, it is not the case that all people are reflectively conscious of the God of Christian theism, but rather that they are inescapably aware of a sense of 'claim', however articulated, which the Christian asserts does in fact originate in God and is evidence of a relationship subsisting between even fallen humanity and God, whether or not it is acknowledged in such terms.

What essentially marks out a person as human, then, is the relation to God. 'His relation to God is not something which is added to his human nature; it is the core and ground of his *humanitas*.' Thus writes Emil Brunner,[3] and he goes on to define this relational understanding of human nature in terms of *responsibility*. 'One who has understood the nature of responsibility has understood the nature of man. Responsibility is not an attribute, it is the substance of human existence'[4] ... 'Responsibility and the knowledge of it – however obscure and distorted it may be – the responsibility precisely of the "godless" human being, can only be understood from man's special relation to God.'[5]

Now clearly this fact of responsibility brings us close to the question of rights, duties, obligations, *etc.* It is because each person is aware not only of his own uniqueness as a creature with a sense of relation and responsibility to the transcendent, but also of the fact that other human beings stand on the same plane, that he instinctively feels he must treat them differently from all else in the cosmos. As Brunner says, 'it is precisely this sense that he has no right to dispose of himself and his fellow-creatures [as things] that gives man the consciousness of his peculiar nature – of his being as man ... Man's being is inseparable from his sense of obligation.'[6]

Thus a Christian discussion of 'human' rights begins with a definition of 'human' that requires God. This will inevitably differentiate it from any secular, humanist view which omits this divine dimension.

2. Rights. C. S. Lewis, in *Mere Christianity*, showed in his opening chapter how much unconscious metaphysical and ethical assumption lies behind common patterns of human speech – particularly when people quarrel. If, following his lead, we take the word 'right' or 'rights', many phrases come tumbling into mind:

'What right have they got to do that ...?'
'You've no right to be here ...'
'We've got a right to know ...'
'I know my rights ...'
'I've got as much right as you ...'
'By rights ...'

If we ask what such usage shows up, the first thing that strikes us is that they all betray situations of conflict. The language of right and rights appears to be most used where there is a breakdown of relationship, a conflict of interests or a dispute over what is fair. This suggests *prima facie* that the whole conflict over human rights is a consequence of our fallenness – a point we shall need to look at later.

The second thing is the point that Lewis himself made. There lies behind such phrases a tacit acknowledgment of some external standard or norm, which can be a source of authority ('By what right?'), a means of gain ('I have a right to a share ...'), or of protection ('my rights'), or a criterion of arbitration ('in the right'). Such a standard or norm has to be independent of the parties in the dispute for it to be worth appealing to. It has to 'transcend' them both.

Now, in Christian thinking, of course, this transcendent norm is God himself – God in his righteousness and justice.[7] In biblical terms, both righteousness and justice in all human affairs derive from God. Indeed, they are intrinsic to God's essential character, so much so that God's very holiness can be said to be manifested in them particularly (Is. 5:16). God is both the ultimate standard of what is 'right', and the ultimate decider of whether or not this standard is being conformed to in human life. The Old Testament expresses these truths poetically rather than doctrinally, in such affirmations as Deuteronomy 32:4; Psalms 89:14; 97:2.

b. The direction of obligation

If responsibility is of the essence of what it is to be human, and if responsibility entails obligation, as we have argued, where is that obligation directed? Humanist oratory and the instincts of most 'people of goodwill' set before our eyes our fellow human being, for whom we are exhorted to care, for no higher reason or motive than that that is what he or she is – another of the same human species as myself. No higher reason can be given, for there appears to have evolved no higher species, and any 'transcendent' authority source is ruled out *a priori*. Two-dimensional humanism, however, cannot logically invalidate within its own framework the stance of either the self-centred individual who thumbs his nose at the rest of humanity or the ideologically genocidal group which claims to be acting for the good of the human race as a whole. On what external or objective grounds can either self-centredness or allegedly utilitarian violence be morally condemned within a humanist framework?

But Christians sometimes argue in similar two-dimensional terms – adding just a dash of doctrine, by speaking of 'fellow creatures', rather than merely fellow humans. It is because we are all God's creatures that we should recognize our obligations to one another.

The catch-phrase, 'the brotherhood of all men', only adds the sentiment of fraternity to the same two-dimensional duty. This, however, can appear as logically inadequate as humanism, for it can do little else but frown upon the person or group who choose to ignore the appeal – however piously clothed. If our alleged obligation is solely to one another horizontally, and located in some intrinsic feature that we have in common, there can be no compelling reason why I should not choose to ignore it – or indeed to boast with the existentialist that my very non-recognition of the said obligation shows my freedom from such 'herd' conformities and the authentication of my own individual existence in doing so.

The Bible, however, does not operate in this way. It does not put our obligation primarily on a horizontal plane, but rather directs it upwards to God. It is not so much the case that I am under obligation to my fellow human beings, as that I am under obligation to God *for* my fellow human beings. (This is not just a petty distinction, but has important consequences, as we shall see.) Thus, God addresses Cain directly with his question, 'Where is your brother Abel?' (Gn. 4:9). Though he might attempt to deny it, or at least to question it, Cain was responsible *to God* for his brother. He could try to deny his responsibility for Abel, but even in doing so he had to answer God. This reinforces our definition of essential humanness as responsibility to God.

What we are not doing, it should be stressed, is falling back on a two-dimensional obligation to our fellows, only this time located merely in some 'religious feature' that we have all in common. For responsibility to God is not just one among many 'attributes' of humanity; it *is* the essential *humanum*. We cannot escape that responsibility, for it is not in our power as creatures. Even to try to deny it is to acknowledge its reality. Thus, as we have just seen, Cain, even in his attempt to disclaim responsibility for his *brother*, by the very act of answering *God*, concedes his accountability to his creator. And inseparable from that primary

251

answerability is the fact that God holds us responsible *for* our fellows. Since we cannot escape the intrinsic fact of our human constitution – responsibility *to* God – neither can we evade its divinely imposed correlative, obligation to God *for* our fellow humans.

This pattern repeats itself throughout Scripture. God does not just lay on humanity a horizontal command to look after one another's interests and welfare. God consistently puts God's own self first – calling for Godward gratitude, loyalty and obedience, which then motivates and sanctions inter-human relations. Leviticus 19 calls for a practical holiness that reflects God's holiness. It is because the responsibility to God is primary, and because social breakdown results from failure in that primary direction, that God sends prophets with a passion for the people's response to God, and not simply social reformers. 'There is … no acknowledgment of God in the land,' complains Hosea (4:1) – so there is nothing surprising about the consequential neglect of human rights and responsibilities that he immediately goes on to list.

The first aspect of the biblical perspective on human rights, then, is that it 'suspends' the horizontal plane of inter-human duties from the transcendent 'hook' of God, by means of the fact and awareness of responsibility to God as constitutive of human nature itself. We are not primarily or solely responsible or obliged to our fellow human being. We *are* responsible *to* God *for* him or her, and that is something we cannot evade on a biblical understanding of what it is to be human.

c. From responsibility to rights

The other side of the issue now arises. Does the fact of responsibility entail equivalent rights in reverse? There is a danger here too of lapsing into a two-dimensional framework – of speaking as if the rights of person B were what he *deserved* from person A because of some intrinsic 'inalienable right' in person B himself, or some horizontal factor between them. But there is a vertical dimension to 'rights' corresponding to what we have emphasized regarding responsibility. To say that B has certain rights is simply the entailment of saying that God holds A responsible to do certain things in respect of B. B has rights *under God*, because God is as concerned with how B is treated as with how A acts. The two are correlatives of the single will of God regarding the well-being of God's human creatures.

To introduce the idea of 'deserts' confuses the issue (as we shall see under section 2, 'The effects of the fall'), and tends to drag the matter back to the horizontal plane again. It is not the case that the concept 'B has rights' means that I have to act towards B in some way because B deserves it of me or I owe it to him. Rather, it means that *God* requires it of me and I owe it to *God* to fulfil the responsibility. B's right in respect of me is a right under God, which has no other validation or independent existence than my responsibility to God in respect of him. What God demands of me to do for B constitutes B's rights.

Indeed, it is in situations where an obligation towards another person is felt most directly that this triangular dimension is most present. When I owe a debt or make a promise to a friend, the debt has to be paid and the promise kept to that friend, assuredly. But the sense of obligation to do so arises not from some inherent feature of the friend, but from God, who has made us both responsible to God for honouring debts and promises. The universal human practice of calling deity to witness in such situations, orally or in written contracts, underlines this.

This exposes the hollowness of the view which says, more or less, 'I accept that I have some responsibility towards other people, but that doesn't give them the right to "demand their rights" from me.' For when, on the Christian view, both responsibilities *and* rights are located in *God*, then 'right' is intrinsically demanding, for if 'they' have a right at all, it is entirely because *God* demands that I fulfil it. You don't need a right to demand your rights! Rights do not exist apart from the demand of God upon someone.

The Cain and Abel incident focuses this point too.

Having faced Cain with his inescapable responsibility, God points to Abel's 'right': 'Your brother's blood cries out *to me* from the ground.' Likewise God hears the (living) cry of the wronged (Ex. 22:22f., 26f.; Ps. 146:7). God sanctions and upholds their right to fair treatment from those whom God holds responsible for giving it. This pattern too is reflected in the Bible whenever there is an issue at stake between a person claiming a right over against someone held to be responsible for providing it. The emphasis is laid upon A's responsibility to God or B's right under God, not primarily on some horizontal factor, such as pity for B's plight, or common nationality (though these may of course be invoked as reinforcements).

A clear example is in Nehemiah 5, where Nehemiah takes up the cause of impoverished farmers, who were being forced to mortgage their land, and eventually to sell their dependants as pledges, to pay off interest to the rich. Nehemiah's appeal to the creditors goes directly to their obligation to God. 'Shouldn't you walk in the fear of our God?' (verse 9). Verse 13 puts the response of the rich also firmly in a vertical mode.

The first two chapters of Amos show this triangular dimension in settings which were not related to Israel as the covenant people (though in one case covenant language is used of a horizontal relationship to show that it had a vertical dimension, since covenants and treaties were 'witnessed' by God). God has observed oppression, and what would now be called violations of human rights, and through the mouthpiece of the prophet God pronounces sentence on the guilty. They are thus held to be accountable *to God* for their treatment of other nations. The nations unjustly treated, conversely, have rights under God which have been denied. The violence of Tyre in disregarding a 'treaty of brotherhood' (1:9) is the story of Cain writ large.

Likewise, in the case of Sodom and Gomorrah the judgment of God falls as a result of the 'outcry [against them] that has reached me' (Gn. 18:20f.). Now who was raising this 'outcry'?[8] Presumably the poor and the needy whom they were failing to help – which is the understanding of the sin of Sodom in Ezekiel 16:49.

> Now this was the sin of your sister Sodom: She and her daughters were arrogant, overfed and unconcerned; they did not help the poor and needy.

It was the cry of the poor, calling God's attention to the neglect of their rights at the hand of the 'arrogant, overfed, unconcerned' Sodomites, whom God held responsible, that brought judgment on the cities of the plain. The vertical dimension of the issue is again made very clear, even though the parties involved, as in Amos 1 and 2, stand outside the covenant of election and redemption through Abraham. They are nonetheless held accountable to God. The issue can legitimately be regarded as a violation of human rights, because God exposes a dereliction of human responsibility.

Another clear example of this aspect of human rights in the Bible is the advice given to King Lemuel by his mother in Proverbs 31:1–9. It is the responsibility of a king to stay sober so that he does not 'deprive all the oppressed of their rights' (verse 5). Rather the king must 'speak up for those who cannot speak for themselves', and 'defend the rights of the poor and needy' (8–9) The rights in question are not something the poor 'deserve' from the king, but simply the substance of what he is responsible under God to do for them, namely to see to it that they are heard and treated justly.[9]

It seems clear, then, that responsibility to God for others and rights under God in respect of others are inseparably correlative. Where one exists, the other cannot be denied.

d. 'Charity' or 'duty'

Now this has its bearing on whether we see our social concern and involvement as charity or duty. There are many well-meaning Christian folk whose view of their social commitment would include a sense of responsibility

– undefined but sincerely felt. 'Being responsible' means giving to charitable causes, or seeking to alleviate human need either financially or by practical involvement. But they would probably resist the suggestion that the recipients of their goodwill had a 'right' to receive such benefit. To make the issue one of human rights would appear to diminish the benefactor's deed, from an act of charity which he *need* not have done, to one of duty which he would have been at fault *not* to have done. Now I am not wishing to question or deny the proper feeling and expression of Christian love through 'charitable giving'. Nevertheless, most people, including myself, would prefer not to have their charity transformed into responsibility or duty like this. It would extinguish any private glow of pride in one's generosity or sacrifice. It would change the felt relationship between benefactor and recipient from one of paternalistic benefaction into one of simple obligation.

But isn't this precisely what a truly biblical under-standing of responsibility in fact *does* do? Responsibility is not a matter of charity but of duty: not primarily (though of course including) a matter of pity for another, but of obligation to God for another, and of the other person's *right*, under God, to my practical concern and action. It is such a regular feature of Old Testament law that it easily escapes our notice, that the injunctions to generosity, material support and impartial justice for the vulnerable and poor in society were not charitable extras, but legal duties. The rich man in the parable of Lazarus was not guilty merely of a neglect of *charity*. He had broken God's *law* (a point which the final warning of the parable makes clear by referring to the law and the prophets).

> Therefore I *command* you to be open-handed towards your brothers and towards the poor and needy in your land.
>
> (Dt. 15:11)

This text is from the Old Testament law, but it is echoed closely in the New Testament as well:

256

> *Command* those who are rich in this present
> world ... to be rich in good deeds, and to be
> generous and willing to share.
>
> (1 Tim. 6:17–18)

e. Responsibility and guilt

Our emphasis on the vertical dimension of both
responsibility and rights also enables us to draw an
important distinction between two shades of meaning in
the popular use of the word 'responsibility' – *viz.* between
responsibility as *implying guilt*, and responsibility as
entailing obligation.

Resistance to claims based on alleged 'rights' sometimes
arises from the feeling that if I acknowledge that some
person has a *right* to my action on his behalf, I somehow
admit guilt for his plight. If I can maintain, however, that
'It's not my fault. I'm not responsible for [= guilty of
causing] the situation,' then I feel free to choose whether or
not to help the victims of it. If I do, it is to the credit of my
generosity. If I don't, I cannot be reproached, for I am not
under any claim of 'rights'.

Now, to what extent we (at any rate we in the West) can
disclaim guilt for the plight of others – particularly in the
realm of international relationships, the world order of
which we are inevitably part, which operates unjustly to
our benefit and to the deprivation of others – is a matter of
complex moral debate. There are questions of direct and
indirect guilt, of corporate and individual guilt, of inherited guilt, and guilt by association, and of 'moral
distance'. It is clearly absurd to imagine that God holds any
one of us individually responsible to him for all the needy
people of the world. Even in biblical terms, morality, like
art, has to draw a line somewhere. But my point is this:
even if, in any given situation, we could legitimately
disclaim all guilt and truthfully say, 'I am not responsible
for [*i.e.* guilty of causing] *the situation,* that does not in itself
answer the question whether or not we have responsibility
to *God* for the *persons* involved in the situation. If such
responsibility exists, then, even though it does not imply

257

guilt, it nevertheless entails obligations on our part and rights under God attaching to the persons concerned.

This is relatively simple to grasp and illustrate at an individual and immediate level. To help the injured at the scene of a road accident is felt to be a moral duty whether or not one is in any way to blame for the accident. We can feel responsible for the care of the injured without feeling responsible (= guilty) for the accident. The Good Samaritan was as little responsible for the plight of the injured traveller as the priest or the Levite, but that had no bearing on his active fulfilment of his responsibility towards the person before him. But we should not regard his act as mere 'charity' – the kindly good-neighbourliness that the parable has often been reduced to. Jesus told the story in answer to a question about a *commandment* – the second greatest in the law, to be precise: 'Love your neighbour as yourself.' The Samaritan was in fact doing no more than the law required, fulfilling his responsibility to God (thereby in effect obeying the first great commandment too) for his fellow man. The barb of the story was that it was a *Samaritan* who thus obeyed the law, whereas representatives of the very groups among the Jews who knew the law best, by their inaction were actually guilty of disobedience. It is vital to see the parable as an illustration of responsible obedience to God's law, not as a shining example of charity.

It becomes harder to get our minds around to this way of thinking of responsibility and rights when the issue is bigger or further away – social or international. It becomes so much easier to go on from the assumption, 'I am not remotely responsible for the circumstances of the urban poor, or of the racially deprived, or of the starving millions,' to the conclusion, 'so there is no claim of human rights as between them and *me*.' The distinction drawn above between responsibility for a situation and responsibility to God for persons *in* the situation at least enables us to show that the conclusion is not logically deducible from the assumption, even if the assumption were wholly true, which is improbable.

2. The effects of the fall

A Christian view of human rights, we have argued, locates them within a three-dimensional framework with God as both giver of responsibility and guardian of rights. But since humanity has chosen to throw off the constraints of God's authority, and since, in the fall, the relationship between humanity and God has been vitiated, what then? If human rights depend upon God, they must have been radically affected by the fall. Indeed so, but here again lies possible confusion.

a. Human rights not forfeited

It is common to speak of the fall in terms of 'forfeiture'. In our rebellion, the human race forfeited life, the blessing of unbroken fellowship with God, marital harmony, the co-operative fruitfulness of nature, *etc.* Standing under condemnation, human beings have no claim, no rights to plead. Our very continued existence on the earth is an act of God's grace. To those accustomed to emphasize this aspect of the fall, talk of human rights is extremely suspect. It sounds like renewed blasts on the raucous trumpet of human arrogance and autonomy. Man, it is said, is a sinner without rights. Any Christian interest in human-rights campaigns they see as infected with liberal and Pelagian ideas of humanity, ignoring the totality of the fall, and amounting to a kind of self-salvationism or old-fashioned 'social gospel'. The fact that the present human-rights arena is so polluted with political hypocrisy and double standards only proves the point of those who see it as entirely the product of human fallenness.

However, the question whether or not humanity has any rights as over against God is quite distinct from the question what rights one person (or group of people) has, under God, over against any other. The theological conclusions in the former realm cannot be pulled over (logically or emotionally) into the latter. And in any case, although it is true that in our fall we forfeited our life and all the blessings mentioned above, it can hardly be said that

259

we forfeited the *right* to them, for we never had such a 'right'. Before the fall just as much as after it, human existence on earth was a matter of God's grace – not of desert (with which 'right' is again being confused in this popular usage), and the blessings humans were meant to enjoy were a matter of divine gift, not of right or claim. 'Man' as a creature of God has had no claim as of right upon God his creator in either his innocence or his guilt. It is mistaken, therefore, to make an alleged loss of rights at the fall a reason for rejecting or suspecting the language of *human* rights.

b. Responsibility remains

Secondly, the fall did not destroy that essential fact of our humanness from which we have derived our view of human rights, namely our responsibility before God. The intimacy of communion with God, the perfection of moral reflection of God's character, these we certainly lost. But even in our fallen state, human beings remain aware of God and capable of being addressed by God, questioned by God, and held accountable to God. And it was in this 'transcendent' dimension of the human constitution that we carefully located the Christian perspective on human rights. For if rights were located only in some common feature inherent in humanity itself, unrelated to our Godward dependence, then it could be said that the fall had so mangled both our understanding of who and what we are, and our relationships with one another, that the idea of and quest for human rights would be vain from the start. Such would be the inevitable conclusion if human rights rested solely on the empirical facts of human relations, which proclaim our fallenness all too loudly. But as long as God holds one fallen human being responsible to God for his fallen brother or sister, then the corresponding rights under God also remain. The fall did not destroy responsibility. It has not, therefore, nullified rights either.

This is true not only in the general sense of the fallenness of all people, however relatively good or bad. It is true also of those who express their fallenness in criminal or antisocial behaviour. Cain, though a 'convicted' murderer, is nevertheless protected by God from random killing (Gn. 4:14f.). He has flouted God and violated his brother, but he has not thereby lost his rights *vis-à-vis* his fellow human beings. We note that this protection is granted *not* because those rights are inherent in Cain himself, but because of the fact that God will still hold *others* responsible to God for how they treat Cain. Cain's right is the substance of other men's accountability to God for him.[10]

Thus, I would disagree with the view of A. Bloom: 'The Bible ... knows nothing of an inherent worth or of "inalienable rights" within a person apart from that individual's decision to do God's will.'[11] For rights do not emerge from doing God's will. They are not the consequence of anything their possessor actually does. They are solely, though necessarily, the correlative of the human responsibility of another person to God. In fact, whether or not I 'receive my rights' – *i.e.* am treated in a way that is right, which in Christian definition means 'in accordance with God's righteousness' – depends on *someone else's* 'decision to do God's will'.

When Amos described the oppressed of his day as 'the righteous', he was making a forensic rather than a moral judgment. In the scale of God's justice, they were those who were 'in the right', as over against the wealthy oppressors who were 'in the wrong' (*i.e.* 'the wicked'). So it was *their* cause (their 'right'), that the prophet maintained in God's name. They were not necessarily any more morally virtuous or pious as individuals. They were quite as fallen as their oppressors. Their rights stemmed not from some intrinsic superior virtue in them, but simply from the fact that God demanded justice on their behalf from those he held responsible. *Rights are not what we deserve but what God requires.*

Micah's question, 'What does the Lord require of you, but to *do* justice ...?' (Mi. 6:8, RSV) states the issue from the same angle. It is human responsibility to obey God's demand that justice be done that is the primary and objective factor. Human right is the obverse of that; it is not an objective, inherent virtue in a person resulting from *his or her* obedience to God. As Bloom more correctly puts it, referring to the 'active' quality of justice in the prophets: 'Human right or social righteousness root in our relationship to God, and not to some independent quality in a person which calls forth such considerations.'[12]

The fall, then, has had no effect on the *fact* of human rights, for it has not affected the fact of our responsibility to God for other people.

c. Pursuit of right intensified

Thirdly, far from obliterating human rights, as we have seen, the effect of the fall has rather been to sharpen the issue and render the pursuit of rights all the more important. It is because of the fall, with its curse upon the earth, and human incompetence, laziness, squandering, injustice and oppression, that people become poor, indebted, and eventually dispossessed of their land. But this only serves to increase the responsibility of a kinsman to help a brother in such straits (Lv. 25:25ff.). It is noteworthy, in view of our earlier argument, that there is no suggestion that the kinsman whose duty it was to help was in any way to *blame* for the brother's plight. The rights of the impoverished kinsman rest neither in the guilt of his fellow kinsman, nor in his own relative virtue, but only in the fact that a situation exists in which God holds one man responsible to assist another, even at sacrificial cost to himself.

It is because of the fall that whole classes in society, or whole nations, are subdued by the tyranny of others. It is because of the fall that those who should be responsible for preventing or rectifying such circumstances fail to do so (judges, kings, priests, *etc.*), thus leading God to speak directly through his prophets – proclaiming the 'right' of the oppressed.

It is because of the fall that some people are constrained to 'insist on their rights', when other people neglect or violate their responsibilities. Separated from God in rebellion and sin, fallen human beings seek to seize their own rights by demand and violence. It is thus characteristic of the great 'reversal' that the fall has wreaked in human life that people typically demand rights and see them as something 'inalienable', passive, to be received and possessed, whereas God demands responsibility and sees rights as something to be given and conferred on others by active obedience.

Christians, therefore, armed with their doctrine of the fall, ought not to be surprised at the conflicts that surround the whole modern issue of human rights. They would have no surprise at all if they took the trouble to read the conflict-laden pages of the prophets. Still less should they stand aloof from the arena on the grounds that people's insistence on their rights, claims and counter-claims, political double-talk, and double standards, proclaim the fallenness of the whole charade. There is *no* area of human life which is *not* affected by the fall. Fallenness is no ground for non-involvement. Sickness too is a product of the fall, but Christians have never made that fact a reason for cynical evasion of the duty of medical care. God only knows the full extent of the fallenness of the world – but that is the world into which Christ sends us, as the Father sent him. It should not engender pessimism or cynicism, only realism.

And the Father who sent the Christ who sends us is the God whose very acts of righteousness and judgment are permeated with the desire to be merciful – to *all* people. Even Sodom had its Abraham and Nineveh its Jonah. If God can be said to be 'responsible', it is only to the demands of the divine nature, *i.e.* to God's own self. God discharges that responsibility in the form of love towards all the fallen human creation. The universality of the love of God as creator, and its indiscriminate prodigality, regardless of relative merit, was expressed by Jesus in Matthew 5:45: 'He causes his sun to rise on the evil and the good, and sends rain on the righteous and the unrighteous.' Jesus uses this feature of God as creator as a model for the exercise of our responsibility – which is what love is. To love your neighbour means to fulfil the requirements of your responsibility to God for him. Those requirements do not cease even when your neighbour becomes your enemy – as Israel had known since the law of Exodus 23:4–5. He still has a right to your love and your prayers (Mt. 5:44) – not as something *he* can demand of you as of desert, but as something *God* demands of you for his sake, and in imitation of God's own 'behaviour pattern'.

To return to the parable of the good Samaritan, it is a familiar point that Jesus turned the lawyer's question, 'Who is my neighbour?' right round by his own question, 'Who proved to *be* neighbour *to* the injured traveller?' As applied to our concern with human rights, the lawyer was really asking, 'Who can be said to have rights upon my "love"? Who has a right to be called my neighbour and thereby expect my charitableness?' But Jesus shows that this was to approach the question from the wrong angle. For such preoccupation with defining the other person's rights will always end up by limiting my responsibility. It becomes, in fact, as it was in this lawyer's case, a means of qualifying and circumscribing the otherwise boundless demand of the 'second great commandment'. And the more my responsibility is confined within conditions and limits, the more my neighbour's rights are diminished. For rights, as we have argued, proceed from responsibility, not *vice versa*. The vicious circle thus completes itself, for to start out trying to define rights is to end up reducing them. It reduces them to the measure of my own fallen perceptions as to what kinds of people I am prepared to accept as neighbours, and as to what degree of responsibility I feel towards them.

The two 'greatest commandments' of the law are in effect God's 'Universal Declaration of Human Responsibilities'. It is because the essence of sin, since the fall, is to neglect *both* of the two fundamental commandments, that human preoccupation with rights is all at the same time so inevitable, so necessary, and yet, apart from God's redemptive action, so frustratingly ineffective.

3. Perspectives from redemption

a. Old Testament

The events by which Israel came into existence as a nation are in themselves a dramatic, historical 'declaration of human rights'. This is so at two levels.

1. *'Right' as the social foundation of Israel*. First, it was an act of righteousness by which Israel was liberated from oppression and slavery. The whole train of events is set in motion by the outcry of Israel against their Egyptian oppressors (Ex. 2:23 – z^e'āqâ again, the cry against injustice). Their right to freedom, to the fruit of their own work, to worship the God of their fathers, even to normal family reproduction and life, were all being violated. But God saw and heard, and God acted in the great deliverance of the exodus, granting freedom to a captive people, restoring them to a 'right' situation and simultaneously executing righteous judgment on the wrongdoers.

Scarcely was the Red Sea crossed, however, than the whole new experience of freedom was consolidated on a covenant basis at Sinai, with the Ten Commandments as a foundational charter. But the Ten Commandments are prefaced by a clear statement of the new freedom, won for the nation by the redemptive power of God ('I am the LORD your God, who brought you out of Egypt, out of the land of slavery', Ex. 20:2). For the two are inseparable – the freedom that redemption achieves, and the responsibility it entails.

In the exodus redemption, God had conferred rights and freedoms on God's people. But, precisely for the purpose of preserving them, these were immediately translated into responsibilities in the form of the Ten Commandments. Thus, those who were now free to worship Yahweh must worship him alone, without idolatry and without abuse of that name whose power the exodus had proclaimed. Those who now had the right to work as free people and the freedom to rest, were put under responsibility to preserve and grant sabbath rest for human and beast. Those who were now free from oppressive violations of their family

265

life were responsible to preserve parental authority and the sexual integrity of marriage. Freed from violence and terror, they were not to kill. With the prospect of land and property of their own, they were not to steal or covet what belonged to a neighbour. Freed from injustice themselves, they were responsible to protect a neighbour under suspicion or on trial from the injustice of untruthful witness.

Read thus, the Decalogue can be seen as a table of human (and divine) rights, expressed, in what we have seen to be the characteristic biblical way, in terms of responsibilities. Equally characteristically, the rights and responsibilities enshrined in it are held within a vertical dimension by their explicit presupposition of the experience of redemption. It was *God's* initiative of grace that had provided the framework of freedom within which the responsibilities and rights could be exercised, and it was to God and under God, by virtue of the covenant, that such exercise would take place.

The rest of the social laws and institutions of the Old Testament can be seen as designed to *maintain* the righteousness upon which the nation was founded. The right of every Israelite lay in the responsibility demanded by God of his fellow Israelite for him or her. The essence of the law was, 'Obey me *by* loving your neighbour.' There is thus an intensification from responsibility for a fellow created human being to responsibility for a fellow redeemed brother. One could go through the Old Testament laws and institutions and compile a fascinating pattern of human rights, inferring them from the kaleidoscopic range of human responsibility embodied in them. It is impossible to do that in an essay which is concerned more with perspective than detail. But, in addition to those associated with the Decalogue, as just outlined, the list would include the rights of dependent persons – women, children, slaves; of the vulnerable and weak – widows, orphans, the poor, immigrants, prisoners of war; of citizens in the face of political power, of animals; of clergy; of newly-weds(!); *etc.*

2. *The covenant right of Israel.* Secondly, the exodus was a

'declaration of right' inasmuch as *Israel had a right to be redeemed*. Now if our minds are still confusing rights with intrinsic deserts, this sounds preposterous. Of course Israel did not *deserve* to be delivered. God would repeatedly impress on them that it was not for any inherent virtue or righteousness that God had redeemed them (Dt. 7:7; 9:4–6). But if we have grasped that a 'right' is not the deserts of its possessor, but rather the entailment of the responsibility of another, then the statement begins to make sense. For God had, in sovereign freedom, chosen to *make God himself responsible for Israel*. In the covenant with Abraham, God not only undertook a responsibility towards Abraham in the form of a promise, God also bound God's own self to God, as it were. In the ritual of the covenant in Genesis 15:9–21, God submitted to the symbolism of the conditional self-curse, a common feature of covenants between men. The ritual implied, 'May my fate be the same as these animals if I fail to fulfil my obligation under the covenant between us.' God's covenant with Abraham was a self-imposed responsibility for Abraham's descendants, which included rescuing them from the enslavement predicted in Genesis 15 and giving them the land of Abraham's sojourn. God undertook responsibility to God's self for Israel.

If God had *not* redeemed Israel, God would have abdicated this divine self-responsibility, thereby denying God's own faithfulness. That would have meant being false to God's own character – in effect, self-destruction. Israel's right was grounded, therefore, in God's 'self-responsibility' – on God's very nature and existence as God. 'I AM WHO I AM,' said God to Moses, as he was sent on his mission, 'and it is just because I am who I am that I have remembered my covenant with Abraham, Isaac and Jacob [Ex. 2:24; 6:4–8] and intend to fulfil it by redeeming my people from slavery.'

Further evidence of the right of Israel comes in Exodus 4:22, where God chooses to confer on Israel the title, 'my first-born son'. Now the right of the first-born son was a clearly defined custom of the ancient world. But it was grounded in the responsibility of the *father* to ensure that

267

the first-born received his proper inheritance. That God should call Israel his first-born showed the responsibility God took upon himself towards them – specifically the responsibility to grant them the land of Canaan as their inheritance. Their right of inheritance to the land was real enough, but it rested not upon their merits but on God's love and faithfulness to the covenant with Abraham. Deuteronomy 7:7f. spells this out.

Now, awareness of this right within Israel could and did become perverted into arrogant presumption Neglecting the demands of the covenant for reciprocal obedience and loyalty, Israel tended to treat their God as a celestial insurance policy for their own convenience and protection. Rights without responsibility again. However, properly appreciated, this right that God had conferred on Israel, as the expression of God's responsibility for them, was the well for the deepest intercession and the rock for the surest confidence of faith to be found in the Old Testament.

The boldness of Moses' intercessions for apostate and idolatrous Israel after the golden calf (Ex. 32:11–13; 33:12–16) is astonishing until we see that it only shows how thoroughly Moses had grasped the motives of the divine mind that lay behind the exodus. God's action had been the discharge of God's obligation to God's self and God's word. Therefore Moses directed the arrows of his intercession to that target. He pleads the right of Israel, assuredly not by appealing to their deserts – for they had none, except judgment – or by evoking pity for their plight, but by reminding God that God's own character and reputation was at stake. 'Remember the Egyptians ... Remember Abraham ... Remember this is *your* people' (*cf.* 32:12–13; 33:13, 16). The right of the nation to existence and freedom had been born of God's faithfulness to God's own self; their right to continued survival issued from the same source or nowhere. That Moses saw this so clearly shows his unique insight into the very heart of God, and explains the prompt and decisive answer to his intercession (33:17). The same understanding characterizes other great Old Testament prayers of intercession (1 Ki. 8:46–53; Ne. 9; Dn. 9:1–19).

The confident claims to be in the right, so frequently found in the Psalms, can also be perplexing, until we realize that they too stand on the same ground. The person who knows himself to be redeemed, and who knows the character, acts and promises of the God who has redeemed him, is enabled to respond to the violation of his personal human rights, or those of the whole redeemed community (and how many of the Psalms writhe with violence, injustice and broken rights!), not without anguish and complaint, but nevertheless with faith and assurance and even praise. Such a person has the certainty that God will vindicate the righteous and judge the wicked – somehow, sometime – and he can claim, even demand, that it should happen ('demanding his rights', as our jargon might put it), precisely because he knows that God, in loyalty to God's own nature and word, cannot ultimately do otherwise. He establishes his own right on the firm ground of God's self-responsibility to be righteous.

To dwell with God under God's protection is the highest human right, granted by God to those God has redeemed and taken into this divine responsibility. To possess that right is to have cause for praise even when secondary human rights are denied. 'In God I trust ... What can man do to me?' (Ps. 56:11). Even when other people do their worst, the redeemed believer can commit his right to God in hope. The Servant of the Lord, suffering every kind of injustice, and ultimately the violation of his right to life itself, yet trusts in the vindication of God (Is. 50:7–9; cf. 53:10–12).

From here the line goes directly to the cross, to the one who voluntarily suffered the injustice of a shabby trial and the rights violation of an innocent execution. In human history there can be no greater violation of human rights than the cross, for there could be no human being to whom we owed a greater responsibility than Jesus, the Son of God. *Yet*, in that act of human denial of right, the righteousness of God was at work. Indeed, it was precisely in the confidence that his Father *was* acting righteously, and that he would be vindicated and exalted – in short, for the joy set before him – that Jesus endured the cross with the faith and words of the psalmists in his heart and on his lips. All men might be liars, all human rights denied, even his disciples prove faithless, but *God* would be true to God, and therein lay his hope. As Messiah he embodied Israel and Israel's right. God would not, could not, abandon him to the grave or let his Holy One see corruption. His right, too, rested on the 'self-responsible' character of God his Father, just as his death was the fulfilment and ultimate cost of that 'self-responsibility'. It was the cross that was the real answer to the intercession of Moses, and the resurrection that was the real foundation of the righteous confidence of the psalmists.

What then of the redeemed Israel of God who stand on this side of the cross and resurrection?

b. New Testament

1. *'The right to become children of God.'* When we thus put the cross and resurrection at the heart of the matter, as we ought, we can see that the primary issue of human rights relates to salvation. The New Testament is absorbed with how a person has the right to enter the kingdom of God, be saved, justified (or whatever other concept may be used), and how wide that right extends.

It answers the first question by a clear denial that the right to be saved has anything to do with merit or desert, and locates it solely in what God has done in Christ *and* in the certainty of God keeping God's own promises. The right of the believer to salvation, in New Testament as in Old, resides in God's covenantal responsibility to honour God's own act of atonement in Christ and the promise of salvation based on it. It answers the second question by extending the gospel promise and the right based upon it to *all* people, and by showing that this too was a right based on God's will. For it had been built into the covenant of redemption from the beginning: 'all peoples on earth will be blessed through you' (Gn. 12:3). The inclusion of the Gentiles was no grudging concession. It was a *right* based

270

on God's faithfulness to the covenant with Abraham. The salvation of the nations 'to the ends of the earth' was seen as being just as much a fulfilment of God's covenant faithfulness as was the exodus or the cross.

John sums up both points: 'To *all* who received him, to those who believed in his name, he gave the *right* (*exousia*) to become children of God' – a right grounded in no intrinsic human factor, but solely in God (Jn. 1:12).

2. *The right to hear the gospel.* If there is no higher right for human beings than to receive the salvation God offers, there can be no higher responsibility upon those who have already experienced it (*i.e.* the redeemed community) than that of taking the gospel to others. Now since the burden of our argument has been that it is responsibility that generates rights, this amounts to saying that the greatest human right of people as yet outside the kingdom of God is to hear the gospel and to have the opportunity of responding to it. The Great Commission (Mt. 28:16–20) is the great declaration of human rights, precisely because it lays the church under the supreme responsibility to God for 'all nations'. Significantly, it grounds both the right of the nations to hear the gospel and the right and responsibility of the disciples to preach the gospel in the ultimate right/authority (*exousia*) of the Lord himself. We have the right to preach because they have the right to hear, because God wants them to be saved. It is the universal will of God to love and save that is the proper foundation for evangelistic responsibility and rights.

It is this that accounts for the sense of compulsion which characterized Jesus' ministry. 'Let us go somewhere else – to the nearby villages – so I can preach there also. That is why I have come' (Mk. 1:38) – as if to say, 'They have as much right to hear the Good News as Capernaum.' Likewise, Paul translates this right of the nations to hear the gospel into a personal indebtedness on his part to all people (Rom. 1:14f.; *cf.* 1 Cor. 9:16f.). He goes directly on from the right of people to be saved, because God is faithful to his promise (Rom. 10:9–13), to the right of people to hear, expressed in terms of the responsibility to preach (Rom. 10:14f.).

3. *The subordination of personal rights.* For three years Jesus taught his disciples that being citizens of the kingdom of God entailed a revolution in their habits of thought and action. 'You are not to be like that' (Lk. 22:26) could be the motto of all this teaching. In the kingdom of God the standards of the world since the fall were to be reversed – no longer the self-righteous demanding of rights, but the giving of rights by acceptance of responsibility and loving service. This could be abundantly illustrated too from the epistles – *e.g.* in the realm of marriage (Eph. 5:21ff.), of rights of conscience (Rom. 14 – 15:3; 1 Cor. 8), and relationships generally (Phil. 2:3ff).

But as well as this internal transformation of 'rights' within the kingdom of God, the disciples learned that the service of the kingdom would require voluntary renunciation of legitimate personal rights, or the subordination of such rights to obedience to Christ. The disciple must 'deny himself and take up his cross', which means being prepared to accept, for the sake of the kingdom, the same utter violation of one's human rights as Christ experienced. To stand within the kingdom of God is to possess the highest right open to humanity. That entails that all other personal rights take a place secondary to the right of those outside to hear the gospel by which they can come to stand where we stand.

Two further things need to be said on this matter.

a. We must be careful not to suggest that if a Christian (or Christian community) chooses to forgo rights or to accept the violation of rights, the rights in question somehow cease to exist. They still remain as a valid expression of responsibility. The rights which a Christian waives, or accepts the denial of, presuppose responsibility before God on someone's part, which is not dissolved by the Christian's action. That Christ *accepted* the injustice of his sentence and execution did not make it any less unjust or lessen Pilate's responsibility.

Thus, a Christian may be willing to forgo or suffer the violation of his own rights but, without inconsistency, uphold the identical rights of others in similar circumstances. What he is doing is holding up before people their responsibility before God for one another and seeking to persuade them to recognize and fulfil it. That is his duty as 'salt' and 'light' in the world. It is therefore no contradiction to acknowledge that the Christian and the church are often called passively to accept injustice and violation of rights *against themselves,* and yet at the same time are committed to the active pursuit of justice in society at large – including such upholding of *other people's* rights. Indeed, it is just these two 'horns' which produce the dilemma faced by Christians in many situations in the world – *e.g.* in industrial disputes where a real issue of justice is at stake, or in legal trials where to defend the rights of one Christian may affect the fate of many more persecuted minorities.

Precisely this point lies behind 1 Corinthians 9. Paul had chosen to waive his right to be materially supported by the churches he ministered to. But that did not mean that the right was not there, or that the Corinthians did not have the responsibility to support him and other ministers, or that other apostles were wrong to avail themselves of this right. Paul staunchly upheld for others (*cf.* Gal. 6:6; 1 Tim. 5:17f.) a right he chose to forgo for himself.

Paul's attitude to his civil rights is also interesting and flexible and equally related to the furtherance of the gospel. He did not hesitate to claim his Roman citizen's right to avoid a flogging in Jerusalem (Acts 22:25), yet in Philippi he submitted to flogging and imprisonment, thereby providing the Philippian jailor, whose whole household was saved as result, with his first piece of Christian service – washing his wounds (Acts 16:33)!

b. Christian acceptance of the violation of our rights for the sake of the gospel also has to be set in the context of our future hope – the eschatological certainty of the final triumph of the kingdom of God. This has two implications. First, it guarantees that all our efforts for the sake of the kingdom – at whatever sacrifice of our own human rights – are ultimately worthwhile. For in striving for human rights – with the perspectives, priorities and motives we

273

have discussed – we are working towards a goal which is guaranteed by the very character of God. We bring to others the gospel of righteousness and peace, in *all* its dimensions, secure in the covenant-based hope of that new heaven and new earth in which righteousness dwells (2 Pet. 3:13) because God dwells there with his people (Rev. 21:3).

Secondly, at the personal level, this hope sustains the Christian suffering injustice in the confidence that his right is lodged with God and cannot finally be denied or destroyed as long as God remains God. This is the faith of the psalmists, vindicated and reinforced by the resurrection. It was also the faith of Paul, who, having suffered multiple violations of his human rights for the sake of the gospel, looked forward with confident joy to the 'crown of *righteousness*, which the Lord, the righteous Judge, will award to me on that day' (2 Tim. 4:8).

Chapter Eleven

When the system fails

The struggle against corruption, dishonesty and injustice[1]

Whenever we seek to use the Bible on any ethical issue, it is important that we do not choose texts at random. We need to have a method. We need to respect the form in which the Bible is given to us, which is that of a story, with a beginning, an end, and a middle. We can envisage this as a line, with all the major parts of the canonical story set out upon it. The four major parts are: creation, fall, redemption in history, and the eschatological hope of new creation. Within the section of redemption in history would be included the story of Old Testament Israel from the call of Abraham, the incarnation of Christ and coming of the kingdom of God, his death, resurrection and ascension, the gift of the Spirit and the life of the church, and finally the second coming.[2] In this chapter we shall think only of Old Testament material along this 'line', since the New Testament material relevant to this issue would need a chapter of its own.

1. Integrity and dishonesty in canonical perspective

a. Creation

For biblical Christian ethics, the creation is the basic platform for all else. It sets the stage and gives us the fundamental orientation and principles for all our thought and behaviour. It is in the creation narratives that we see the basic structure of reality as God wants us to understand and relate to it. That structure is like a triangle of relationships, between God, humanity and the earth.

God's original intention is clearly that God would dwell with human beings on earth. God wanted a mutual relationship between God and human beings, and between human beings themselves, within the context of the created, material environment, which God had declared 'good'.

In all these respects there was a transparency of relationships. We read that Adam and Eve were naked but not ashamed. They had nothing to hide from God, or from each other. There was an absence of dishonesty or corruption because there was no need to dissemble or deceive. There were no goals or objectives that required such means for their achievement.

b. The fall

It is noticeable that the first attack of the serpent in Genesis 3 was on the *truthfulness* of God. Satan's strategy was to corrupt human relationship with God by corrupting our view of God, and corrupting our goals and desire. By questioning the *truthfulness of God*, he assailed the whole foundation of *human honesty*. If God cannot be trusted, why need men and women be honest or truthful? Our view of the deity makes an enormous difference to the standards we adopt in this or in any other ethical field. Religions in which deities are themselves duplicitous and untrustworthy in behaviour and relationships provide no cultural disinfectant for the same tendencies among fallen humanity.

Then Satan suggests a new goal for humanity – to be as gods. This was not a desire that was wholly alien or rebellious. God had made human beings in God's own image, to be like God in the world. But that role was corrupted into a desire to be *as* God.

The immediate result of the serpent's corruption of human perception of God, and of our desires for ourselves, is to introduce deception and dishonesty into the rest of human and divine relationships. Where is the man now? Hiding from God and making excuses, using his mind to rationalize and excuse his sin and defend himself and to blame others. Thus sin has corrupted every dimension of human life:

1. The spiritual relationship with God, in which we are basically dishonest and cannot face the truth about ourselves.

2. The mental realm, in which the human mind is darkened and reason employed for corrupt ends.

3. The physical dimension, both in that the human body becomes subject to decay and death and victim to the ravages of sin and oppression, and in that the whole physical environment is now under the curse of God.

4. The social realm: the story of Genesis 1 – 11 quickly goes on to show how the sin of Adam and Eve not only estranged them as individuals, but soon gave rise to other social expressions of evil, including jealousy, anger, murder, vengeance, corruption, violence, pride, strife and division.

All this should remind us that when we are up against corruption and dishonesty, we are dealing with an area which has the original fingerprints of Satan himself. Our fallenness shows its very essence in corruption and dishonesty. That is why it is such a difficult and usually costly matter to stand against it in the world. It is also one of the areas of human character deformity that is among the last to be truly converted and transformed even among Christians.

c. Redemption in history

1. *The patriarchs.* God initiated redemption in the history of humankind with the call of Abraham. God's intention is not just to redeem individuals, but to create a new community, a people through whom God could reveal himself and ultimately bring salvation and blessing to all nations of the earth.

The passages outlining the covenant between God and the patriarchs are familiar to us (*cf.* Gn. 12:1–3; 15:1–21; 17:1–27). But we should notice that God's redemptive activity and purpose are very closely linked with ethical implications in this context. A key passage in this respect is

Genesis 18:18ff. The context is God's declared intention to judge Sodom and Gomorrah. An 'outcry' has been raised against them (18:20); this is the same word as is used of the Hebrews crying out under oppression from Egypt. It indicates that the sin of Sodom included not only the kind of sexual perversion and atrocities that chapter 19 describes, but also social injustice, *i.e.* economic as well as moral corruption. This is confirmed by Ezekiel's verdict on the sin of Sodom (see Ezk. 16:49). In contrast with this comes God's comment on the role and function of Abraham in the divine purposes. God reaffirms his purpose of salvation to all nations through the family of Abraham (verse 18), and then immediately points out the ethical challenge: 'so that he will direct his children and his household after him to keep the way of the LORD by doing what is right and just, so that the LORD will bring about for Abraham what he has promised him' (verse 19). God's answer to the corruption and evil of a Sodom and Gomorrah was a new community which would reflect the very righteousness and justice of God in its own life. The battle against corruption, the battle for social justice, goes back to the very source of God's redemptive purpose – the covenant with Abraham – earlier even than the law of Moses itself. We who are the spiritual heirs of Abraham (as Paul clearly teaches) also inherit his mission and social demand as it is unambiguously expressed in this verse.

2. *The law.* The natural focus for our issue here is, of course, the ninth commandment: 'You shall not give false testimony against your neighbour.' But before we go into that further, we should note the historical context of the Decalogue itself. It is given *after* the deliverance of Israel out of the corrupt oppression of Egypt into freedom. The exodus was a comprehensive act of deliverance, which answered Israel's need in four dimensions – political, economic, social and spiritual. It was also an act of justice – God's justice. In it God both judged the guilty oppressor, and vindicated a suffering people, setting them now in a situation of justice and freedom from exploitation. The law in general, then, and the Decalogue in particular, are given

in order to maintain and preserve that freedom, to enable the people to live out the state of righteousness which God had achieved for them as an act of redemptive grace. Obedience to the laws was a matter of grateful response to the saving acts of God. Having experienced justice, they were to do justice, in this and every area of life.

Two main strands flow from the ninth commandment, especially if it is taken in conjunction with the eighth, against stealing.

The first is *judicial integrity*. The law is primarily concerned with protecting the integrity of the courts in Israel. Injustices are bound to arise within a society, conflicts of interest, disputes and damages, *etc.* So long as there is an authentic source of redress and justice in the local legal assembly, things can be put right and justice restored. But if the courts themselves are corrupted, by partial or corrupt judges, or by false and malicious witnesses, or by bribery and influence, then justice is lost altogether. Thus, this commandment is supported by a number of similar exhortations concerning judicial procedure. It is clearly something which God, the God of justice, is passionately concerned about (Ex. 23:1–8; Lv. 19:5; Dt. 16:18–20; *cf.* 2 Ch. 19:4–11).

Secondly, *commercial honesty*. Dishonesty is something most commonly seen in the world of trade, from the local market-place or shop to the modern international economic system. Israel was no exception. Here also God, the God of truth, demands scrupulous truth and honesty in all dealings (Lv. 19:35f.; *cf.* Pr. 11:1).

The assumption in all these laws and others like them is that covenant loyalty to Yahweh demands covenant integrity in all social dealings within Israel itself. Any form of corruption and dishonesty is by definition a denial of the character of the God they worshipped.

3. *The narratives.* It would be impossible to list all the narratives in the Old Testament which have something to do with corruption and dishonesty. A quick glance through Judges, Samuel and Kings should provide plenty of examples! However, one passage is rather interesting – the

279

account of Samuel's farewell speech at the anointing of Saul to be king, in 1 Samuel 12. Samuel has had a very long ministry as judge, prophet and military leader. Here he is handing in his accounts, so to speak, and he wants the record to be quite clear. The significant thing is that he desires confirmation from the people that his tenure of high office has been free from any kind of corruption. His questions and the people's replies show the high standard that was expected of public leadership in Israel, even in those early days.

> 'Here I stand. Testify against me ... Whose ox have I taken? Whose donkey have I taken? Whom have I cheated? Whom have I oppressed? From whose hands have I accepted a bribe to make me shut my eyes? If I have done any of these, I will make it right.'
>
> (1 Sa. 12:3)

The people then affirm that Samuel has done none of these things. He has not used theft or extortion to gain personal profit from public office (an endemic temptation of our day); nor has he favoured bribery to gain personal profit from his exalted judicial power. The sad thing was that this high standard of public integrity, which for Samuel was simply a matter of obedience to the redeemer God of Israel (verses 3, 5, 6), was not maintained by his own sons, and this was one of the motives behind the popular demand for a king. Unfortunately for Israel, many of the kings that followed turned out to be even more corrupt and oppressive than any son of Samuel, as Samuel indeed explicitly warned them (1 Sa. 8:10–18).

4. *The prophets.* It is very clear that the prophets had as a major concern the failure of society in this area. Their pages bristle with accusations against oppression, corruption and dishonest dealings at every level of society. As background for this, it is important to understand what had been happening in Israel since the time of Solomon, especially.

First, there had been a shift *of economic power.* The

original economy of Israel, as evidenced in the land-division texts of Joshua and Numbers, along with the various pentateuchal land laws, and the social picture in Judges, was one of a broad agricultural basis of relatively equal, free, land-owning peasant farmers, with no bureaucratic or centralized state structure or heavy external taxation. The land, which ultimately belonged to Yahweh himself, was intended to be shared out equitably to all households so that all families had viable means of economic self-support.[3] However, partly as a result of the extension of trade and merchandise at the height of Solomon's empire, and partly through royal favours and the inroads of a wealthy court élite, there had emerged a smaller, wealthy class who could buy up land, pressurizing poorer kinsmen into debt, and then use the legal means of redemption procedures to take over their land (the corruption of an economic instrument intended for relief into one of effective exploitation). Thus they added 'field to field' (Is. 5:8; *cf.* Mi. 2:1f.). Where legal redress failed, who could stand in the way of a king and queen like Ahab and Jezebel? The fate of Naboth (1 Ki. 21) was probably tragically typical of many another.

Secondly, there had been a shift of *judicial power*. The economic change inevitably affected other areas of social power and influence. Under the original Israelite system, it seems that most forms of basic power and decision-making in society lay in the hands of 'the elders'. The social definition of this group most probably was that it comprised the senior males in each land-owning household. Possession of household and land was probably the qualification for the varied role of 'elder'. The legal assembly in Israelite towns and villages was composed of elders in the community. It thus had an originally 'democratic' flavour – a group of senior local people settling their own disputes with broad equality. However, as increasing numbers of local peasant farmers were dispossessed of their land, or had their families broken up by debt-bondage (*cf.* Mi. 2:8f.), there would have been a corresponding decrease in the number of those qualified to

281

participate in the judicial process. The courts became dominated by the wealthy minority, who clearly looked after their own interest and denied redress and justice to the increasingly exploited poorer farmers. Not only did they not uphold the traditions of Israel's existing covenant law, but they could pass other laws which legalized their oppression (Is. 10:1f.). Thus we find in the prophets a vigorous protest against the mockery of justice that had taken root in Israel's courts (cf. Is. 1:17, 23; 5:22f.; Je. 7:6; 22:16–17; Am. 2:7ff.; 5:7, 10–15; Mi. 3:8–11; 7:2–4).

Hosea finds that the rot has penetrated the whole of society – not just the courts. He complains that there is no ḥeseḏ in the land (Ho. 4:1ff.). The word means 'faithfulness' or 'loyalty to the demands of a given relationship'. It is a frequently mentioned characteristic of God, translated 'loving kindness', 'steadfast love', 'unfailing love', 'covenant faithfulness', etc. But in Hosea it is used for reciprocal human relationships. The prophet is saying that all social integrity has broken down. There is no longer any convention of honesty, truth or dependability. Significantly, he regards this as a failure to know, or acknowledge, God. The book of Hosea depicts a society revelling in a most corrupted and perverted religion (which he calls 'a spirit of prostitution'), which has its counterpart in social corruption and violence. Corrupt religion and corrupt society go hand in hand.

Similarly, in the southern kingdom of Judah and in the following century, Jeremiah, possibly on the occasion of his first visit to the capital from his country village, is utterly appalled at the total lack of social or commercial honesty in Jerusalem – from the lowest in society to the highest and most educated (Je. 5:1–5).

5. *The Psalms.* The prophets called for religion to come out of the sanctuary and into the market-place and court assembly ('the gate' was the location of both). They refused to accept the current religious cult of the people, not primarily because it was apostate or idolatrous (in some cases it was outwardly orthodox worship of Yahweh – as in Is. 1), but because it had lost all touch with the moral and

social demands of the covenant faith. So the prophets rejected the worship of a corrupt society. But this was not because the traditions of Israel's worship were themselves irrelevant to the matter of social morality. On the contrary, there is a strong emphasis on this in the Psalms. Indeed, it could be said that concern for truth, integrity and trust-worthiness is one of the major ethical notes of the Psalter. A few examples must suffice: Ps. 5:9ff.; 12:1ff.; 15:2f.; 24:3f.; 34:12f.; 50:16–20; 52:2–4; 58:1ff.; 82. One fails to detect anything like the same passionate concern for integrity, or anger over its absence, in much Christian worship and hymnody.

6. *The Wisdom tradition.* Concern for social righteousness is also a regular feature of the Wisdom literature in the Old Testament. There is plenty in the Proverbs about the duties of those in any kind of authority – political or judicial (*cf.* 16:10, 12–15; 17:15; 18:5; 20:8, 26; 22:22; 28:3, 16; 29:14; 31:1–9). But specifically on the issue of honesty and corruption, the main thrust is found in the sages' concern for the value of *words and speech.* Often this is expressed using the figure of the lips or the tongue (*cf.* 12:19, 22; 14:5; 18:6–8, 20f.). The same concern for economic honesty in trade is found here as in the law and the prophets (Pr. 11:1).

In Job's great self-defence, one of the planks of his argument is his claim to have exercised judicial impar-tiality without corruption during his previous public life (Jb. 29:12–17). Though he had been a man of great substance, and therefore with a great potential for 'influence', he had refused to use it for corrupt ends (Jb. 31:21). On the contrary, all his judicial and social power had been engaged in pursuing justice and relieving hardship (31:5f., 13f., 16–20, 38–40). Even if we take Job to be a figure of powerful dramatic fiction, the story is a challenging picture of what was expected of 'the righteous man' in Israelite society. It is a picture of great moral force.

Similar pictures of model righteousness are to be found in Ezekiel 18. There is much in common between these pictures and the self-defence of Samuel which we looked at earlier.

d. Eschatological hope of vindication

What could you do when justice failed? In the second part of this chapter we shall look at a few models of how individual or minority groups reacted in the face of oppression or corruption. But of course it might turn out that nothing could be done, no redress seemed possible, the forces of evil seemed to triumph. What then?

In such cases in the Old Testament, in the face of extreme injustice, the righteous person is sometimes seen 'committing his cause to the LORD', in fervent hope of future vindication. He refuses to fight back, convinced that ultimately God will vindicate his cause and 'judge', *i.e.*, in Old Testament terms, put things right. Indeed, God has to do so to vindicate God's own name as a just God. This eschatological perspective is important, in that it releases the wronged sufferer from the need to achieve his own vengeance or to engage in desperate measures of self-vindication. The matter ultimately can be left confidently in God's hands.

There are examples of this in the Psalms, but the most profound case is that of the suffering servant figure in Isaiah. Here is someone to whom all human justice is denied and who himself is tempted to think that his whole effort is in vain. Yet he puts his 'right' in God's hands (Is. 49:4). Even in the face of personal violence he refuses the option of retaliation, looking for God's vindication (Is. 50:6–9). The final servant song (Is. 53) shows that the hoped-for vindication did in fact come. This motif of the patient enduring of injustice in the hope of God's eschatological vindication is an Old Testament perspective which the New Testament clearly applies by way of example to Christians in situations of unjust suffering (1 Pet. 2:19–23; note the last line of verse 23). The same idea is present in the very name 'Son of Man', which in its context in Daniel 7 includes the fact that the saints of the Most High will suffer all kinds of unjust persecution, but will ultimately receive vindication and a kingdom through their representative figure, the Son of Man. This hope

284

sustained Jesus at the time of his hideously corrupt and unjust trial.

2. Models of response to political power and oppression

As we saw in chapter 9, there is no single answer to the question, 'What is the biblical attitude to the state?' The Bible does not deal in broad generalities like that. One of the necessary features of the historical nature of the biblical revelation is that there are development and change in the nature of both the people of God themselves and also of the state as such. This is particularly true in the Old Testament. However, what we do have is quite a variety of concrete responses, from widely differing periods of Israel's history, to the problems of corrupt power and social injustice. When the system fails to be what the law of God required, what can ordinary people do? Here we can look at just a few fascinating examples, to which doubtless the reader could add many more.

a. Parabolic approaches to specific moral issues

There are two interesting events in the reign of David when an appeal was made to him on behalf of some person whom he had wronged. In each case the means of approach to the centre of political power was a parable.

1. *Nathan's parable* (2 Sa. 12:1–10). The case here is that David has used his power and means as king for morally evil ends – first in an act of lustful acquisition, and then in deliberate planned murder. In a sense the injustice was irremediable. But the point of Nathan's parable is to bring David to see the enormity of his acts and to induce repentance. It was successful in its objectives.

2. *Joab's parable* (2 Sa. 14:1–24). The case here is that of David's exclusion of Absalom from Jerusalem – a policy which was clearly unpopular, and arguably unfair, though David with hindsight would have argued that it was politically sensible. Again, the parabolic approach achieved its objective, namely a change of mind on the part of David,

and a change of situation for one allegedly wronged individual.

Though we may not feel inclined to go and tell stories to the present generation of oppressive authorities, there may yet be something to learn from this parabolic approach to those in power. The main point seems to be that they got the attention of the king in such a way that he was morally 'hooked' by his own response. He was forced to act by being made to accept the validity of a moral case. Also, the action was limited and well within the bounds of possibility.

> [These parables] gained the attention and involvement of the king as 'the one who *ought* to act': morally and politically they implicated him. Both were practical *ad hoc* interventions in immediate events, not abstract political theory. Both were successful in their intended effect, to bring about a change of heart and mind in the king. They required, in fact, repentance, moral in the first case, political in the second.
>
> These parabolic appeals to authority serve as a motive and model for Christian involvement in politics. As 'salt' and light', Christians should persistently present to authority moral arguments with persuasive force and practical relevance. This should characteristically be on behalf of the weak, powerless and those wronged by injustice or callous neglect, as in Nathan's and Joab's action. And it is most likely to be effective at the level of specific issues and achievable, limited objectives.[4]

b. Prophetic responses to corrupt power

We move now from the time of a relatively godly and approachable king, David, to a very different situation: the reign of Ahab and Jezebel in the northern kingdom of Israel in the ninth century BC. Though still nominally the head of the covenant nation (or part of it), Ahab had in effect become an apostate king, and worse, under the influence of his foreign wife Jezebel, had become actively hostile to the worshippers of the true faith of Yahweh. There was an insidious combination of religious persecution to the death (1 Ki. 18:4) and social and economic persecution of those who tried to maintain the rights and freedoms of Israel's original land-tenure laws (the case of Naboth in 1 Ki. 21). It was a dangerous time to be a Yahweh worshipper. Only 7,000 were left in the entire nation. What should be the response of such a minority to a violently unjust and oppressive state system?

1. *Elijah's* response is well known and easy to identify with. It was simple, implacable, uncompromising opposition in the name of God. He was, in a sense, God's man on the outside. He came from outside – beyond the Jordan, in Gilead. He mostly stayed outside, beaming in from time to time to attack or declare judgment. He challenged both the religious apostasy, in his great showdown between Yahweh and Baal on Mount Carmel, and also the economic injustice of the treatment of Naboth. Undoubtedly he saw the two things as closely linked together. The faith of Yahweh was a liberating ideology born out of the experience of actual deliverance from slavery, and given concrete social substance in laws and institutions of unparalleled justice and equity. The faith of Baal, especially in the form imported by Jezebel, sanctioned the exploitation of the masses by the royal élite to whom all land and all power belonged. Elijah was a prophet of Yahweh – extremely zealous for the name of Yahweh, he claimed. His calling therefore was one of prophetic denunciation and incessant critique.

Was he 'successful'? In the case of Jezebel, Elijah's message seems to have had no effect other than to stir up her hatred and fury still further. But in Ahab's case, Elijah was clearly a niggling thorn in what shreds were left of Ahab's Israelite conscience. We may gather this from Ahab's sullen reactions to Elijah's disconcerting habit of materializing before him: 'Is that you, you troubler of Israel?' (18:17); 'So you have found me, my enemy!' (21:20).

287

In the end it had some effect, for Ahab came to some measure of repentance and humility (21:27–29).

2. *Obadiah:* not the prophet, but the politician whom we meet in 1 Kings 18:1–16. The chapter begins with Elijah coming in from the outside to face Ahab again – the hero figure, one man for God against the world. Suddenly in verse 3 we meet somebody else previously quite unknown who has been in there all the time – right in the heart of Ahab's vicious regime – Obadiah. He is painted for us by the skilful Hebrew narrator in three quick but very revealing strokes.

First, he held very high political office. The term (literally) 'over the king's house' meant chief palace administrator, and probably included some such office as treasurer or chancellor. He was a key person in Ahab's government. But second, he had preserved his faith in Yahweh – ever since his childhood (verse 12). He had even been able to keep his own name, which means 'One who serves or worships Yahweh'. And we are told that his faith was not just nominal but 'devout' – 'he served the LORD' greatly. Third, he was using the privilege and access of his office to preserve the lives of some of God's prophets, doubtless at great personal risk in view of Jezebel's attitude and acts (verse 4).

In Obadiah, God had a man on the inside and used him for God's own purposes, all the while Elijah was off on the outside, by the brook Cherith and with the widow of Zarephath. In fact, Obadiah's calling to a political career at the very heart of the viciously anti-Yahwistic court, and to serve God there, was far more risky than the brief encounters of Elijah. It must have been a nerve-racking strain. At the end of the story, the 100 prophets of Yahweh owed more to Obadiah than to Elijah. Without his 'inside' help, they would not have been alive and well (though perhaps rather thinner) in their caves when Elijah summoned them to slay the disgraced prophets of Baal. So his calling obviously required a lot of courage. But it was courage of a different sort from that of Elijah. Unlike Elijah, Obadiah does not strike one as a naturally brave and

288

blustery man. His reaction to Elijah's request to go and make an appointment with Ahab is a panic-stricken jumble of objections, with a single repeated theme: 'He'll kill me!' Yet such was God's man on the inside serving the Lord at the head of the civil service of a hostile, apostate despot.

The moral of this double-sided picture is surely that there can be more than one position from which to serve God in relation to unjust and corrupt secular authority. God will certainly have those who present God's challenge and critique from the outside – the prophetic voice denouncing evil in the name of God's justice. But God will also have those who are called to work within the system, yet preserve their faith and their integrity. The point is that each needs to avoid the temptation to criticize the standpoint of the other – as might easily have happened between Elijah and Obadiah, but we read no trace of it. Elijah could have done what so many Christians do when fellow Christians get directly involved in politics or government, *i.e.* accused Obadiah of compromise, 'ruining his witness', betraying his faith, *etc*. Likewise, Obadiah could have urged Elijah to keep quiet, arguing that all his prophetic blasts from the outside did not make things any easier for believers in the corridors of corrupt power.

Although there is no trace of conflict between the two in the Old Testament text, we need to recognize, of course, that in practical politics there is almost bound to be a tension between the stances they represent. Again, it is probably Obadiah's role that will eventually become the most difficult to sustain. What if Jezebel had ordered *him* to do the actual killing of the prophets of Yahweh? Or to bow the knee to Baal? Then we have to turn, perhaps, to the stories of Daniel, Shadrach, Meshach and Abednego (Dn. 3 and 6) for reflection on the limits of co-operation with pagan government.

c. Prayer and practical political involvement

Skimming over the centuries again, we arrive at the time of the exile in the sixth century BC. Now the enemy is no longer an internal apostate monarchy, but an external

289

pagan state which has overrun and destroyed the country and its capital and taken most of the population into captivity. How are the faithful remnant to react to such a situation? Again, as we saw in chapter 9 above, the Old Testament affords us several examples which show us a variety of possible responses, all involving prayer.

1. *Jeremiah*. The response of Jeremiah is at first sight most remarkable. In his letter to the exiles, in Jeremiah 29, when the dust of their departure has scarcely settled, he tells them to *pray for Babylon!* This is the same prophet who, along with others, speaks oracles of God's dire doom and judgment upon Babylon for all their arrogant iniquities and corruption. Yet here he says that the proper response for the exiles to make is to 'seek the shalom of the city, pray for it, for in its shalom shall you find shalom'. And as they did so, they should get on with the ordinary things of life – homes, marriage, business, *etc.* Cope with the situation you are in; be pragmatic; settle down, but as you do so, pray. Pray not only for yourselves and your hope for deliverance, but also for your persecutors and enemies. For prayer puts things in perspective – divine perspective. To pray for Babylon is to recognize a higher power than Babylon. Its authority is derived, controlled and temporary.

2. *Daniel*. The book of Daniel portrays him as a man who had great natural ability, academic and administrative. But it also describes him as a man of prayer. His long and eventually fruitful relationship with the pagan king Nebuchadnezzar leads me to believe that his prayers were frequently *for* Nebuchadnezzar – in obedience to the advice of Jeremiah, whose writings he pored over deeply (Dn. 9:2). For Daniel, prayer and practical politics were not mutually exclusive.

His prayer life was not an escape from the dirty world of politics in which he daily lived, but rather the source of the power by which he made that world a bit cleaner. The patience of such a policy of prayer and practical service, even for a pagan state, over a lifetime, eventually led to the conversion of the head of state himself (Dn. 4). Later still, we find that it is the incorruptible integrity of Daniel which makes him so attractive and useful to Darius, but so obnoxious to his political opponents (Dn. 6:3–5). Their vicious conspiracy against Daniel is typical of those who find their way to corrupt gain blocked by the principles and integrity of a superior. In reality, not every case of violent persecution of the just by the unjust ends up as happily as the story of Daniel and the lions' den. That is where the eschatological vision becomes so relevant – as indeed it is so powerfully presented in the later chapters of Daniel for those who were going to have to undergo even fiercer persecution but without the service of lion-taming angels.

3. *Nehemiah.* Another outstanding example of prayer and pragmatic seizing of opportunities would be Nehemiah. Again it is interesting to find such a devout believer high up in the service of a pagan king (*cf.* Joseph, Obadiah, Daniel). Presented with a desperate situation, we find that he prays fervently, and then looks out for an opportunity to take practical action. When it turns up, he prays again, then moves in with an obviously well-thought-out plan. As well as praying, he had done his homework, so that when the king asked his question, Nehemiah had a prompt, practical and prepared answer, complete with costings and projected time-scale (Ne. 2:1–9). The rest of the book shows Nehemiah continuing this double-edged (prayerful and practical) approach to his problems, internal or external. Scripture encourages us not to despise the use of whatever practical means lie at our disposal, alongside the battle waged in prayer.

Here, then, are several models of response to political power when it has descended to varying degrees of corruption and injustice: the parabolic approach of small-scale 'pressure-point' political appeal on specific moral issues; the prophetic approach which brings all human life under the dynamic word of God's judgment; the need for practical political involvement on the part of devout believers with courage and integrity; the balance of profound prayer and pragmatic ability to seize the given moment and its opportunity for the cause of the Lord and his people and his justice. There may well be other approaches to be discovered, if the reader feels stimulated to re-read the Old Testament from this angle, on the look-out for such cases.

It seems that one approach, however, is not offered as an option to us: that is the refusal to respond at all, to opt out of the struggle altogether. Such an attitude is simply to acquiesce in the grip of evil. In the battle between integrity and corruption, truth and falsehood, justice and oppression, there is no neutrality, and never has been since the day Adam and Eve chose to believe a lie.

Select bibliography

Bahnsen, G., *By This Standard: The Authority of God's Law Today* (Tyler: Institute for Christian Economics, 1985).
—— 'Christ and the Role of Civil Government: The Theonomic Perspective', Part I, *Transformation* 5.2 (1988), pp. 24–31; Part II, 5.3 (1988), pp. 24–28.
—— *Theonomy in Christian Ethics* (Phillipsburg: Presbyterian and Reformed, 1977, 1984).
Barker, W. S., and Godfrey, W. R. (eds.), *Theonomy: A Reformed Critique* (Grand Rapids: Academie, 1990).
Barclay, O. R., 'The Theology of Social Ethics: A Survey of Current Positions', *EQ* 62 (1990), pp. 63–86.
Barclay, O. R., and Sugden, C., 'Biblical Social Ethics in a Mixed Society', *EQ* 62 (1990), pp. 5–18.
Bauckham, R., *The Bible in Politics* (London: SPCK, 1989).
Barton, J., 'Approaches to Ethics in the Old Testament', in J. Rogerson (ed.), *Beginning Old Testament Study* (London: SPCK, 1983), pp. 113–130.
—— 'Understanding Old Testament Ethics', *JSOT* 9 (1978), pp. 44–64.
Birch, B. C., *Let Justice Roll Down: The Old Testament, Ethics and the Christian Life* (Louisville: Westminster John Knox, 1991).
—— 'Old Testament Narrative and Moral Address', in G. M. Tucker, D. L. Petersen and R. R. Wilson (eds.), *Canon, Theology and Old Testament Interpretation: Essays in Honor of Brevard S. Childs* (Minneapolis: Fortress, 1988), pp. 75–91.
Birch, B. C., and Rasmussen, L. L., *Bible and Ethics in the Christian Life* (Minneapolis: Augsburg, 1976).

293

Boecker, H. J., *Law and the Administration of Justice in the Old Testament and Ancient East* (ET London: SPCK, 1980).

Brueggemann, W., *The Land: Place as Gift, Promise and Challenge in Biblical Faith* (Philadelphia: Fortress, 1977; London: SPCK, 1978).

—— *The Prophetic Imagination* (Philadelphia: Fortress, 1978).

Clements, R. E., 'Christian Ethics and the Old Testament', *The Modern Churchman* 26 (1984), pp. 13–26.

—— (ed.), *The World of Ancient Israel: Sociological, Anthropological and Political Perspectives* (Cambridge: Cambridge University Press, 1989).

Dearman, J. A., *Property Rights in the Eighth-Century Prophets: The Conflict and its Background* (Atlanta: Scholars Press, 1988).

Gammie, J. G., *Holiness in Israel: Overtures to Biblical Theology* (Philadelphia: Fortress, 1989).

Geisler, N. L., *Christian Ethics: Options and Issues* (Grand Rapids: Baker, 1989; Leicester, IVP, 1990).

—— 'Dispensationalism and Ethics', *Transformation* 6.1 (1989), pp. 7–14.

Gnuse, R., 'Jubilee Legislation in Leviticus: Israel's Vision of Social Reform', *BTB* 15 (1985), pp. 43–48.

—— *You Shall Not Steal: Community and Property in the Biblical Tradition* (Maryknoll: Orbis, 1985).

Goldingay, J., 'The Old Testament as a Way of Life', in *idem, Approaches to Old Testament Interpretation* (Leicester: IVP, 1981; updated edn., Leicester: Apollos, 1991), pp. 38–65.

—— *Theological Diversity and the Authority of the Old Testament* (Grand Rapids: Eerdmans, 1987).

Gottwald, N. K., *The Tribes of Yahweh: A Sociology of the Religion of Liberated Israel 1250–1050 BCE* (Maryknoll: Orbis, 1979; London: SCM, 1980).

Gowan, D. E., 'Wealth and Poverty in the Old Testament: The Case of the Widow, the Orphan and the Sojourner', *Interpretation* 41 (1987), pp. 341–353.

Harrelson, W., *The Ten Commandments and Human Rights* (Minneapolis: Fortress, 1980).

House, H. W., and Ice, T. (eds.), *Dominion Theology: Blessing or Curse?* (Portland: Multnomah, 1988).

Janzen, W., *Old Testament Ethics: A Paradigmatic Approach* (Louisville: Westminster John Knox, 1994).

Kaiser, W., 'God's Promise Plan and His Gracious Law', *JETS* 33 (1990), pp. 289–302.

—— 'New Approaches to Old Testament Ethics', *JETS* 35.3 (1992), pp. 289–297.

—— *Toward Old Testament Ethics* (Grand Rapids: Academie, 1983).

Longenecker, R. N., 'Three Ways of Understanding Relations between the Testaments: Historically and Today', in G. F. Hawthorne and O. Betz (eds.), *Tradition and Interpretation in the New Testament: Essays in Honor of E. Earle Ellis for His Sixtieth Birthday* (Grand Rapids: Eerdmans; Tübingen; Mohr, 1987, pp. 22–32).

Mason, J., 'Biblical Teaching and Assisting the Poor', *Transformation* 4.2 (1987), pp. 1–14.

Miller, P. D., Jr, 'The Place of the Decalogue in the Old Testament and Its Law', *Interpretation* 43 (1989), pp. 229–242.

Mott, S., 'The Contribution of the Bible to Economic Thought', *Transformation* 4.3–4 (1987), pp. 25–34.

O'Donovan, O., *Resurrection and Moral Order: An Outline for Evangelical Ethics* (1986; 2nd edn. Leicester: Apollos; Grand Rapids: Eerdmans, 1994).

Ogletree, T., *The Use of the Bible in Christian Ethics* (Minneapolis: Fortress, 1983; Oxford, Blackwell, 1984).

Patrick, D., *Old Testament Law* (Louisville: John Knox, 1985; London: SCM, 1986).

Rogerson, J. W., 'The Old Testament and Social and Moral Questions', *MC* 25 (1982), pp. 28–35.

Schluter, M., and Clements, R., 'Jubilee Institutional Norms: A Middle Way between Creation Ethics and Kingdom Ethics as the Basis for Christian Political Action', *EQ* 62 (1990), pp. 37–62.

—— *Reactivating the Extended Family: From Biblical Norms to Public Policy in Britain* (Cambridge: Jubilee Centre, 1986).

Sider, R. L., 'Toward a Biblical Perspective on Equality: Steps on the Way Toward Christian Political Engagement', *Interpretation* 43 (1989), pp. 156–169.

Stackhouse, M. L., 'What Then Shall We Do? On Using Scripture in Economic Ethics', *Interpretation* 41 (1987), pp. 382–397.

Walsh, J. P. M., *The Mighty from Their Thrones: Power in the Biblical Tradition* (Minneapolis: Fortress, 1987).

Wenham, G. J., 'Law and the Legal System in the Old Testament', in B. N. Kaye and G. J. Wenham (eds.), *Law, Morality and the Bible: A Symposium* (Leicester: IVP, 1978), pp. 24–52.

Wilson, R. R., 'Approaches to Old Testament Ethics' in G. M. Tucker, D. L. Petersen and R. R. Wilson (eds.), *Canon, Theology and Old Testament Interpretation: Essays in Honor of Brevard S. Childs* (Minneapolis, Fortress: 1988), pp. 62–74.

Wright, C. J. H., *God's People in God's Land: Family, Land and Property in the Old Testament* (Exeter: Paternoster; Grand Rapids: Eerdmans, 1990).

—— *Knowing Jesus through the Old Testament* (London: Marshall Pickering, 1992; Downers Grove: IVP, 1995).

—— *Living as the People of God: The Relevance of Old Testament Ethics* (Leicester: IVP, 1983) = *An Eye for an Eye: The Place of Old Testament Ethics Today* (Downers Grove: IVP, 1983).

Wright, D. F., 'The Ethical Use of the Old Testament in Luther and Calvin: A Comparison', *SJT* 36 (1983), pp. 463–485.

Notes

1. The use of the Bible in social ethics

1. First published as *The Use of the Bible in Social Ethics*, Grove Booklets on Ethics 51 (Nottingham: Grove Books, 1983), and in *Transformation* 1.1 (1984), pp. 11–20.
2. For further elaboration on this point, see chapter 2 below.
3. This incident is more fully discussed in chapters 9 and 11 below.
4. Such a study is attempted in more detail, though only in relation to the Old Testament material, in chapter 9 below.
5. For fuller discussion of these three 'angles' of Old Testament ethics, see C. J. H. Wright, *Living as the People of God: The Relevance of Old Testament Ethics* (Leicester: IVP, 1983) = *An Eye for an Eye: The Place of Old Testament Ethics Today* (Downers Grove: IVP, 1983), Part One.
6. For further expansion of the ways in which Israel was socially, economically and politically different from the surrounding culture, and the implications of their distinctiveness for ethics, see chapter 6 below.
7. On the theology of the land, see further chapter 7 below. On the wider range of Old Testament economic ethics, see C. J. H. Wright, *God's People in God's Land: Family, Land and Property in the Old Testament* (Exeter: Paternoster; Grand Rapids: Eerdmans, 1990).
8. A more detailed exegetical study of the jubilee year is provided in chapter 8 below .
9. For further development of this theme, see C. J. H. Wright, *God's People in God's Land*, pp. 110–114, and *idem, Knowing Jesus through the Old Testament* (London: Marshall Pickering, 1992), pp. 107–116.
10. These convictions underlie my approach to understanding the wholeness of Jesus' identity and mission in the light of the Old Testament Scriptures, in *Knowing Jesus through the Old Testament*.
11. A recent helpful setting-out of both viewpoints, in discussion with each other, is provided in a symposium of articles in *EQ* 62 (1990).

2. The authority of Scripture in an age of relativism

1. This chapter was first published in Martyn Eden and David F. Wells (eds.), *The Gospel in the Modern World: A Tribute to John Stott* (Leicester and Downers Grove: IVP, 1991), pp. 31–48.

2. Oliver O'Donovan, *Resurrection and Moral Order: An Outline for Evangelical Ethics* (1986; 2nd edn. Leicester: Apollos; Grand Rapids: Eerdmans, 1994), p. 122.
3. For further discussion of the biblical theology of the land and its distinctiveness from quasi-religious use of the Gaia hypothesis, see chapter 7 below.
4. Walter Brueggemann, *The Land: Place as Gift, Promise, and Challenge in Biblical Faith* (Philadelphia: Fortress, 1977; London: SPCK, 1978), is a most stimulating survey of the land tradition in the Scriptures, emphasizing the redemptive historical dimension and yet showing how the theme can be fruitfully applied today.
5. O'Donovan, *Resurrection and Moral Order*, p. 61.
6. C. J. H. Wright: 'Response to the Theological Overviews' (of the presentations in the Social Concern Track at the Lausanne II conference in Manila), *Transformation* 7.1 (1990), p. 17.
7. O'Donovan, *Resurrection and Moral Order*, p. 67.
8. This has never been true of all missionaries, of course. Many missionaries and mission societies have made enormous efforts to understand and respond positively to other cultures. Some cultures and small human communities owe their survival to missionary advocacy and protection in the face of other forces that would have destroyed them. Much highly valued early anthropological research and ethnography were done by missionaries.
9. H. R. Niebuhr, *Christ and Culture* (New York: Harper and Row, 1951).
10. See C. J. H. Wright, *Living as the People of God: The Relevance of Old Testament Ethics* (Leicester: IVP, 1983) = *An Eye for an Eye: The Place of Old Testament Ethics Today* (Downers Grove: IVP, 1983). The presuppositions and practical methodology of my paradigmatic approach are more fully explained in the final section of chapter 4 below.
11. Vern S. Poythress, *Science and Hermeneutics: Implications of Scientific Method for Biblical Interpretation* (Grand Rapids: Academie; Leicester: Apollos, 1988).
12. Thomas S. Kuhn: *The Structure of Scientific Revolutions* (2nd edn., University of Chicago Press, 1970).
13. Poythress, *Science and Hermeneutics*, p. 43.
14. Millard C. Lind, 'The Concept of Political Power in Ancient Israel', *The Annual of the Swedish Theological Institute* 7 (1968–69), pp. 4–24.
15. One does not need to agree with the sociological positivism and ideological motivation of Norman Gottwald to accept the thrust of his detailed analysis of the close functional relationship between Israel's social, economic and political structures and ideals on the one hand and the total shape of their religious beliefs on the other. In *The Tribes of Yahweh: A Sociology of the Religion of Liberated Israel 1250–1050 BCE* (Maryknoll: Orbis, 1979; London: SCM, 1980), he has shown with massive evidence how distinctive the Israelites actually

were from their surrounding culture, both in values and in practice. Chapter 6 below provides a survey and critique of Gottwald's work, assessing its relevance to our ethical understanding of the relevance of Israel.

16. John Goldingay, *Theological Diversity and the Authority of the Old Testament* (Grand Rapids: Eerdmans, 1987). I am thinking particularly of chapter 3, 'A Contextualizing Study of "the People of God" in the Old Testament'. See also chapter 9 below, 'The People of God and the State'.

17. In *Living as the People of God = An Eye for an Eye*, chapter 8, 'Society and Culture'.

18. *Cf. ibid.*, chapter 7, 'Law and the Legal System', and also G. Wenham, 'Law and the Legal System in the Old Testament', in B. N. Kaye and G. J. Wenham (eds.) *Law, Morality and the Bible* (Leicester: IVP, 1978), pp. 24–52.

19. John Goldingay is again very helpful in stressing the importance of the concrete particularity of Old Testament laws and institutions. They prevent us from being content with abstract generalities. 'Thus either the Bible's statements tell us how to live, or (when they do not do this) these actual statements are the model for and the measure of our attempts to state how we are to live. This means we do not ignore the particularity of biblical commands (and apply them to our own day as if they were timeless universals). Nor are we paralysed by their particularity (and thus unable to apply them to our day at all). We rejoice in their particularity because it shows us how the will of God was expressed in their context, and we take them as our paradigm for our own ethical construction.' *Approaches to Old Testament Interpretation* (Leicester: IVP, 1981), p. 55.

20. Another example of a paradigmatic approach to the ethical interpretation of the Old Testament is offered in the most recent monograph on the subject: W. Janzen, *Old Testament Ethics: A Paradigmatic Approach* (Louisville: Westminster John Knox, 1994). Janzen offers a more internally nuanced exposition of various paradigms within the ancient Israelite tradition than my more over-arching use of the term for Israel as a whole. He explores the central familial paradigm, with its key components of life, land and hospitality, and then goes on to describe separately the priestly, wisdom, royal and prophetic paradigms of moral behaviour and concludes with an examination of their impact on Jesus and the New Testament. He discusses a number of differences from my own approach, but is broadly in agreement with its assumptions and method.

21. Review in *TSFB* (March–April 1985).

3. The ethical authority of the Old Testament, part 1

1. This chapter was first published in *TB 43.1* (1992), pp. 101–120,
2. R. N. Longenecker, 'Three Ways of Understanding Relations between the Testaments: Historically and Today', in G. F. Hawthorn and O. Betz (eds.), *Tradition and Interpretation in the New Testament: Essays in Honor of E. Earle Ellis for his Sixtieth Birthday* (Grand Rapids: Eerdmans; Tübingen: Mohr, 1987), pp. 22–32.
3. See K. Froehlich, *Biblical Interpretation in the Early Church* (Philadelphia: Fortress, 1984), pp. 62–64.
4. See Longenecker, 'Relations between the Testaments', p. 27.
5. See Froelich, *Biblical Interpretation*, p. 82.
6. See *ibid.*, pp. 98ff.
7. Fuller discussion of the theonomist position is included in chapter 4 below.
8. A very helpful discussion of this feature of Luther, with illustrations and full bibliographical detail, is provided by D. F. Wright, 'The Ethical Use of the Old Testament in Luther and Calvin: A Comparison', *SJT* 36 (1983), pp. 463–485. See also G. O. Forde, 'Law and Gospel in Luther's Hermeneutic', *Interpretation* 37 (1983), pp. 240–252; D. G. Bloesch, *Freedom for Obedience: Evangelical Ethics in Contemporary Times* (New York: Harper and Row, 1987), chs. 7–8.
9. J. Calvin, *Institutes* 2:7:12.
10. *Ibid.*, 2:7:13; 2:8:7.
11. J. Calvin, *Commentaries on the Four Last Books of Moses Arranged in the Form of a Harmony, vols.* I–IV (ET Edinburgh: Calvin Translation Society, 1852–55).
12. See further D. F. Wright's discussion in 'Ethical Use', and also in 'Calvin's Pentateuchal Criticism: Equity, Hardness of Heart and Divine Accommodation in the Mosaic Harmony Commentary', *CTJ* 21 (1986), pp. 33–50.
13. W. Robert Godfrey provides a helpful critique, from within the Reformed tradition itself, of the theonomists' claim to Calvin, pointing out significant difference of approach and exegesis, in 'Calvin and Theonomy', in W. S. Barker and W. R. Godfrey (eds.), *Theonomy: A Reformed Critique*, pp. 299–312. The theonomist position is examined further in chapter 4 below.
14. A most helpful and illuminating collection of essays on Anabaptist biblical hermeneutics is provided by Willard Swartley (ed.), *Essays on Biblical Interpretation: Anabaptist–Mennonite Perspectives* (Elkhart, In.: Institute of Mennonite Studies, 1984).
15. Timothy George, *Theology of the Reformers* (Nashville: Broadman; Leicester: Apollos, 1988), p. 276.
16. See H. Poettcker, 'Menno Simons' Encounter with the Bible', in Swartley, *Essays*, pp. 62–76 (70f.).

17. See W. Klassen, 'The Relation of the Old and New Covenants in Pilgram Marpeck's Theology', in Swartley, *Essays*, pp. 91–105. Klassen asks whether Marpeck was a Marcionite and concludes that he was not. Though he stressed the discontinuity of the old and new covenants, he placed a high value on the devotional use of the Old Testament.

18. W. Eichrodt, *Theology of the Old Testament*, vol. 2 (London: SCM, 1967), pp. 316–379.

19. J. Hempel, *Das Ethos des Alten Testaments*, BZAW 67 (1938, rev. edn. 1964).

20. J. Barton, 'Understanding Old Testament Ethics', *JSOT* 9 (1978), pp. 44–64; and 'Approaches to Ethics in the Old Testament', in J. Rogerson (ed.), *Beginning Old Testament Study* (London: SPCK, 1983), pp. 113–130. A similar critique with reflections on critical method in the field of Old Testament ethics is found in H. McKeating, 'Sanctions against Adultery in Ancient Israelite Society, with Some Reflections on Methodology in the Study of Old Testament Ethics', *JSOT* 11 (1979), pp. 57–72.

21. Barton, 'Approaches', p. 128.

22. J. W. Rogerson, 'The Old Testament and Social and Moral Questions', *MC* 25 (1982), pp. 28–35.

23. R. R. Wilson, 'Approaches to Old Testament Ethics', in G. M. Tucker, D. L. Petersen and R. R. Wilson (eds.), *Canon, Theology and Old Testament Interpretation: Essays in Honor of Brevard S. Childs* (Philadephia: Fortress, 1988), pp. 62–74.

24. R. E. Clements, 'Christian Ethics and the Old Testament', *MC* 26 (1984), pp. 13–26 (17).

25. *Ibid.*, p. 22.

26. B. C. Birch and L. L. Rasmussen, *Bible and Ethics in the Christian Life* (Minneapolis: Augsburg, 1976).

27. B. C. Birch, 'Old Testament Narrative and Moral Address', in Tucker, Petersen and Wilson, *Canon*, pp. 75–91.

28. B. C. Birch, *Let Justice Roll Down: The Old Testament, Ethics and the Christian Life* (Louisville: Westminster John Knox, 1991), p. 34

29. It is almost impossible to select from Brueggemann's enormous output. Among his most stimulating books, however, must be included *The Land: Place as Gift, Promise and Challenge in Biblical Faith* (Philadelphia: Fortress, 1979; London: SPCK, 1978), and *The Prophetic Imagination* (Philadelphia: Fortress, 1978).

30. It would extend this article inordinately to include any adequate discussion of the use of the Old Testament in liberation theology (of many varieties) or in feminist writings of recent years. I am conscious of this gap, which would, however, require a separate chapter to fill.

31. N. K. Gottwald, *The Tribes of Yahweh: A Sociology of the Religion of Liberated Israel 1250–1050 BCE* (Maryknoll: Orbis, 1979; London: SCM, 1980).

32. I have summarized and critiqued Gottwald's approach and assessed its contribution to biblical ethics in C. J. H. Wright, 'The Ethical Relevance of Israel as a Society', *Transformation* 1.4 (1984), pp. 11–21, which appears as chapter 6 below.

4. The ethical authority of the Old Testament, part 2

1. This chapter first appeared in *TB* 43.2 (1992), pp. 203–231.
2. *Living as the People of God: The Relevance of Old Testament Ethics* (Leicester: IVP, 1983) = *An Eye for an Eye: The Place of Old Testament Ethics Today* (Downers Grove: IVP, 1983).
3. Walter C. Kaiser, Jr, *Toward Old Testament Ethics* (Grand Rapids: Academie, 1983).
4. Walter C. Kaiser, Jr, 'New Approaches to Old Testament Ethics', *JETS* 35.3 (1992), pp. 289–297.
5. See chapter 3 above.
6. Kaiser, 'New Approaches', p. 295.
7. Walter C. Kaiser, Jr, 'God's Promise Plan and His Gracious Law', *JETS* 33 (1990), pp. 289–302.
8. For example, it is the framework of J. N. D. Anderson's discussion of the role of the law for Christian ethics in *Morality, Law and Grace* (London: Tyndale Press, 1972), pp. 118ff.
9. I myself joined in the attack in my earliest wrestling with the task of applying Old Testament law in 'Ethics and the Old Testament', *Third Way* 1.9–11 (May–June 1977), articles subsequently reprinted as a booklet, *What Does the Lord Require?* (Nottingham: Shaftesbury Project, 1978).
10. This is a term and a method also used by Michael Schluter and the Jubilee Centre in its application of biblical materials to social issues, as discussed below.
11. Kaiser has developed these ideas further than the earlier book *Toward Old Testament Ethics*, in *Toward Rediscovering the Old Testament* (Grand Rapids: Zondervan, 1987), pp. 155–156.
12. Kaiser, 'God's Promise Plan', pp. 296f.
13. These points are made in John Goldingay's chapter 'The Old Testament as a Way of Life', in *Approaches to Old Testament Interpretation* (Leicester: IVP, 1981; updated edition, Leicester: Apollos, 1990). As well as discussing the problem of the 'specificness' of Old Testament commands, Goldingay tackles the diversity and apparent limitations of Old Testament moral standards.
14. Goldingay, *Approaches*, p. 55
15. John Goldingay, *Theological Diversity and the Authority of the Old Testament* (Grand Rapids: Eerdmans, 1987), ch. 3. The insights and structure of this chapter of Goldingay's book underlie my own 'The

People of God and the State in the Old Testament', *Themelios* 16.1 (1990), pp. 4–10, reprinted as *The People of God and the State: An Old Testament Perspective*, Grove Ethical Studies 77 (Nottingham: Grove Books, 1990), and appearing as chapter 9 below.

16. Goldingay, *Theological Diversity*, ch. 5.

17. Goldingay, *Approaches*, p. 55. A recent attempt to take seriously even those narratives in the Old Testament which seem ethically remote from us and therefore indirect in their ethical relevance is by W. Janzen, *Old Testament Ethics: A Paradigmatic Approach* (Louisville: Westminster John Knox, 1994). Janzen directs our attention in the opening chapter to five stories, each of which seems to claim to model right behaviour in given circumstances: Abraham and Lot (Gn. 13); Phinehas' slaying the idolaters (Nu. 25); David and Abigail (1 Sa. 25); David and Saul (1 Sa. 24); and Naboth and Elijah (1 Ki. 21). These provide starting-points for each of the five major paradigms Janzen explores later in the book, namely, familial, priestly, wisdom, royal and prophetic. By including stories which are not all at first sight (to us) ethically appealing, Janzen emphasizes that it is not the individual characters of the Old Testament that are 'models' simply as individuals, or in all that they do. It is the stories that generate, composite, person-like paradigms. Paradigms, for Janzen, are mental images – in the Old Testament context, Israel's 'inner image of a loyal family member, of a dedicated worshipper, of a wise manager of daily life, of a just ruler, or an obedient proclaimer of the prophetic word' (p. 20); ... 'a personally and holistically conceived image of a model that imprints itself immediately and non-conceptually on the characters and actions of those who hold it' (p. 28).

18. Daniel P. Fuller, *Gospel and Law, Contrast or Continuum? The Hermeneutics of Dispensational and Covenant Theology* (Grand Rapids: Eerdmans, 1980), provides a full account of Darby's pilgrimage and the development of his theological system, followed by an exegetically very thorough examination and critique of the conflict between these opposing systems .

19. Most influentially, *The Scofield Bible*.

20. Norman L. Geisler, 'Dispensationalism and Ethics', *Transformation* 6.1 (1989), pp. 7–14.

21. *Ibid.*, p. 7.

22. Geisler cites Jas. 2:10; Rom 6:14; 2 Cor. 3:7, 11; Eph. 2:15; Rom. 10:4; Gal. 3:25; Heb. 7:11; 8:1–2.

23. Geisler, 'Dispensationalism', p. 9.

24. *Ibid.*, p. 10.

25. *Ibid.*

26. Similarly, theonomist reconstructionism is the main target of the book by H. Wayne House and Thomas Ice (eds.), *Dominion Theology: Blessing or Curse?* (Portland: Multnomah, 1988), which includes helpful chapters setting out a dispensational view of the law,

especially chapters 6 and 7, 'Are Christians Under the Mosaic Law?' and 'Should the Nations Be Under the Mosaic Law?'

27. Norman L. Geisler, *Christian Ethics: Options and Issues* (Grand Rapids: Baker, 1989; Leicester: IVP, 1990).

28. Dispensationalists are aware of this criticism, but some argue that such negative pietism is not intrinsic to the dispensational system as such. There is a place for Christian social involvement, but not on the scale, or with the expectations, of the reconstructionist agenda. And for dispensationalists, such social involvement is generated via the New Testament and the Great Commission; it does not take its authority or its shaping from the Old Testament. 'Dispensationalists are often accused of being defeatist, just sitting around waiting for the rapture. It is unfortunate but true that pietism has infected many in the dispensational camp. However, social and cultural impotence is not organic to dispensationalism. The believer is called to a ministry of exposing evil during the night (Ephesians 5:11) ... If dispensationalists are not properly involved in issues today, it is not inherent to their theology; rather it is unfaithfulness to their calling.' House and Ice (eds.), *Dominion Theology*, pp. 241, 243.

29. The most thorough critique of theonomy, which pays attention to its theology, eschatology, ethical agenda and historical roots, comes from a symposium of Reformed 'cousins' from the faculty of Westminster Theological Seminary, William S. Barker and W. Robert Godfrey (eds.), *Theonomy: A Reformed Critique* (Grand Rapids: Academie, 1990).

30. Rushdoony's most significant work, out of his enormous output, is probably *Institutes of Biblical Law* (Phillipsburg: Presbyterian and Reformed, 1973), which is an exposition of the Decalogue as the blueprint for society. Greg Bahnsen's major contributions have been *Theonomy in Christian Ethics* (Phillipsburg: Presbyterian and Reformed, 1977, 1984) and *By This Standard: The Authority of God's Law Today* (Tyler: Institute for Christian Economics, 1985). An extensive, annotated bibliography of the prolific writings of these and other members of the theonomist, reconstructionist camp is provided by House and Ice (eds.), *Dominion Theology*, pp. 425–444.

31. Greg Bahnsen, 'Christ and the Role of Civil Government: The Theonomic Perspective', Part I, *Transformation* 5.2 (1988), pp. 24–31; Part II, 5.3 (1988), pp. 24–28 .

32. 'Standing law' is Bahnsen's way of distinguishing 'policy' imperatives that were clearly intended to have continuing force over time for classes of people from those which were equally clearly specific to individuals in unique historical contexts (*e.g.* the command to Abraham to sacrifice Isaac, or to Joshua to invade Canaan).

33. I have explored some of the implications of this as regards the mission and ethics of Jesus himself in C. J. H. Wright, *Knowing Jesus*

through the Old Testament (London: Marshall Pickering, 1992; Downers Grove: IVP, 1995).

34. Two recent books provide extensive and illuminating critiques of theonomic/reconstructionist/dominion theology and proposals. House and Ice (eds.), *Dominion Theology*, is from a dispensationalist perspective, and so confronts theonomism head-on at every level – theologically, exegetically, eschatolologically, ethically and socially. Barker and Godfrey (eds.), *Theonomy*, is perhaps even more telling in that it attacks theonomy from the same theological perspective on which it is founded. The points I make above are supplementary to the major exegetical and hermeneutical arguments of the latter volume.

35. On the administration of justice in Israel and the ancient Near East, and the role of written law within it, *cf.* Hans Jochen Boecker, *Law and the Administration of Justice in the Old Testament and Ancient East* (ET London: SPCK, 1980), pp. 21–52; Gordon Wenham, 'Law and the Legal System in the Old Testament', in B. N. Kaye and G. J. Wenham (eds.), *Law, Morality and the Bible: A Symposium* (Leicester: IVP, 1978), pp. 24–52; also C. J. H. Wright, *Living as the People of God: The Relevance of Old Testament Ethics* (Leicester: IVP, 1983) = *An Eye for an Eye: The Place of Old Testament Ethics Today* (Downers Grove: IVP, 1983), pp. 168ff., and *idem, God's People in God's Land: Family, Land and Property in the Old Testament* (Exeter: Paternoster; Grand Rapids: Eerdmans, 1990), pp. 76–81.

36. G. Wenham, 'Law and the Legal System', p. 35.

37. I have explored this more fully in *God's People in God's Land*; see particularly ch. 3, 'The Family and Israel's Relationship to Yahweh'.

38. See G. Wenham, 'Law and the Legal System', pp. 38ff., and C. J. H. Wright, *Living as the People of God = An Eye for an Eye*, pp. 163–168.

39. *Cf.* my comments on the limitations of the law in *Living as the People of God = An Eye for an Eye*, pp. 171ff.

40. Bahnsen, 'Christ and the Role of Civil Government', Part I, p. 25.

41. The Foundation for Christian Reconstruction, PO Box 1, Whitby, North Yorkshire, England YO21 1HP.

42. Some of their published theological work is referred to below. Much of it still exists as unpublished papers, or as biblical/theological sections in specific, issue-related publications available from 3 Hooper Street, Cambridge, England CB1 2NZ.

43. The fullest statement of their position is set out in *Reactivating the Extended Family: From Biblical Norms to Public Policy in Britain* (Cambridge: Jubilee Centre, 1986). In this they give a concise survey of Israel's kinship system and the political and economic structures that went along with it. Then they set out their hermeneutical method of moving from that descriptive work into normative ethics. Finally they move on to concrete proposals for social reform in Britain that would, in their view, be a starting-point for bringing

society more into line with the objectives and priorities of the biblical paradigm. I reviewed this work in 'Kin Deep', *Third Way* 10.1 (January 1987), pp. 29–32

44. The Jubilee Centre has launched a campaign under the banner of 'relationism' to bring relational concerns much more into focus in the course of public, political, economic and social policy-making. Their proposals are set out in M. Schluter and D. Lee, *The R Factor* (London: Hodder and Stoughton, 1993), and the biblical and hermeneutical foundations of the whole project are set out in C. Townsend and J. Ashcroft, *Political Christians in a Plural Society: A New Strategy for a Biblical Contribution* (Cambridge: The Jubilee Policy Group, Jubilee Centre, 1994).

45. See M. Schluter and R. Clements, 'Jubilee Institutional Norms: A Middle Way between Creation Ethics and Kingdom Ethics as the Basis for Christian Political Action', *EQ* 62 (1990), pp. 37–62.

46. On the history, background and contemporary significance of messianic Judaism, see Arthur F. Glasser, 'Messianic Jews – What They Represent', *Themelios* 16.2 (January 1991), pp. 3f.; Walter Riggans, *The Covenant with the Jews: What's So Unique About the Jewish People?* (Eastbourne: Monarch, 1992); David H. Stern, *Messianic Jewish Manifesto* (Jerusalem: Jewish New Testament Publications, 1988).

47. Stern, *Manifesto,* describes a spectrum of different answers, from absolute yes to absolute no, to the question whether messianic Jews should keep the Torah as understood in Orthodox Judaism, and seems personally to favour the position that it is desirable but not essential.

48. Stern, *Manifesto,* pp. 146ff. See also Daniel Juster, *Jewish Roots: A Foundation of Biblical Theology for Messianic Judaism* (Rockville: Davar, 1986), ch. 3.

49. Stern is so concerned about the importance of a right Christian understanding of the abiding relevance of the Torah that he devotes a lengthy chapter of his book to it. 'The lack of a correct, clear and relatively complete Messianic Jewish or Gentile Christian theology of the Law is not only a major impediment to Christians' understanding their own faith, but also the greatest barrier to Jewish people's receiving the Gospel' (*Manifesto*, p. 125). Lamenting the lack of interest in the Law among Christians in general he goes on: 'It means, first, that most Christians have an overly simplistic understanding of what the Law is all about; and, second, that Christianity has almost nothing relevant to say to Jews about one of the three most important issues of their faith. In short, *Torah* is the great unexplored territory, the *terra incognita* of Christian theology' (p. 126) .

50. I have not been able to find published material on social ethics from messianic Jewish sources, but gather the above comment from conversations with some members of the community in Britain.

51. See chapters 1 and 6 in this volume particularly, and also C. J. H. Wright, *Living as the People of God = An Eye for an Eye*, and *God's People in God's Land*.
52. I am in agreement here with Kaiser, 'God's Promise Plan', pp. 293–295.
53. R. E. Clements draws attention to this broad adaptability of Old Testament law which, though he does not use the term 'paradigmatic', is similar in effect to the point I am making. 'What is remarkable in fact is the way in which the Old Testament has provided a system of *tora*-instruction, which has proved to be remarkably adaptable to a vast range of human social and political systems. Societies of dramatically different economic, political and cultural types have found within the Old Testament a richly viable source of social and moral teaching.' 'Christian Ethics and the Old Testament', *MC* 26 (1984), p. 22.
54. See C. J. H. Wright, *Living as the People of God = An Eye for an Eye*, chapter 7.
55. This is not the place for a full bibliography of these enormous fields, but a helpful survey of them is provided by R. E. Clements (ed.), *The World of Ancient Israel: Sociological, Anthropological and Political Perspectives* (Cambridge: Cambridge University Press, 1989).
56. See, for example, Wayne Meeks, *The Moral World of the First Christians* (Philadelphia: Westminster, 1986; London: SPCK, 1987), as well as the various books recently emerging on the economic and political context of the ministry and ethics of Jesus: *e.g.* M. Borg, *Conflict, Holiness and Politics in the Teaching of Jesus* (New York: Edwin Mellen, 1984); and D. E. Oakman, *Jesus and the Economic Questions of His Day* (New York: Edwin Mellen, 1986).

5. Ethical decisions in the Old Testament

1. This chapter was first prepared as a paper for the 1990 conference of the Fellowship of European Evangelical Theologians, and then published in *EJT* 1.2 (1992), pp. 123–140.
2. O. O'Donovan, *Resurrection and Moral Order: An Outline for Evangelical Ethics* (1986; 2nd edn. Leicester: Apollos; Grand Rapids: Eerdmans, 1994).
3. This point is further discussed, with quotation from O'Donovan, in chapter 2 above.
4. A very lucid account of utilitarianism is to be found in R. Higginson, *Dilemmas: Christian Approach to Moral Decision-Making* (London: Hodder and Stoughton, 1988), chapters 2 and 8.
5. This is not universally accepted among scholars of Israelite and comparative ancient Near Eastern law, but it is a view with strong support. I have discussed the issue, with full bibliography, in *God's People in God's Land: Family, Land and Property in the Old Testament*

(Exeter: Paternoster; Grand Rapids: Eerdmans, 1990), pp. 156–160.
6. *Cf.* David M. Clemens, 'The Law of Sin and Death: Ecclesiastes and Genesis 1 – 3, *Themelios* 19.3 (May 1994), pp. 5–8.
7. These connections have been thoroughly explored by R. E. Clements, *Abraham and David* (London: SCM, 1967).
8. John G. Gammie, *Holiness in Israel: Overtures to Biblical Theology* (Philadelphia: Fortress, 1989), pp. 33f.
9. I have discussed more fully these dimensions of motivation for Old Testament ethics in *Living as the People of God: The Relevance of Old Testament Ethics* (Leicester: IVP, 1983) = *An Eye for an Eye: The Place of Old Testament Ethics Today* (Downers Grove: IVP, 1983), chapter 1, and also, with particular reference to their influence on the ethical teaching of Jesus, in *Knowing Jesus through the Old Testament* (London: Marshall Pickering, 1992), chapter 5.
10. See J. A. Soggin, 'Cultic-Aetiological Legends and Catechesis in the Hexateuch', in *Old Testament and Oriental Studies, Bib et Or* 29 (1975), pp. 72–77.
11. In detail, in *God's People in God's Land*, chs. 2 and 3; and in a more applied way, in *Living as the People of God* = *An Eye for an Eye*, ch. 8.
12. In *Living as the People of God* = *An Eye for an Eye*, chapter 9.
13. For a representative survey of the theonomist view, see Greg Bahnsen, 'Christ and the Role of Civil Government', in *Transformation* 5.2 and 5.3 (1988), and for a comparable dispensationalist view, see Norman Geisler, 'Dispensationalism and Ethics', *Transformation* 6.1 (1989). See also the critical discussion of both in chapter 4 above.
14. On my understanding of paradigmatic application, see also chapters 1, 2 and 4 above.

6. The ethical relevance of Israel as a society

1. This chapter was originally given as a paper at a meeting of the Tyndale Fellowship Ethics Study Group, and published in *Transformation* 1.4 (1984), pp. 11–21.
2. N. K. Gottwald, *The Tribes of Yahweh: A Sociology of the Religion of Liberated Israel 1250–1050 BCE* (New York: Orbis, 1979; London: SCM, 1980). Earlier work includes: S. W. Baron, *A Social and Religious History of the Jews* (New York: Columbia University Press, 2nd rev. edn., vol. 1, 1952). H. G. May, 'A Sociological Approach to Hebrew Religion', *JBR* 12 (1944), pp. 98–106; M. Weber, *Ancient Judaism* (New York: Free Press; London: Collier-MacMillan, 1952); S. Yeivin, 'Social, Religious and Cultural Trends in Jerusalem under the Davidic Dynasty', *VT* 3 (1953), pp. 149–166; E. Neufeld, 'The Emergence of a Royal-Urban Society in Ancient Israel', *HUCA* 31 (1960), pp. 31–53, and many others, cited in Gottwald.
   Since Gottwald's magisterial work, the field of sociological study

of the Old Testament has grown rapidly. Several recent contributions and critiques are collected in three symposia: N. K. Gottwald (ed.), *The Bible and Liberation: Political and Social Hermeneutics* (Maryknoll: Orbis, 1983); D. N. Freedman and D. F. Graf (eds.), *Palestine in Transition: The Emergence of Ancient Israel, The Social World of Biblical Antiquity* 2 (Sheffield: Almond, 1983); and R. E. Clements (ed.), *The World of Ancient Israel* (Cambridge: Cambridge University Press, 1989). For a survey of sociological approaches to ancient Israel from 1880 to 1960, see F. S. Frick and N. K. Gottwald in Gottwald (ed.), *The Bible and Liberation*, pp. 149–165. See also R. R. Wilson, *Sociological Approaches to the Old Testament* (Philadelphia: Fortress, 1984); and A. D. H. Mayes, *The Old Testament in Sociological Perspective* (London: Marshall Pickering, 1989). For a more critical view of the contribution of sociology, see G. A. Herion, 'The Impact of Modern and Social Science Assumptions on the Reconstruction of Israelite History', *JSOT* 34 (1986), pp. 3–33; and D. Jobling, 'Sociological and Literary Approaches to the Bible: How Shall the Twain Meet?' *JSOT* 38 (1987), pp. 85–93.

3. G. E. Mendenhall, 'The Hebrew Conquest of Palestine', *BA* 25 (1962), pp. 66–87; and *The Tenth Generation: The Origins of the Biblical Tradition* (Baltimore and London: Johns Hopkins University Press, 1973). Mendenhall himself has since disassociated himself from the methods and conclusions which Gottwald built upon his work, in 'Ancient Israel's Hyphenated History', in Freedman and Graf (eds.), *Palestine in Transition*, pp. 90–103.

4. See also, on the subject of kinship in Israel, F. I. Andersen, 'Israelite Kinship Terminology and Social Structure', *BT* 18 (1967), pp. 19–26; C. U. Wolf, 'Some Remarks on the Tribes and Clans in Israel', *JQR* 36 (1946), pp. 287–295; and *idem*, 'Terminology of Israel's Tribal Organisation', *JBL* 65 (1946), pp. 45–49.

5. *Cf.* G. E. Mendenhall, 'The Census Lists of Numbers 1 and 26', *JBL* 77 (1958), pp. 52–66.

6. G. E. Mendenhall, 'The Relation of the Individual to Political Society in Ancient Israel', in J. M. Myers *et al.* (eds.), *Biblical Studies in Memory of H. C. Allman* (New York: N. Gluckstadt Press, 1960), p. 92.

7. See A. Phillips, 'Some Aspects of Family Law in Pre-Exilic Israel', *VT* 23 (1973), pp. 349–361; and *idem*, 'Another Example of Family Law', *VT* 30 (1980), pp. 240–243.

8. The jubilee year is discussed, with more detailed exegesis of Leviticus 25, in chapter 8 below.

9. *Cf.* J. L. McKenzie, 'The Elders in the Old Testament', *Biblica* 40 (1959), pp. 522–540; G. Bornkamm, '"Elders" in the Constitutional History of Israel and Judah', *TDNT* VI, pp. 655–661; C. U. Wolf, 'Traces of Primitive Democracy in Ancient Israel', *JNES* 6 (1947), pp. 98–108; C. J. H. Wright, *God's People in God's Land: Family, Land and Property in the Old Testament* (Exeter: Paternoster; Grand Rapids:

Eerdmans, 1990), pp. 78–81.

10. Gottwald, of course, would complain that in putting it that way I have lapsed into supernaturalist, religious idealism. He himself would put it the other way round – namely, that Yahweh was conceived as a certain kind of God because he was the religious symbol of the total social system and its struggle to emerge and sustain itself. 'Yahweh', for Gottwald, was only a 'social servomechanism' (*The Tribes of Yahweh*, p. 704), 'Israel's cipher for the enduring human project' (p. 706).

11. On the subject of the relationship between the church, as the messianic community of believing Jews and Gentiles, and Israel of the Old Testament era, *cf.* C. J. H. Wright, *Knowing Jesus through the Old Testament* (London: Marshall Pickering, 1992); and *idem*, 'A Christian Approach to Old Testament Prophecy Concerning Israel', in P. W. L. Walker (ed.), *Jerusalem Past and Present in the Purposes of God* (Carlisle: Paternoster; Grand Rapids: Baker, 2nd edn., 1994), pp. 1–19.

12. R. B. Sloan, Jr, *The Favorable Year of the Lord: A Study of Jubilary Theology in the Gospel of Luke* (Austin: Schola Press, 1977). *Cf.* also, on the same theme, S. H. Ringe, *Jesus, Liberation, and the Biblical Jubilee: Images for Ethics and Christology* (Philadelphia: Fortress, 1985).

13. *Cf.* on this issue J. Goldingay, *Approaches to Old Testament Interpretation* (Leicester: IVP, 1981; updated edn., Leicester: Apollos, 1990), pp. 51–55, and the literature there cited.

14. Again, one must point out that Gottwald sees this in purely social terms, and would not regard the religious features of Israel as of continuing relevance, but poses an unbridgeable 'religion gap'. The last section of his work, Part XI, 'Biblical Theology or Biblical Sociology?', is eloquently hostile to conventional religion, including Christianity, and what he calls 'the mystifying idealistic and supernaturalistic dregs of biblical theology' (*The Tribes of Yahweh*, p. 702). His major accusation is that it has betrayed the original function of the religion of ancient Israel, which was to inspire and sustain its bid for social freedom and politico-economic equality. Instead, religion has become identified with structures and processes of oppression and injustice, 'a mystifying accompaniment of class rule' (p. 706). Sadly, one has to admit that his analysis and accusation ring true for many aspects of the church, both in the contemporary world and throughout its post-biblical history. But the answer, surely, is that our theology must recapture its authentic, biblical social thrust, if we believe that the living God of Israel is still our God, not that we should abandon our theology altogether, or trade it in for a wholly materialistic brand of sociology. Gottwald unfortunately treads the well-worn reductionist path of turning a thesis which has great descriptive and analytic power into an exclusive theory of causation, *i.e.* that Yahwism was wholly caused

by the social struggle of Israel, and was nothing but 'the symbolic side' of that struggle (cf. pp. 642–649) .

15. Cf. J. A. Kirk, *Theology Encounters Revolution* (IVP, 1980), chapter 9, 'Is There Revolution in Revelation?', and J. Goldingay, 'The Man of War and the Suffering Servant: The Old Testament and the Theology of Liberation', *TB* 27 (1976), pp. 79–113.

16. This point has been mentioned also in chapter 4 above, particularly in discussion of the kind of specific social reform and action undertaken by the Jubilee Centre. The social shape of Israel helps us to articulate social objectives and to critique actual social policy proposals from government or other sources. It provides an orientation and direction for the more detailed stuff of practical Christian political involvement.

7. Theology and ethics of the land

1. This chapter was first presented as a paper at a World Evangelical Fellowship conference on Ethics and the Environment, at the Au Sable Institute, Michigan, USA, and subsequently published as 'Biblical Reflections on Land', *ERT* 17 (1993), pp. 153–167.

2. C. J. H. Wright, *God's People in God's Land: Family, Land and Property in the Old Testament* (Exeter: Paternoster; Grand Rapids: Eerdmans, 1990). Still probably the most thorough and stimulating monograph on this theme is the seminal work of W. Brueggemann, *The Land: Place as Gift, Promise and Challenge in Biblical Faith* (Philadelphia: Fortress, 1977; London; SPCK, 1978).

3. Ron Elsdon makes the theme of the goodness of creation the thread running through his survey of biblical material in both Testaments on this issue in his book *Green House Theology: Biblical Perspectives on Caring for Creation* (Tunbridge Wells: Monarch, 1992).

4. James Lovelock, *Gaia: A New Look at Life on Earth* (Oxford: Oxford University Press, 1979). For a survey and critique of New Age ecological views and their influence on recent Christian thought, see Loren Wilkinson (ed.), *Earthkeeping in the Nineties: Stewardship of Creation* (Grand Rapids: Eerdmans, rev. edn., 1991), pp. 181–199, and *idem*, 'New Age, New Consciousness and the New Creation', in W. Granberg-Michaelson (ed.), *Tending the Garden: Essays on the Gospel and the Earth* (Grand Rapids: Eerdmans , 1987), pp. 6–29 .

5. I have immensely enjoyed reading James Gleick, *Chaos: Making a New Science* (Harmondsworth: Penguin, 1987), with its fascinating account of the mysteries of living and dynamic systems, inorganic, organic and human, and the progress being made in understanding some of their inner simplicities. Gleick refers in passing to Lovelock's hypothesis, but his book is not interested in the religious or philosophical aspects of its topic, but is a historical and descriptive account of 'chaos theory' in several branches of science.

6. *Cf.* Stephen Bishop, 'Green Theology and Deep Ecology: New Age or New Creation?' *Themelios* 16.3 (April 1991, pp. 8–14 .

7. *Cf.* Constance Cumbey, *The Hidden Dangers of the Rainbow: The New Age Movement and Our Coming Age of Barbarism* (Shreveport: Huntingdon House, 1983), and Dave Hunt, *Peace, Prosperity and the Coming Holocaust* (Eugene, Oreg.: Harvest House, 1983).

8. It is important to distinguish between *personalizing and personifying* nature. The Old Testament frequently personifies nature as a rhetorical device, a figure of speech, for greater effect. For example, the heavens and earth are summoned to bear witness to God's address to his people (*e.g.* Dt. 30:19; 32:1; Is. 1:2; Ps. 50:1–6), they declare his glory (Ps. 19), they rejoice at his judgment (Pss. 96:11–13; 98:7–9). Most vividly, the land itself 'vomited out' the previous inhabitants for their wickedness, and did the same to the Israelites when they followed suit (Lv. 18:25–28). But the point of this rhetorical personification of nature is to underline either the personal character of the God who created it and is active in and through it, or to express the personal and moral nature of human beings' relation to God. It is not ascribing personhood to nature or natural forces in themselves. In fact, to *personalize* nature in that way results in both *de*personalizing God and *de*moralizing the relationship between humanity and God. To accord to creation the *personal* status and honour that are due only to God (or derivatively to humans who bear his image) is a form of idolatry as ancient as the fall itself (*cf.* Rom. 1:21–25), though now given new characteristically twentieth-century dress in the New Age movements.

9. Stephen Hawking discusses various versions of the anthropic principle (though he disagrees with them) in *A Brief History of Time* (London, *etc.*: Bantam Press, 1988), pp. 124ff. Simply put, the principle is saying that this universe *had* to be as it is and has been since the beginning for creatures such as ourselves to emerge. It is a non-theological, non-purposive way of expressing the theological affirmation that the universe was created for the purpose of the arrival of humanity within it.

10. 'The Historical Roots of our Ecologic Crisis', *Science* 155 (1967), pp. 1203–1207.

11. See C. J. H. Wright, *Living as the People of God: The Relevance of Old Testament Ethics* (Leicester: IVP, 1983) = *An Eye for an Eye: The Place of Old Testament Ethics Today* (Downers Grove: IVP, 1983), chapter 4.

12. This is a deep and complex issue, which the conference itself was not able to resolve. One question is whether the curse on the earth is ontological (*i.e.* affects the very nature of the cosmos as it now is), or funtional (*i.e.* affecting only our human moral relationship with the earth and with God). The former view allows its adherents to attribute destructive natural phenomena such as earthquakes to the curse, though the chronological problem remains that the natural

causes of such events long pre-date the arrival of the human species. Another question is whether features of nature which we as human beings find 'unpleasant', such as carnivorous species, are the result of the fall or were always part of 'the way things were' long before humans existed, let alone sinned. *Cf.* the response to Stephen Bishop's article by Michael Roberts, in *Themelios* 17.1 (October 1991), p. 16.

13. A detailed survey of the material is given by G. von Rad, 'The Promised Land and Yahweh's Land in the Hexateuch', in *The Problem of the Hexateuch and Other Essays* (London: SCM, 1966; Philadelphia: Fortress, 1984), pp. 79–93.

14. For further elaboration of what is meant by a paradigmatic approach to Old Testament ethics, see my *Living as the People of God = An Eye for an Eye*, and chapters 1, 2 and 4 above.

15. Detailed discussion of the points following will be found in C. J. H. Wright, *Living as the People of God = An Eye for an Eye*, pp. 76–87. For a fuller and more technical study of Israel's economic system, *cf. idem, God's People in God's Land: Family, Land and Property in the Old Testament* (Exeter: Paternoster; Grand Rapids: Eerdmans, 1990). Israel's economic history has received several specific investigations recently, including J. A. Dearman, *Property Rights in the Eighth-Century Prophets: The Conflict and its Background* (Atlanta: Scholars Press, 1988) and Robert Gnuse, *You Shall Not Steal: Community and Property in the Biblical Tradition* (Maryknoll: Orbis, 1985).

16. These may include harsh climatic conditions in one place; differences of soil fertility; lack of children; illness; effects of war in border regions; *etc.* The point is that poverty is not necessarily the result of injustice and oppression by the rich, even though that is the major reason highlighted by the prophets. The economic laws of Israel, however, were concerned to redress impoverishment, regardless of its causes.

17. A very thorough survey of this material is provided by John Mason, 'Biblical Teaching and Assisting the Poor', *Transformation* 4.2 (1987), pp. 1–14.

18. Elsdon, *Green House Theology*, pp. 102–107, gives some staggering statistics in relation to these two wars alone, in a book which is an excellent survey of the subject.

19. The inadequacy of this New Testament section of the paper can be rectified by the excellent symposium edited by Calvin DeWitt, *The Environment and the Christian: What Can We Learn from the New Testament?* (Grand Rapids: Baker, 1991).

20. This is a point strongly developed by O. O'Donovan in *Resurrection and Moral Order: An Outline for Evangelical Ethics* (1986; 2nd edn. Leicester: Apollos; Grand Rapids: Eerdmans, 1994).

21. Still the best survey of this whole theme, with constant suggestive attention to its contemporary relevance, is Brueggemann, *The Land.*

Various aspects of the issue are also explored in C. J. H. Wright, *God's People in God's Land.*

22. At the end of 2 Pet. 3 :10, I prefer the textual reading that the earth 'will be found' to the emendation reflected in several English translations 'will be burned up'. I also find Bauckham's interpretation of this convincing, namely that the earth will be 'found out', *i.e.* exposed and laid bare (*cf.* NIV) before God's judgment so that the wicked and all their works will no longer be able to hide or find any protection: Richard J. Bauckham, *Jude, 2 Peter*, Word Biblical Commentary (Waco: Word, 1983), pp. 316–322. The purpose of the conflagration described in these verses is not the destruction of the cosmos *per se*, but rather its purging and new creation.

23. Francis Bridger, 'Ecology and Eschatology: A Neglected Dimension', *TB* 41.2 (1990), pp. 290–301 (301). This article was a response and addition to an earlier one by Donald A. Hay, 'Christians in the Global Greenhouse', *TB* 41.1 (1990), pp. 109–127.

24. William Cowper, 'The Task', Book 6, lines 733, 763–774, 791–797.

8. The jubilee year

1. This chapter was first published as 'Jubilee, year of', in *The Anchor Bible Dictionary*, ed. D. N. Freedman *et al.* (New York: Doubleday, 1992), vol. III, pp. 1025–1030.

2. *E.g.* J. Mason, 'Biblical Teaching and Assisting the Poor', *Transformation* 4.2 (1987), pp. 1–14; S. C. Mott, 'The Contribution of the Bible to Economic Thought', *Transformation*, 4.3–4 (1987), pp. 25–34; S. H. Ringe, *Jesus, Liberation, and the Biblical Jubilee: Images for Ethics and Christology* (Philadelphia: Fortress, 1985); J. H. Yoder, *The Politics of Jesus* (Grand Rapids: Eerdmans; Exeter: Paternoster, 1972; 2nd rev. edn., 1994).

3. A preliminary sketch of its relevance is offered above in chapter 1.

4. For further details, see chapter 6 above, and also *cf.* C. J. H. Wright, 'Family', in *The Anchor Bible Dictionary.*

5. *Cf.* C. J. H. Wright, *God's People in God's Land: Family, Land and Property in the Old Testament* (Exeter: Paternoster; Grand Rapids: Eerdmans, 1990), chapter 3.

6. See, for example, J. J. Finkelstein, 'Ammisaduqa's Edict and the Babylonian "Law Codes"', *JCS* 15 (1961), pp. 91–104: *idem*, 'Some New Misharum Material and its Implications', *B. Landsberger Festschrift, AS* 16 (1965), pp. 233–246; C. H. Gordon, 'Sabbatical Cycle or Seasonal Pattern', *Orientalia* n. s. 22 (1953), pp. 79–81; J. Lewy and H. Lewy, ' The Origin of the Week and the Oldest West Asiatic Calendar', *HUCA* 17 (1942–43), pp. 1–152; and J. Lewy, 'The Biblical Institution of deror in the Light of Akkadian Documents', *EI* 5

(1958), pp. 21–31.

7. *E.g.* E. Ginzberg, 'Studies in the Economics of the Bible', *JQR* n. s. 22 (1932), pp. 343–408; R. Westbrook, 'Jubilee Laws', *Israel Law Review* 6 (1971), pp. 209–226.

8. *E.g.* H. Schaeffer, *Hebrew Tribal Economy and the Jubilee as Illustrated in Semitic and Indo-European Village Communities* (Leipzig, 1922); S. Stein, 'The Laws on Interest in the Old Testament', *JTS* n. s. 4 (1953), pp. 161–170; R. North, *Sociology of the Biblical Jubilee* (Rome, 1954); J. van der Ploeg, 'Slavery in the Old Testament', *VTS* 22 (1972), pp. 72–87; A. van Selms, 'Jubilee, Year of', *IDB*, Supplement, pp. 496–498.

9. N. K. Gottwald, *The Tribes of Yahweh: A Sociology of the Religion of Liberated Israel* (New York: Orbis, 1979; London: SCM, 1980), p. 264.

10. Other scholarly work on the jubilee includes the following: S. B. Hoenig, 'Sabbath Years and the Year of Jubilee', *JQR* 59 (1969), pp. 222–236; N. P. Lemche, 'The Manumission of Slaves – the Fallow Year – the Sabbatical Year – the Jobel Year', *VT* 26 (1976), pp. 38–59; E. Neufeld, 'Socio-Economic Background of Yobel and Semitta', *RSO* 33 (1958), pp. 53–124; C. J. H. Wright, 'What Happened Every Seven Years in Israel? Old Testament Sabbatical Institutions for Land, Debts and Slaves', *EQ* 56 (1984), pp. 129–138, 193–201; G. C. Chirichigno, *Debt-Slavery in Israel and the Ancient Near East* (Sheffield: JSOT Press, 1993).

11. A. Trocmé, *Jesus-Christ et la revolution non-violente* (Geneva, 1961); ET *Jesus and the Nonviolent Revolution* (Scottdale: Herald, 1973), as cited and discussed by Yoder, *Politics*, pp. 60–75.

12. Yoder, *Politics*, p. 71.

13. R. B. Sloan Jr, *The Favorable Year of the Lord: A Study of Jubilary Theology in the Gospel of Luke* (Austin: Schola, 1977).

14. Ringe, *Jesus, Liberation*.

15. A thorough attempt to apply the relevance of the Old Testament's patterns regarding the extended family to modern Western society is made by M. Schluter and R. Clements, *Reactivating the Extended Family: From Biblical Norms to Public Policy in Britain* (Cambridge: Jubilee Centre, 1986).

9. The people of God and the state

1. The content of this chapter was first prepared as a paper at a consultation on the church and state, co-sponsored by the World Evangelical Fellowship and Partnership in Mission – Asia, held in Hong Kong in October 1988. It was subsequently published in *Themelios* 16.1 (1990), pp. 4–10, and reprinted under the same title as Grove Ethical Studies 77 (Nottingham: Grove Books, 1990).

2. C. J. H. Wright, *Living as the People of God: The Relevance of Old Testament Ethics* (Leicester: IVP, 1983) = *An Eye for an Eye: The Place of*

Old Testament Ethics Today (Downers Grove: IVP, 1983), chapter 5, 'Politics and the World of Nations', pp. 103–108.

3. For a helpful discussion of this issue, see Paul Marshall, *Thine is the Kingdom: A Biblical Perspective on the Nature of Government and Politics Today* (Marshalls, 1984), pp. 41f.

4. John Goldingay, *Theological Diversity and the Authority of the Old Testament* (Grand Rapids: Eerdmans, 1987), chapter 3.

5. E. Voegelin, *Israel and Revelation* (Baton Rouge: Louisiana State University Press 1956), p. 140; quoted in Goldingay, *Theological Diversity*, p. 61.

6. W. Brueggemann, *The Prophetic Imagination* (Philadelphia: Fortress, 1978), chs. 1–2 .

7. The question how and when Israel established itself in Canaan (by conquest, infiltration, revolt, or a mixture of these) is still a much debated area among historians of the period. See F. S. Frick, *The Formation of the State in Ancient Israel: A Survey of Models and Theories* (Sheffield: Almond, 1985) and J. J. Bimson: 'The Origins of Israel in Canaan: An Examination of Recent Theories', *Themelios* 15.1 (1989), pp. 4–15.

8. N. K. Gottwald, *The Tribes of Yahweh: A Sociology of the Religion of Liberated Israel 1250–1050 BCE* (Maryknoll: Orbis, 1979; London: SCM, 1980). For an appreciation and critique of this important work and its impact on Old Testament ethics, see chapter 6 above.

9. Goldingay, *Theological Diversity*, p. 66, with references to the work of Mendenhall, Gottwald and other sociologists of Israel.

10. Brueggemann, *Prophetic Imagination*, pp. 16f. (his italics).

11. 'Yahweh was regarded as political leader both of Israel and of the world, a concept which in itself was not unique, however, as the rule of divinity was a belief held by all ancient Near Eastern peoples.' Millard C. Lind, 'The Concept of Political Power in Ancient Israel', *ASTI 7* (1968-69), pp. 4–24.

12. *Ibid.*, pp. 12f. Lind adduces Gideon's resistance to proffered kingship (Jdg. 8:22f.), Samuel's critique of monarchy as an essentially enslaving burden (1 Sa. 8:10–18), and Jotham's fable (Jdg. 9:7–15) in which monarchy is mocked as 'a socially useless, even harmful institution'.

13. Gregory Baum, referring to Norman Cohn's historical study of such movements in Europe, *The Pursuit of the Millennium* (London, 1957), in his own article, 'Exodus Politics', in B. van Iersel and A. Weiler (eds.), *Exodus – A Lasting Paradigm*, *Concilium* 189 (1987), pp. 109ff. This volume includes helpful surveys of the use of the exodus paradigm in various theological traditions.

14. Michael Walzer, *Exodus and Revolution* (New York, 1985). His approach is also summarized in Baum, 'Exodus Politics'.

15. In *Prophetic Imagination*, chapter 2. Brueggemann lists the characteristic features of the Solomonic era as 'an economics of affluence

(1 Kgs. 4:20–23), politics of oppression (1 Kgs. 5:13–18; 9: 15–22) and a religion of immanence and accessibility (1 Kgs. 8:12–13)'.

16. G. H. Wittenberg, 'King Solomon and the Theologians', *JTSA* 63 (June 1988) (special issue on church and state and the problem of legitimacy), pp. 16–29. Brueggemann also finds implicit criticism of the golden age of Solomon in the texts themselves which catalogue it, texts which he claims conceal a social criticism designed to lead the reader to enquire exactly what kind of shalom it was under Solomon which brought the people such satiety. See 'Vine and Fig Tree – A Case Study in Imagination and Criticism', *CBQ* 43 (1981); 'The Bible and Mission', *Missiology* 10.4 (1982), pp. 397–411; 'Trajectories in Old Testament Literature and the Sociology of Ancient Israel', *JBL* 98 (1979), pp. 161–185.

17. Goldingay, *Theological Diversity*, p. 70.

18. *Ibid.*, pp. 85f.

19. *Ibid.*, pp. 72f.

20. Goldingay has some perceptive comparisons between the various stages of Israel's development and the history of the Christian church from its familial origins to its present 'post-exilic' (post-Enlightenment) tensions: *Theological Diversity*, p. 83.

21. I have reflected on this dimension of these chapters in *Tested by Fire: Daniel 1–6 in Today's World*, The Word for Today (London: Scripture Union, 1993).

22. I have discussed these responses to the state further in *Living as the People of God = An Eye for an Eye*, pp. 122–130.

23. Brueggemann, *Prophetic Imagination*, p. 75.

24. Baum, 'Exodus Politics', p. 115. He goes on to suggest paradigms such as reconciliation between estranged brothers, for example, as a more helpful and equally biblical way of looking at such conflicts as Northern Ireland and Israel–Palestine.

25. Goldingay, *Theological Diversity*, pp. 91f.

10. Human rights

1. This chapter was first published in the Grove Booklets on Ethics series, 31 (Nottingham: Grove Books, 1979).

2. This comment on Ps. 139 is derived from Emil Brunner, *Man in Revolt: A Christian Anthropology* (ET London: Lutterworth, 1939), p. 89.

3. *Ibid.*, p. 94.

4. *Ibid.*, p. 50. One might want to modify this slightly to say that responsibility is the normal, mature expression of the human relationship with God. Otherwise one might be in danger of denying human status to those of defective or nil rationality and responsibility, such as infants or imbeciles. But a child has a relational awareness of his parents long before he can rationalize or

act responsibly upon it. The same must be allowed for the relationship between God and persons for whom we cannot use normal means and measures of judgment but whom we still regard as human.

5. *Ibid.*, p. 73.
6. *Ibid.*, p. 19.
7. See C. J. H. Wright, *Living as the People of God: The Relevance of Old Testament Ethics* (Leicester: IVP, 1983) = *An Eye for an Eye: The Place of Old Testament Ethics Today* (Downers Grove: IVP, 1983), pp. 133–147, for an analysis and discussion of the Old Testament words for 'righteousness' and 'justice'.
8. The word used, z^e'*āqâ*, is that frequently used for the cries and complaints of anyone suffering injustice . It is the cry of the Israelites in Egypt, and in the many other afflictions they underwent. 'The word "outcry" ... is a technical legal term and designates the cry for help which one who suffers a great injustice screams ... With this cry for help ... he appeals for the protection of the legal community. What it does not hear or grant, however, comes directly before Yahweh as the guardian of all right' (*cf.* Gn. 4:10). G. von Rad, *Genesis, A Commentary* (London: SCM, 3rd rev. edn., 1972), p. 211.
9. See the helpful discussion of this passage and its relevance to political authorities in R. Bauckham, *The Bible in Politics: How to Read the Bible Politically* (London: SPCK, 1989), pp. 41–52.
10. This must obviously have some bearing on the issue of human rights in the realm of judicial punishment. When a person breaks the law, I do not cease to be responsible to God for him. In fact, in executing a just punishment upon him I am discharging a responsibility towards God in respect of him. Not to do so is to incur guilt myself. But equally, his right to humane as well as just punishment is grounded in the fact that I am still responsible before God for the manner and extent and conditions of the punishment I inflict (*cf.* Dt. 25:1–3).
11. A. Bloom, 'Human Rights in Israel's Thought: A Study of Old Testament Doctrine', in *Interpretation* 8 (1954), pp. 422–432 (p. 425).
12. *Ibid.*, p. 429.

11. When the system fails

1. This chapter was originally given as a paper to the Theological Research and Communications Institute (TRACI), in Delhi, India, and subsequently published as 'No Neutrality in the Struggle against Corruption and Dishonesty: An Old Testament Perspective', in Bruce Nichols and Christopher Raj (eds.), *Mission as Witness and Justice: An Indian Perspective* (New Delhi: TRACI, 1991), pp. 157–170. Though some of its content overlaps a little with earlier chapters, it illustrates further the method of comprehensive use of the Old

Testament material advocated in chapter 1 above.
2. See the full description of this approach in chapter 1 above.
3. For full details, see chapter 6 above.
4. *Living as the People of God: The Relevance of Old Testament Ethics* (Leicester: IVP, 1983) = *An Eye for an Eye: The Place of Old Testament Ethics Today* (Downers Grove: IVP, 1983), p. 120.